The Call of the Desert

The Call of the Desert

A BIOGRAPHY OF

LITTLE SISTER MAGDELEINE
OF JESUS

Kathryn Spink

Foreword by Jean Vanier

DARTON · LONGMAN + TODD

First published in 1993 by
Darton, Longman and Todd Ltd
1 Spencer Court
140–142 Wandsworth High Street
London SW18 4JJ

Reprinted 1994

ISBN 0–232–51973–0

A catalogue record for this book is available
from the British Library

Cover photograph by Pierre A Pittet,
PO Box 82, 1213 Onex-Geneva,
Switzerland

Phototypeset in 10/12 pt Ehrhardt by Intype, London
Printed and bound in Great Britain
at the University Press, Cambridge

Contents

Illustrations

Little Sister Magdeleine in her tiny office with Pope John Paul II during his visit to the general fraternity in 1985.

The two foundresses, Little Sister Magdeleine and Mother Teresa, together at Tre Fontane in 1975.

Little Sister Magdeleine and Little Sister Jeanne with the 'Shooting Star' on arrival in Moscow.

One of the many attempts to reproduce Our Lady of the Whole World, with the double gesture of Mary offering her child and the infant Jesus reaching out to give himself to the world.

Little Sister Magdeleine at Tre Fontane in 1976, in front of a picture of Charles de Foucauld donated by Pope Paul VI.

The plaster model of the infant Jesus preserved as Little Sister Magdeleine left it in her rooms at Sidi Boujnan.

Little Sister Magdeleine at work in Tre Fontane in 1972.

Foreword

This is a remarkable book about a remarkable woman. It is the story of a woman who, up to the age of forty, seemed condemned to a life of ill health, but who was called by Jesus to travel throughout the world amidst great hardship in order to create little fraternities of love, and to found a new religious congregation. She was a woman of undaunted faith and courage who refused to accept the 'impossible' because of her trust in the 'Master of the impossible', as Brother Charles de Foucauld liked to call Jesus. She was a woman with human defects and weaknesses, but one who knew she was loved by God and called by God to announce a message of love to people all over the world. She was a woman who lived poorly in every way to reveal the riches of the heart of Jesus.

Little Sister Magdeleine was clearly raised up by God for our times to bring the good news of love to people in those places of pain, rejection, isolation and misery where God (and the Church) appears to be conspicuously absent. Little Sister Magdeleine is essentially a lover: a lover of Jesus who revealed himself to her in an intimate way, with the immense tenderness and vulnerability of a child; a lover of people: of the Muslim people she first met in Algeria, of people who seemed far from God, of all those Little Sisters who followed in her footsteps; a lover of all those she encountered, the rich as well as the poor, the powerful and powerless alike, the wise and the foolish. Many people were touched by her penetrating, compassionate eyes.

Little Sister Magdeleine was, however, a very demanding lover. If she accepted without judgement and with great understanding those who seemed far from her own deep religious beliefs, she was sometimes difficult and demanding with her Little Sisters, intolerant of their faults and if she sensed in them any lack of love.

This seemingly weak, frail woman was possessed by an incredible energy of love which constantly pushed her forward through, over, above and around obstacles of all kinds, enabling her to accomplish her mission of love, to reveal the compassionate, forgiving, healing face of God to those who felt abandoned by God.

If her energies went out far and wide to all people of all faiths or of no faith, with a tremendous yearning for unity, she herself was firmly anchored in her own Church, the Roman Catholic Church. She was a passionate lover of this Church, seeking recognition by the Church and the Pope, wanting the fraternities to be earthed in the Church. Her love for the Church and for the gospel message sometimes pushed her to challenge church leaders, calling them lovin֊ to greater faith in the message of Jesus. She was passionately obedient and demanded obedience, just as she was surprisingly free and startlingly creative and audacious.

In this book Kathryn Spink reveals not only the prophetic aspects of Little Sister Magdeleine and how she was led by God in all the details of her travels, but also the shadow side of her strength and gifts; moments of impatience and quick judgements. This book shows how human she was. It is refreshing and consoling to see those weaknesses. Each one of us has a shadow side to our gifts and strengths; none of us is perfect. But Jesus constantly reminds us, as he did Paul: 'My strength is manifest in your weakness'. The work of God can be more perfectly revealed as our own flaws and inconsistencies are manifested. Little Sister Magdeleine is both more human and more divine than we may have suspected. She was loved and chosen to be an instrument of God's love, just as she was. She trusted in that. What a comfort for each one of us who is in contact with our own darkness and so prone to discouragement! We are all called to be instruments of God, just as we are, wherever we are. We do not have to be perfect in the sense of being flawless. Little Sister Magdeleine shows that God wants us to be humble and trusting to the point of audacity.

I first met the Little Sisters of Jesus in 1954. My parents frequently visited their fraternity in a poor, inner city area of Montreal. I was impressed by their presence in that part of the city, and by their own poverty and simplicity of life. The house they lived in was so completely different to other convents which we were used to seeing in Quebec. Their dress was extremely simple. They were living close to and in solidarity with the poor, without any special protection or security. Neighbours out of work, over-burdened, oppressed by the stress of everyday life came in and out of their kitchen. Little Sister

Monique worked in a factory. My parents went to their fraternity every Thursday evening for an hour of quiet adoration in their little chapel. This became a precious moment for renewal and spiritual nourishment for them; it introduced them to the prayer of silent adoration of Jesus in the Blessed Sacrament.

Since then I have visited the fraternities in many places of pain and misery throughout the world. I have climbed staircases of broken-down apartment blocks in the black areas of Boston and Chicago where a smiling Little Sister would welcome me and lead me to the chapel where another was in silent adoration, enveloped in peace. I have met them in the congested slum areas of Beirut amongst the Palestinian people or in a little boat fraternity in the waters of Hong Kong. I have visited them in Cape Town, Rio de Janeiro, Lisbon and so on. Through these Little Sisters, Jesus is presented to the poor, the weary, the isolated and the oppressed.

Yes, I can vouch that the Little Sisters throughout the world are seeking to live out the vision Little Sister Magdeleine announced and lived, proclaiming the good news of love, not so much by their words as by their compassion, understanding and smiles.

I must have met Little Sister Magdeleine for the first time in the early seventies, at Tre Fontane. After that, each year, and often more than once a year, when I went to Rome, the Little Sisters welcomed me to stay with them. When Little Sister Magdeleine was there, she would invite me to a meal with her and the General Council. She was deeply interested in l'Arche and in our people. I too was passionately interested in all she shared with me. I was touched by her love for people, her trust in them, no matter what their faith or lack of faith, their political opinions, or their origins. In each of them she saw the light of God. Once the International Council of l'Arche spent ten days at Tre Fontane. I remember her joyous, childlike laughter when, on the last day, we mimed the life of the Little Sisters to the hundred or so Little Sisters present. I also remember visiting her shortly before her death: she was so fragile, truthful, beautiful. She died as she had lived, in poverty, but so rich in faith and trust.

It was a gift of God for me personally to know her and to have been loved by her; a gift of God also for many of our communities of l'Arche and Faith and Light to be close to fraternities of the Little Brothers and the Little Sisters of Jesus.

The attraction of our communities to them is not just an accident, a coincidence or a piece of luck. Although our communities may be different to the fraternities in many ways, we are attracted to each other by a common spirituality: the spirituality of the Gospels as they were lived and announced by Brother Charles. The Gospels proclaim that the Word made flesh is not only attracted to the weak, the captives and the oppressed in order to announce to them the good news of love, of peace and of liberation, but that God is present in them, identifies with them. In their trust, their love and their simplicity, they reveal to the rich and the powerful, to those who wish to serve them, the vulnerable, loving face of Jesus. In their pain and weakness, they reveal the weakness and pain of the Word made flesh. If at times they are violent, depressed, difficult to relate to, they are also healers of our wounds, our brokenness and our egoism. Through communion with them, they can mysteriously lead us into communion with God. The spirituality of Brother Charles is to be present simply and poorly with the poor, to be close to them, to live in solidarity with them, to see them as a sacrament of God, an icon of Jesus, poor and humble. In this way we discover that small is beautiful, that we do not have to do big or heroic things, but to live a life where we put a primacy on faithful relationships with people and with Jesus. That is why the life of Jesus, Mary and Joseph in Nazareth is a model for the fraternities of the Little Brothers and Sisters, as well as for l'Arche and Faith and Light.

Little Sister Magdeleine and the Little Brothers and Sisters have helped l'Arche and Faith and Light to be what we are called to be: little oases of love, peace, joy, and forgiveness, not hidden away on mountain tops, apart from others, but in and with others, integrated into villages and city neighbourhoods; little signs of love, support and faith for neighbours and friends.

The message of Brother Charles and Little Sister Magdeleine is prophetic. They reveal to the world and to the Church the true face and heart of Jesus. Like the gospels, they reveal that God is in love with people. Today, as yesterday, God yearns that his tender, forgiving, empowering, joyful love be revealed to all people, especially to those who are most abandoned, forgotten, disregarded; to those in slums, in prisons, in psychiatric hospitals, or in desolate war-torn areas; to all those crushed because of their race, their religion, their handicap or for other reasons. But this love is not revealed by words alone. Words can easily become a double message, propaganda, manipulation, empty promises, hypocrisy if they are not accompanied by authentic presence and concrete gestures. Love is revealed by love. Love is revealed through presence, proximity, compassion and joyfulness, through one's face, hands, eyes, one's whole body.

By inspiring Little Sister Magdeleine to go to the ends of the earth with all the folly of her travels and new foundations, Jesus is revealing an important but often forgotten aspect of the Church: the Church is not called to be a fortress of power, certitude and judgment into which people must enter in order to be saved. As in the vision of Ezekiel (Ezek. 47), the Church is called to be the Temple from which flow living, healing waters. These waters flow over all of humanity, cleansing, nourishing, giving life and life in abundance. These waters are called to flow into the most broken areas of our own hearts and of humanity, where sin, death and despair abound. The fraternities of Little Sisters are not places of security, separated from the broken, but close to them, so that the Sisters too may discover these living waters, be cleansed by them, drink from them, and thus become in their turn sources of living water for others.

Little Sister Magdeleine also reveals that the path to unity between all followers of Jesus, the true road of reform and spiritual growth for each person, community, religious order or parish is in, through and with the poor.

I am grateful to Kathryn Spink for the way she has revealed to us the mind and heart of Christ through the story and person of Little Sister Magdeleine. I am grateful to Little Sister Magdeleine and to all the Little Sisters who have followed her footsteps; without their 'yes' to Jesus poor and humble, without their fidelity, Little Sister Magdeleine would not have been the beautiful and loving person she was.

Jean Vanier
June, 1993

Acknowledgements

A special debt of gratitude is owed to the Little Sisters of Jesus for introducing me to their foundress and accompanying me on an extraordinary journey. I would particularly like to thank all those Little Sisters who, in fraternities in Algeria, England, France and Italy, gave so generously of their hospitality, energy and understanding. I would also like to express my thanks to Father Voillaume, to the Little Brothers of Jesus, to Jean Vanier and to the many friends of Little Sister Magdeleine I met along the way. Finally my sincere thanks go to Cherry Fisher and Teresa de Bertadano for their discernment and support, and to the many others who in their various ways have contributed to the writing of this book. They are too numerous to name but their collaboration has been greatly appreciated.

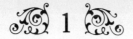

1

The Call of the Desert

TOWARDS THE YEAR 1888, a young man serving as a military doctor with the French troops in North Africa fell off his horse and broke his leg. Following a period of convalescence, Joseph Hutin was sent by the army authorities to Zagouan, a small town in Tunisia, with strict orders not to remount his horse for six months. It was a time, however, when French army doctors were virtually the only source of medical aid for the people of the small Tunisian towns and their surroundings. Joseph Hutin tended not only to the needs of the military but also to those of the civilian population. One day a Muslim boy aged five or six was brought to him, suffering from diphtheria. Without the appropriate serum the child would die, but the serum could only be obtained from Tunis and Tunis was some sixty kilometres away from Zagouan. As the Muslim boy's life was slipping quietly away and no other volunteer presented himself for a journey which could only be made on horseback, Joseph Hutin, knowing full well what the personal consequences of his action might be, galloped to the Tunisian capital in a desperate attempt to save the child. He returned with the serum and the small boy from Zagouan, about whom no one else had cared sufficiently to make the journey, recovered. Joseph Hutin, however, suffered severe physical consequences and at the age of only thirty was invalided out of the army.

The Hutin family came originally from the Lorraine area in the east of France but Joseph Hutin, on his return from Africa, was obliged to move about quite frequently in pursuit of treatment and cures for his medical condition. It was in Nice that in June 1888 he married Rennié Eugenie Elisa Florentine whom he called Jeanne. They had six children – four boys and two girls – the youngest of whom, the future Little Sister Magdeleine, was born on 26 April 1898. Because of her fragile state she was baptised the same day as Elisabeth Marie Madeleine but she was known always as Madeleine.

1

Hers was not an easy childhood. After an early period of relative comfort, the family's financial circumstances deteriorated. Joseph Hutin's army pension was a barely adequate means of financial support and various other ventures on which he subsequently embarked came to nothing. Both Joseph and his wife were devout Catholics. The government of France during the years 1905–9 was staunchly anticlerical and committed to a policy of closing churches, convents and similar institutions. During that period Joseph Hutin worked as director at the école Pigier, a college for shorthand and typing in Paris, but his Christian faith conflicted with official policy. The Hutins liked to receive the sacraments daily at a time when frequent communion was not common practice. The doctor was obliged to attend mass almost in secret and at some distance from where he lived and worked, and eventually the kind of dual existence he was leading became intolerable for the man of integrity he manifestly was. Little is known of his employment after that period. In later life his daughter Madeleine would make reference to the circumstances and events which led most obviously to her own vocation, but there were details of her childhood and background which she quite simply never thought to mention and about which those around her did not think to ask.

What is known is that during and after the 1914–18 war the Hutin family was based primarily in Aix-en-Provence and that the fighting brought extraordinary tragedy to the family. The Hutins had already lost two of their children. One son, Charles, had died in 1893, having lived for only one month. Another, Maurice, died of diphtheria in 1902 at the age of only six. Before the First World War the Hutins had had a family home in Seuzey, Meuse, where they used to spend their holidays, but the house was destroyed in the bombing raids and Madeleine's elderly paternal grandmother was killed by the Germans outside her home in October 1914. Then, on 8 January 1916, André, the brother to whom Madeleine had been particularly close, was killed in action, aged twenty-one. The family was still reeling under the shock of losing him when only six months later the news came through that Jules, their elder son who was twenty-seven years old and a Jesuit scholar, had also been killed. He had been shot in the heart during an attack on Assevilliers. Finally, on 15 February 1918, Madeleine's elder sister Marie, by then a young nun belonging to the Congregation of the Sacred Heart, died of meningitis following an attack of Spanish influenza, which ran rife in France at that time. The story was afterwards told of how Joseph Hutin had had a premonition of this particularly tragic sequence of events. When news reached him of the declaration of war he is said to have knelt down with his head in his hands and predicted: 'Today there are six of us. When the war ends there will be three of us.' By the time the fighting stopped Madeleine Hutin was left, the sole survivor of the Hutins' six children.

When asked years later about the roots of her vocation, Little Sister Magdeleine would say that she thought she was born with a love of Africa. She would speak of how even as a small child whenever she saw little African children, of which there were many in France at the time, she would be drawn quite spontaneously to them. She would speak too of how her favourite game used to be to make up a tent, together with one of her brothers, out of all the blankets she could lay her hands on. Her family in general had shown her what it was to love, but her father in particular had communicated to her his love for the people of North Africa for whom he had developed a special affection during his time there. It was an affection which he retained long after he had returned to France. He kept in touch with a number of North African families. The deprivation of the Muslim nomads had touched him deeply and he still wanted to send them what assistance he could. During his wife's occasional absences, he and his daughter would hardly eat. Joseph Hutin would make up a saucepan of potatoes and that would last them for several days. He was, in his youngest daughter's eyes, a saint, who never expressed any regret for the action which many regarded as foolhardiness and who, together with his wife, had also imbued her with a profound Christian faith without, she would insist, any particular merit on her part. So it was that 'well before her first communion' and 'almost from the age of reason' she felt a calling to the religious life. The response to that call, however, was to be delayed for twenty years: four of them, as she would subsequently explain, as a consequence of the war which decimated her family. Ten more because of tubercular pleurisy which left her so weak that her time was frequently divided between bed and *chaise-longue*. There were lighter moments in her childhood: pranks she got up to with her brother André, moments when she discovered and developed a love of animals. Among the carefully posed Victorian-style photographs presided over by her somewhat stern-looking father with his ample beard and a mother dressed for so many years of her life in the black of mourning, there are some pictures taken of her as a small child showing her playing with horses or milking a goat. She herself would recall training a cockerel to pull a small cart. She also displayed a gift for playing the piano, to such a degree that her father, concerned about where her talent might lead in life, put a stop to her practising. Despite this and despite the fact that she had no talent for singing she retained her love of music, and as an adult would sometimes be caught playing scales with her fingers on a table.

At the age of only a few months Madeleine had already shown signs of ill health. In fact she had very nearly died of double bronchial pneumonia. Madame Hutin made a promise then that if her daughter recovered she would say the rosary every day. The child survived and Madame Hutin kept her promise. Sometimes she would have completed the whole rosary by four o'clock in the morning. Poor health was to remain a handicap to Madeleine, however. At the time when her brother Maurice fell fatally ill, the Sacred Heart nuns had advised Joseph Hutin that if his youngest child remained at home, she too would contract diphtheria. The Sacred Heart sisters took the child into their care. During a period when government policy was to close convent schools in France, in her early teens she was sent for a while to a boarding school in Spain but there she fell ill once more and her father was obliged to collect her and bring her home. Because of the family's financial circumstances the Congregation of the Sacred Heart undertook to educate Madeleine free of charge. At that time the sisters directed their energies primarily into educating girls of a certain social standing. More often than not the girls with whom Madeleine mixed had servants to perform such menial tasks as fetching and carrying water. It was a time when it was regarded almost as 'dishonourable' not to have a maid and to go to the market oneself. Madeleine came to know what it was to be despised for being poor. In general the Hutin family were looked down upon as poor relations and friends by people of whom she would later say, 'They had little moral value but who kept up a façade of nobility and wealth.' 'There was a period in my life when I suffered greatly as a result of the disdain of the rich for the poor,' she acknowledged in a letter she wrote in 1947. She found a compensatory affection and joy on the other side of the social barrier.

It was while Dr Hutin was collecting water from the wash-house because there was no running water in the modest two-room lodgings he and his wife and daughter were occupying at Montigny-les-Metz for two months in the summer of 1921, that he encountered the father of another family whose circumstances were not dissimilar to his own. This family too originated from Meuse, had lost everything and was struggling, as the Hutins were, to obtain government compensation with which to reconstruct their house. The two daughters were aged nine and fourteen; Madeleine was twenty-two by then but she loved young people and she became firm friends with Renée and Paulette in the course of the annual summer holiday visits which the Hutins made to Montigny-les-Metz to escape the heat of the South of France. The younger girls would take every possible opportunity to chat with Madeleine and her mother. They were, as the adult Paulette later recalled, 'so welcoming and kind'.

At school Madeleine had been so quiet and withdrawn that her contemporaries had nicknamed her 'the mummy', but, by her own account, the death of her sister in 1918 in some mysterious way injected a different and more animated and outgoing personality into her. She would explain in a letter written in February 1949,

> I was twenty years old, with the most timid, withdrawn disposition in the world. In one minute, at her deathbed, as if by lightning, a second nature juxtaposed itself to the first without replacing it, and I left the room in which she died a different person from the one who entered it.

Yet at a time when ill health was regarded as an obstacle to entering a religious congregation, Madeleine's tubercular pleurisy appeared to frustrate the vocation she felt she had. By her own assertion she had the kind of temperament which needed physical exercise. From 1918 until 1928, however, she knew all the frustrations of illness. Her father treated her and was understandably solicitous for her well-being, in general requiring her to live the life of an invalid. He was a quiet man of few words but very good-hearted. Montigny-les-Metz was a working-class suburb of Metz. There were those amongst the local residents who did not dare to approach him because of his profession but those who knew him found him very unpretentious and self-effacing. As a doctor, he formed part of the board of medical certification at Lourdes so he took his family there each year. He had himself a great devotion to Lourdes and to the Virgin Mary. The Hutin family took with them a statue of the Virgin when they travelled. In Montigny-les-Metz Paulette noticed that often Mr Hutin would close the curtains to his room in the early afternoon. She had assumed it was for the doctor to take an afternoon rest but when she suggested this to Madame Hutin she was told that Joseph Hutin was preparing himself for his death.

In 1925 Madeleine's mother fell ill with the flu whilst the family was in Montigny-les-Metz for their holiday. Her husband contracted it also. His temperature soared and within a very short space of time, he died at the age of sixty-seven. As a tertiary of the order of St Francis he was given a poor man's burial. Few people knew the family in Montigny-les-Metz so only a handful of mourners attended the ceremony. Ten years later his wife, who took flowers to the grave every Saturday while she was in Metz, had his body laid to rest beside that of his mother in La Meuse. Even in her grief, at a loss as how to make the necessary arrangements in a place she knew only through relatively brief holidays, Madame Hutin did not complain, but her last child became particularly precious to her. Madeleine was left alone with a mother who had survived two world wars but suffered such a succession of tragic bereavements that to inflict on her another loss would have been cruel in the extreme. Madeleine had been a compassionate child, so much so that even the 'poor pieces of iron which the blacksmith reddens in the fire and hammers with all his might' tugged at her heart-strings. Following the death of her father, she took good care of herself not for her own sake but for her mother's, sometimes hiding her medicines in her friend's house so that her mother would not be alarmed. She was conscious in her adult life that much of what she herself was able to do was due to the fact that her mother had surrounded her from babyhood with both strength and tenderness. It was inconceivable that she should abandon her mother now that she was Madame Hutin's only source of comfort and support. It was to this fact that Little Sister Madeleine later attributed a further six years' delay in pursuing her vocation. 'Twenty years of waiting,' she would exclaim. 'Only one who had undergone such an experience could really know what those words meant in terms of fluctuating feelings of faith, trust and anguish.'

In 1927 Madeleine's young friends at Montigny-les-Metz also lost their father. From then onwards the two mothers and their three children spent their holidays under the same roof. The girls would later remember Madeleine for her extreme cheerfulness, as one who took the blows life dealt her in her stride without over-dramatising them. Frail though she was in health, she was also quite heavy at that time. On one occasion she collapsed and on regaining consciousness announced to them that she felt sick, '. . . but as sick as a whale that has just swallowed a man'. It was enough to warrant her being nicknamed 'whale' for many years thereafter. The 'whale' had a tiny black toy terrier as a companion. Its antics were a source of great amusement to her and she used to carry it about in her coat pocket. Always short of money herself, Madeleine was already deeply concerned for the poor. A ten-franc note discovered one day on the pavement had to be placed in the poor box in the church. She was worried in case it was a poor person who had lost what was in those days a not inconsiderable sum. Enthusiastically committed to church activities, she organised the tombola at the parish fêtes and in general could be relied upon to enlist people to engage their energy and talents for a good cause. A born organiser and tenacious in the extreme, she was not someone to whom people could easily say 'No'. New experiences were looked upon as an opportunity to learn. She was good with her hands, a gifted painter of religious subjects, with a strong artistic sense and a dynamism which carried others along with her. She was frank, forthright and persistent in a way that meant she was sometimes rebuffed, but Paulette would many years later recall how Madeleine was liked because others sensed that she liked them: 'She had such a personal way of loving people.'

Madame Hutin's solicitous concern for her daughter's welfare meant that Madeleine was not allowed to go out unless her temperature was as it should be. Yet she managed never to waste a moment. What she did, she did with meticulous care. One stitch out of place in her needlework or embroidery had to be immediately undone. She had inherited her mother's attention to detail. During the First World War Madame Hutin had compiled a list of those things which should be kept by the door at night:

1. a gas mask,
2. a pocket torch,
3. failing that, a candle to light the way downstairs where it must be extinguished to avoid unnecessary consumption of air,
4. identity papers, the book in which births and deaths are registered, official documents in a bag or portfolio.

Her daughter had a similar tendency towards meticulous precision and the predisposition to commit details to paper. Watching her tidy her cupboard was an experience which some would remember years later. Everything had to be removed and laid out on the floor. Then Madeleine, kneeling, or squatting on her heels (a position of which

7

she was particularly fond), would label each object, place them in boxes and restore them to their proper place so that even when she was away, travelling, she was able to tell people precisely where they would find a particular item. Despite her perfectionism and her determination to see her plans implemented she was not cross when others fell short of expectations. Asked one day whether she never got angry she responded: 'Haven't you ever noticed, when I'm angry, my chin or my lip trembles a bit...' Her friends had noticed the occasional tremble but on the whole remembered her for her restraint.

With the war damages they received from the government, the Hutins built a house in Metz and continued to return to the suburb of Montigny-les-Metz each year. The parish priest, a Canon Zimmerman who was equally committed to parish fêtes and whose spiritual direction she valued greatly, became her confessor and friend. He immediately recognised in her a person of extraordinary qualities, predicting that she would either become an exceptional person or be damned. Madeleine, by her own assertion, was not given to prayer in quite the same form as her mother who was inclined to pray for specific causes. With hindsight Paulette, who later entered the religious life herself, defined Madeleine's prayer as that of a contemplative. She was constantly there on her prie-dieu in the church. She caught chills very easily and would have to keep clearing her throat to avoid coughing and alarming her mother, and her young friend was struck by how, in her fragile state, she prayed with great intensity. An atmosphere of extraordinary peace seemed to surround her. Yet she was not one to force others to prayer or to inflict upon them the religious fervour which she undoubtedly felt herself. She was interested in anything to do with missionary activity, was deeply impressed by the work which a Father Baeteman was undertaking amongst lepers at the time. Her own father had also shown her how to look after the sick. At the same time she travelled a good deal between Aix and Montigny-les-Metz, frequently making diversions to visit friends. One such friend from Aix-en-Provence was surprised one day to discover that Madeleine had spent several evenings in a casino and befriended some of the artistes. She had sensed beyond the glitter and glamour the distress of some of their lives and had brought them at very least a little understanding. Her head was, she acknowledged, bursting with ideas, but she did not seem quite able to find a life that corresponded with her vocation. Those close to her knew that she had a religious calling. They sensed too that she was searching for the form that religious life was to take, and did not know quite which way to turn.

For all the gaiety, energy and optimism which others discerned in her, when many years later Little Sister Magdeleine came to publish the history of the congregation she was to found, she referred to this period of uncertainty as 'dark years' in which, she claimed, there was but one point of light. The only illumination of a period which she chose to present, in terms which were characteristically extreme, as one of otherwise unmitigated shadow was the reading of a biography by René Bazin of Charles de Foucauld, the explorer and priest frequently described as a hermit. Completed in 1921, *Charles de Foucauld, explorateur du Maroc, ermite au Sahara*, was a book which belonged very much to its day in its reflection of French colonialist interests and the contemporary mood of missionary expansionism in the Roman Catholic Church. Written very shortly after Charles de Foucauld became the unresisting victim of Algerian rebels in Tamanrasset, Southern Algeria, it recorded his life at a time when the need was felt in certain quarters to alert the French people to the moral and spiritual responsibilities which colonialism carried with it. Charles de Foucauld had been born in Strasbourg in 1858 into a wealthy and influential Christian family. Orphaned at an early age, and brought up by his grandfather, in his teens his faith began gradually to slip away from him. In preparation for a military career he entered the St Cyr School for Officers and began a period of indolent self-indulgence during which he could find no meaning to his life. For twelve years he lived neither denying nor believing in anything. On the death of his much loved and admired uncle, Charles de Foucauld squandered his inheritance on an endless succession of parties and social activities and became in general a source of shame to his family.

He did, however, complete his studies at the Cavalry School at Saumur and served for a while with the French army in North Africa. In 1882 he went absent without leave and embarked on a hazardous exploration of Morocco. The work he undertook, disguised as a poor Jewish rabbi from Central Europe, on this reconnaissance expedition subsequently won him a gold medal from the French Geographical Society. It also brought him into close contact with the Moroccan people whose welcome, prayerfulness and faith in God touched him deeply as indeed it touched Madeleine Hutin's father during his years in North Africa. Charles de Foucauld wrote of how, during further reconnaissance work in the south of Algeria and Tunisia, 'Islam

9

produced in me a profound upheaval. . . . The sight of such faith, of those souls living in the continual presence of God gave me a glimpse of something greater and more real than worldly pursuits.' The experience was to be the catalyst for the rediscovery of his faith. Advised by his spiritual director to go on pilgrimage to the Holy Land, there the mystery of the life and death of Jesus was brought powerfully home to him. Above all, it was the message of Nazareth which touched him, the village which in St John's Gospel (1:46) provoked the question: 'Can there any good thing come out of Nazareth?', the place where Jesus led for thirty years a hidden life of extreme simplicity, working as a poor carpenter. It was not in the quiet seclusion of a chapel that Jesus of Nazareth became an overwhelming reality for Charles de Foucauld but in the noisy, bustling streets of a village in Palestine. There he was overwhelmed by the message of the incarnation, by renewed belief in the reality of a God who loved the world so much that he became one with humankind, a poor man amongst the poor.

In 1890 Charles de Foucauld entered the Trappist monastery of Notre Dame des Neiges where he became Brother Marie-Alberic. A few months later he moved to the Monastery of Akbès in Syria where he was found to be an exemplary member of the Order. In 1897, however, at his own insistence and with the co-operation of his superiors who had recognised in him a vocation which was in some way different and exceptional, he left the Trappists. His desire to identify himself with Jesus of Nazareth drew him irresistibly back to the Holy Land, where for three years as a servant of the Poor Clares in Nazareth he lived a life of extreme poverty, sleeping in a shed, cleaning floors, seeking out the most menial tasks and spending long hours in silent adoration of the Blessed Sacrament and meditation on the Scriptures. The Gospels were the key to his understanding of the life of God made man, and the Gospels taught him that the prime commandment was to love God with all his heart and mind and soul. The requirement to love took precedence over all else. The mystery of the humility of a God who had not merely been content to assume the human condition but chose to become the least of men so moved him that in the language of his day he referred frequently to this abasement of Jesus as 'abjection' and he sought himself to be the least considered. The love for God became for him inseparable from a life of poverty, labour, struggle and love of his fellow human beings. 'For me', he wrote during his time in Nazareth, 'it is not possible to say I love you without feeling an impelling desire to imitate you, and above all to share all the pains ... and hardships of your life.' He found the presence of Jesus in the Eucharist and to the end of his days sustained the desire to remain in the presence of the exposed Sacrament for as long as possible, but he also recognised Jesus in his fellow human beings. Charles de Foucauld himself claimed that the words of Jesus in St Matthew's Gospel, 'Whatsoever you do to the least of these my brethren, you do to me', turned his life upside-down. They were also the unifying factor in his life. Gradually the conviction grew in him that to love Jesus meant sharing in his work of salvation and redemption, and becoming in his footsteps the brother of all people but especially of those who did not yet know the love of Christ. At the age of forty-three he was ordained into the priesthood, a vocation which he had hitherto feared might remove him from his ideal of poverty and his desire to occupy the last place, but which now he accepted as a means of bringing Jesus in the Eucharist to the most forsaken. The most forsaken, he believed, he would find in the Sahara. 'I'm getting ready to go to the Sahara to continue "the hidden life of Jesus of Nazareth",' he wrote in a letter shortly after his ordination, 'not to preach but to live in solitude the poverty and humble work of Jesus, whilst trying to do good to souls, not through words but through prayer, through offering holy Mass, through penance and through the practice of charity.'

At Beni-Abbes, not far from the Algerian border with the Morocco he loved, he settled amongst the isolated people of the desert, wanting to live a life of prayer centred upon the presence of Jesus in the Eucharist, but wanted, too, to be a brother to all the local inhabitants. He placed himself at the disposal of the poor soldiers, of the local slaves, of passing travellers regardless of their religious commitment. Accordingly the Arabs began to call the humble dwelling he built there the *khaoua*, meaning 'fraternity'. It was an appellation which appealed to the man who by then was calling himself 'Brother Charles'. To his cousin, Marie de Bondy, he wrote: 'I want all the inhabitants, Christians, Muslims and Jews to get used to seeing me as their brother. They begin to call this house the "fraternity" and it is so good to hear that.'

To the south of Beni Abbes lay desert terrain into which no other priest would venture but where the Touareg led their nomadic existence. Word came to Brother Charles of a Touareg woman who rescued her injured enemies from a battlefield, took them into her

11

home, nursed them back to health and then had them repatriated to Tripoli. It was a gesture which found a resonance in Charles de Foucauld who felt increasingly impelled, despite his personal reluctance to leave Beni Abbes, to make the journey through the desert to the mountainous part of the Ahaggar in the extreme south of Algeria. Charles de Foucauld saw the desert as a profound and necessary ingredient of the spiritual journey. In the desert, he claimed, there was an emptying of the self. Its vast arid expanses had a way of disposing of everything within one that was not of God. The soul was emptied leaving room for God alone. In biblical history the Hebrews had gone through the desert, Moses had lived in it before he received his mission. St Paul, en route to Damascus, had traversed the desert. 'It is indispensable,' asserted Charles de Foucauld.

> It is a time of grace. It is a period through which every soul wanting to bear fruit has to pass of necessity. Silence is needed, that recollectedness, that forgetfulness of all creation wherein God builds his Kingdom and forms the inner spirit – the intimate life with God – the conversation of the soul with God in faith, in hope, in charity.

Later, he maintained, the soul would bear fruit in the exact measure by which the inner self had been formed.

After a year's journeying of some 1,500 kilometres through the desert, for part of the time in the company of the French military columns which patrolled the desert, Charles de Foucauld had come into contact with many of the Saharan peoples. Finally he settled at Tamanrasset. Dressed in a flowing white *gandourah*, on his breast was sown a red heart, surmounted with a cross. The symbol was a reflection of his deep devotion to the Sacred Heart of Jesus and 'so that I remember God and men and women and love them.' He befriended the Touareg people, learning their language in order to understand and draw closer to their culture. He transcribed the poems sung round the Touareg campfires in the desert night, in an effort to transmit the history and the 'soul' of this nomadic people, and he worked with meticulous care on a translation of the Gospels into Tamahaq, the written language of the Touareg, and on a French-Touareg dictionary. The years 1906–7 brought a great famine to the area, during which Charles de Foucauld shared all that he had in an attempt to alleviate the suffering of the poverty-stricken people around him. It was at this point, however, that he himself fell gravely ill, largely as a result of under-nourishment and disregard for his own welfare. His illness became the means by which he learned what it was not just to give but to receive. The Touareg brought him goats' milk and nursed him back to health and through reciprocity the friendship deepened. The 'hidden life' for Charles de Foucauld did not mean a life removed from people and the potential for such friendship. What was 'hidden' in the life of Jesus of Nazareth was the mystery of the incarnation. Even when in 1911 Charles de Foucauld built a 'hermitage' more than 2,000 metres up in the mountains of the Ahaggar it was not so much in pursuit of solitude as of the tribes who brought their flocks and herds to graze on the high mountain pastures.

Charles de Foucauld had long dreamed of founding a congregation which would be the realisation of his ideal, the life of Nazareth. He had written both constitutions and rules for a community of Brothers and Sisters. He had even started to build with the idea of 'making ready a nest' for them. Among his written resolutions the expressed intention to do everything he could to 'establish and develop the Little Brothers and Little Sisters of the Sacred Heart of Jesus' was a frequently recurring refrain. Yet he remained alone in his life of rigorous poverty and commitment to his 'apostolate of kindness', proclaiming the gospel not by words but by example and endeavouring to live each day as if that evening he would be called upon to die a martyr's death.

In 1904 he wrote:

> Unless the grain of wheat falls into the ground and dies it remains alone. I am not dead, therefore I am alone. Pray for my conversion so that in dying I may bear much fruit . . . Jesus wants me to build this double family [Little Brothers and Little Sisters]. How can I work to this end? By imploring, by offering myself, by dying, by sanctifying myself, by loving Him . . . Our Lord is in a hurry. This hidden life of Nazareth, so poor, so abject and recollected is not imitated.

When in 1914 the First World War broke out, Charles de Foucauld's initial impulse was to return to France to serve as an ambulance man on the front line. At that stage the French military authorities directed him to remain in the Ahaggar. Even there, however, the conflict had its repercussions. Two years later, he moved into a *bordj* or fortress constructed in Tamanrasset for the protection of the local population.

13

As the hostilities in the area increased, he was advised to place himself under the protection of a nearby French military post. Despite the danger, however, he opted not to abandon the people of Tamanrasset and on 1 December he was murdered by a group of Senoussist Touaregs, partisans of the Sultan Ahmoud.

To follow Jesus in the way advocated by Charles de Foucauld during his lifetime would have been to go against the tide of contemporary European attitudes, marked as they were by considerations of industrial power, colonial expansion and, in the religious context, by missionary activity which was frequently not altogether free of associations with conquest, superiority and power. Only a few years after his death, however, in René Bazin's account of the life and death of Charles de Foucauld Madeleine Hutin found the ideal for which she had been yearning. Charles de Foucauld was for her, she would later explain, the incarnation of all the love for Muslims instilled into her by her father, and it was as if his life gave expression to all that she was quietly harbouring within her. The terms in which Little Sister Magdeleine described retrospectively the nature of her early vocation were on the whole imprecise. She spoke of being drawn to Africa, to the desert, to Islam, of a love of the poor, of a calling to the religious life. She told of how she had felt herself called to a succession of different vocations each of which would in time be fulfilled by the various orientations of the congregation she later founded. As a very small child she had been strongly attracted to gypsies, so much so that her grandmother had told her she would end her days in a gypsy caravan. She would run to them when others chose not to notice their presence and she felt deeply the disdain with which they were for the most part treated. In 1931 she visited a leper hospital in Valbonne. Much later she would refer to how her close contact with the lepers had awakened in her dreams of a calling associated with them. Father Voillaume, founder of the Little Brothers of Jesus and close companion of her spiritual journey, described her initial calling as a 'missionary vocation'. It is from her description of her own response to the life by René Bazin, however, that the nature of her vocation may perhaps best be inferred. What she saw in the life of Charles de Foucauld that so attracted her was the concrete, living expression of the gospel message, total poverty, a life buried at the very heart of people whom all others had forsaken and, above all, love in all its fullness. Having read his biography, all she believed she had to do was follow in the footsteps of a man who had given his life to the poor of the Sahara in a way that was radically different from the methods of other contemporary religious congregations, namely not by remaining apart and in a sense above those to whom he was committed but by sharing their lives as one of them. Charles de Foucauld had been prepared to go to the ends of the earth to 'cry the gospel with his life' and if necessary to die in the process.

There is evidence to suggest that Madeleine Hutin and Charles de Foucauld were not dissimilar in temperament. The walls of the narrow building which Charles de Foucauld constructed out of stones and baked clay and branches in Tamanrasset, Algeria, at a time when the village consisted of just 'twenty fires', and in which he lived and prayed for nearly eleven years, are adorned with snippets of his writings and the meticulous plans he made for other structures. These and other handwritten accounts bear witness to the same neatness, precision, practical ability and attention to detail as characterised the work of Madeleine Hutin. In his rule for the congregation he had hoped to found, he covered every contingency with extraordinary exactitude. The plan for the 'fraternity' specified every door and window and even the distance that should be left between the bars at the windows. He also stipulated that there were to be no newspapers in the house, not even old newspapers, yet he himself received as many as thirty newspapers every fortnight, keeping himself closely informed of the progress of world affairs.

What interested Madeleine Hutin about Charles de Foucauld was his love for Jesus but she also shared with him the kind of extreme temperament and conviction that was willing to die in the gospel cause and even yearned for such a death as an expression of love and a means by which she would draw closer to the object of her love. If Charles de Foucauld had written of his readiness to cry the gospel with his very life, for Madeleine Hutin also belief in the gospel message was not a question of mere words but rather of rendering it concrete. She read the spiritual writings of Charles de Foucauld and resolved to allow herself to be guided by him. Ill and bound by her duty to her mother as she was, she prayed nonetheless that the day of her departure for the Sahara or the Ahaggar might come quickly. Marriage and the possibility of a family of her own does not appear to have entered into her thinking. Why could one not have for God incarnate in Christ, she reasoned, a love that was as absolute and ardent as that which went into setting up a home and family? There was, she later acknowledged, no doubt in her mind that she was being

15

called to become one of the Little Sisters Charles de Foucauld had wanted so much. It was merely a question of when. The God to whom she frequently referred as the 'Master of time and of the impossible' was apparently in no hurry but to her the waiting seemed interminable.

She was distressed because, as she explained in the introduction to the diaries and documents she published in 1981 under the title of *Du Sahara au monde entier* (*He took me by the Hand*), the life was welling up in her and she did not understand at the time that illness and suffering, 'far from being sterile, could be the most marvellous and fruitful way of serving and giving of oneself'. She would have reached such an understanding by the time in July 1941 she gave a succession of talks to sick people in sanatoria in the region of Hauteville. She would also be able to speak of her own experience of illness as a young person: 'Like you, I have known long sleepless nights, harsh hours of fever, endless stays in bed at a time when I was young and life was bubbling up in me ... I knew those long periods of anguish during which everything is called into question.' It was as if her youthful existence as others perceived it, that of the dynamic, cheerful young woman who was so actively involved in working for others and who derived much pleasure from life in all its diversity, were quite distinct from the inner life she later chose to describe: that of the invalid, waiting for the impossible fulfilment of a vocation, who in some sense already knew the desert emptiness which she was convinced only God could fill. In later life she wrote of how throughout that period she longed only for the day when she would leave for the Sahara. Others said she spoke of Charles de Foucauld but only very little. Her private preoccupation did at times find its way into her church activities, providing the theme for a 'tableau vivant' she produced. It depicted the successors to Charles de Foucauld: on a pure white altar stood a beautiful monstrance, while at the foot of the altar was a group of Little Brothers and Little Sisters with, beyond them, a group of Arabs, old and young. When she spoke of her 'dream' however, in which, as Little Sister Magdeleine would later explain, the desert nomads, gypsies and lepers were somehow mingled without any apparent logic, she all too frequently met with ridicule.

Despite the fact that she felt no real vocation to be a teacher, Madeleine took up a position as headmistress of a boarding school run by the Sacred Heart nuns in Nantes. The nuns were in need of someone to fill the post and the time had come for their former pupil to repay the moral debt she owed them for the boarding school education she had received free of charge. She had not been to university and in later life would lay no claims to great intellectual competence but she had the necessary diplomas and in 1917 or 1918 had passed her baccalaureate, which in those days was quite a rare achievement for a girl. Her qualifications were apparently adequate to enable her to take charge of a school, and with a heavy heart Madeleine Hutin parted from her friends in Aix-en-Provence and moved to Nantes, taking her mother with her. Those who, even in regretting her departure, predicted that she would soon be achieving great things in Nantes, were to be proved correct. Despite her denial of any natural attraction to the teaching profession Madeleine had a gift for inspiring her young pupils. She was of average height, but broad shouldered with a physique which belied her actual frailty and gave her a natural authority. By her own admission, she knew what it was to be passionately interested in learning and the pursuit of knowledge. It was simply that for her the call of the desert was stronger than her love for family, native land or study.

The Sacred Heart school in Nantes proved to be fertile ground for her ready supply of ideas. In later life she would claim that from her earliest years she had recognised the incomprehension that existed between the different social classes, nations and races by virtue of what she saw as a 'grave lack of the justice and charity of Christ'. Those educated by the Sacred Heart sisters had a reputation for forming something of a clique with an 'old girls' network that guaranteed them a wide range of openings in life. During the eight years she spent in a position of authority at the Sacred Heart boarding school in Nantes she set about making it open to a wider range of social classes. Founded in 1840, it had both an old and a new chapel, both of which featured prominently in the projects of its new directress. The Sacred Heart school was set in sizeable grounds beyond which lay a housing estate for, among other people, railway employees. The housing estate was some distance from any parish church. It did not take Mlle Hutin long to decide that the residents of the estate should at least have the opportunity to attend mass on Sunday if they felt so inclined, and to make up her mind that the solution was simple: they should be welcome to attend a public mass in the private chapel hitherto reserved for the Sacred Heart pupils. The nuns were duly subjected to Madeleine Hutin's most persuasive powers. Authority from the archbishop was less readily forthcoming. Repeatedly, Madeleine applied for interviews only to be refused until finally her persistence eroded even the resistance of the Church authorities. In the spacious new chapel, together with a chaplain, she initiated meetings for the local men. Film shows were laid on and it was Madeleine Hutin who operated the projector.

The old disused chapel was to have its role in the raising of funds needed for a school for the children of the local workers, an idea which was yet another of her innovations. The staff of the Sacré Coeur were in agreement provided the wherewithal could be found to pay the teachers. After consultations with experts in the field, Madeleine Hutin settled on the idea of raising the necessary funds by breeding Angora rabbits for their fur. The old chapel would provide the ideal accommodation for them. For all the energy she put into these various enterprises, however, Charles de Foucauld, the desert and the people of Africa remained unforgotten. In Nantes Madeleine met Father Baeteman, a missionary and Lazarist priest who had just returned from Abysinnia (Ethiopia) where he had been obliged to conceal his religious status in order to be able to remain there. Father Baeteman had written a book, *Camouflé du Bon Dieu*, relating the experiences he had undergone disguised as a travelling merchant in the most dangerous conditions. She was captivated by what was said of and by him. Her classroom and her office were adorned with evocative pictures of the Sahara desert: sand-dunes, palm-trees, camels and, presiding over all this, the smiling face of the man to whom she referred at the time as 'Father de Foucauld'. Little Sister Magdeleine herself described such displays as naive evidence of her impatience. Others accused her of Utopian dreams but no one actually dared to ask her to take them down, despite strict rules relating to the hanging of posters in the school.

Every evening a Polish Sister, Sister Boichak, would open up a small concealed door into the sacristy which gave access directly behind the tabernacle. Madeleine Hutin would go there to ask God for the opportunity to go to the Sahara and to die there. Whenever she asked Sister Boichak to lend support to her prayers, the older woman would invariably respond that for Madeleine at her age, in her frail condition, it would be madness. And Madeleine would equally invariably reply that what was madness in human eyes was often divine wisdom. At the age of eighty even if she were far more seriously ill, she protested, she would still be coming to the chapel every night to ask for the same grace. Father de Foucauld, she would point out, had said that Jesus was Master of the impossible. Such exchanges would conclude with the retort that her Father de Foucauld would end up turning her head. Madeleine wrote for a number of years to Mgr Nouet, the Apostolic Prefect of the Sahara in the small Algerian town of Ghardaia, telling him of her aspiration to come to the desert. In France Father Baeteman gave her his support and encouragement. He believed in her vocation in defiance of all opposition, telling her each time they met that she must not encroach on Providence but that he was certain that she would leave one day for Africa. The Abbé Chancerelle, however, a priest whom Madeleine recognised as remarkable for his humility and spiritual qualities and who for some seven years gave her spiritual guidance, was less obviously encouraging, testing her belief in her vocation to the limits. In his prudence he considered that it would be madness for her to pursue such a calling, even going so far as to forbid all reading and correspondence which might be likely to stimulate it. By 1935, however, Madeleine's persistence had begun to raise doubts in his mind.

Finally, what Little Sister Magdeleine referred to as 'the hour of God' came, just at the point when she had almost resigned herself to never fulfilling her religious vocation. By what seemed to her a stroke of divine irony the way was opened via the very thing which had always seemed to her the greatest obstacle: her ill health. Nantes with its damp rainy climate did not suit her. In March 1935 she began to experience violent pains in her left shoulder. In the course of a year the pain became so intense that she was obliged to give up all her activities. The doctors she consulted were divided in their opinions except when it came to one thing. They were unanimous in advising her to leave Nantes and go and live in a dry, warm climate. Some advised the south of France. A friend in Aix-en-Provence was dismayed when Madeleine returned there crippled with rheumatic pain: 'She confided her worries to me very simply, she feared paralysis and trembled at the prospect... because for all her extraordinary faith, she was still very human.' In May 1936, however, after examining a fresh X-ray, her doctor in Nantes gave her even more explicit instructions. He told her that she was suffering from an acute and deforming form of arthritis with decalcification and atrophying of the shoulder muscles. The shoulder would soon have to be immobilised in plaster. Then, little by little, the other joints would be deformed and she would probably be confined to an invalid bed for many years...

unless she went to live in a country where it never rained such as . . .
'the Sahara', Madeleine Hutin found herself interrupting.

After twenty years of waiting, the doctor was now advising her to
leave immediately. Her condition was already very advanced. A swift
departure would be the only means not of curing the existing damage
but, at least, of preventing it spreading further. Bearing a medical
certificate to this effect, Madeleine resorted once more to the Abbé
Chancerelle. Having read it, the priest paced up and down the room
and spoke to her with a vehemence she had not hitherto witnessed in
him. In the doctor's diagnosis he saw the sign for which for several
years he had been asking God in confirmation of her vocation. He
told her to leave at once for Algeria without even asking herself what
she was going to do there. She was to take a boat from Marseille to
Algiers where she would doubtless find a priest who would ask her
to help him. She was to follow him. But that would not be the end
of it. Little Sister Magdeleine would retain throughout her life the
image which the Abbé Chancerelle offered her next and use it herself
repeatedly to express the childlike helplessness with which she followed the path that was to be shown her. 'The Good Lord', the Abbé
told her, 'will take you by the hand and you will let him do it,
obeying him blindly without the least resistance.' 'God', Little Sister
Magdeleine would often subsequently explain, 'took me by the hand
and I followed him blindly.'

She saw the Abbé's final directive as the underlying explanation for
her long and difficult wait and the prophetic basis on which the future
foundation was constructed:

> 'Always remember this: it is because humanly speaking you are
> no longer capable of anything, that I can tell you with such
> assurance that you must go, because at least, if you ever do
> anything, it will be the Good Lord who has done everything
> because without him, you will be able to do nothing, nothing,
> absolutely nothing.'

Some five or six years later when the elderly Abbé was at death's door
he was still reproaching himself for having obstructed Madeleine's
vocation for so long. Once the doctor's diagnosis had been given,
however, it was as though the necessary 'open sesame' had been
provided in all quarters. Madeleine Hutin's health would still have
made it difficult for her to leave for Algeria on her own, but working
in the same school in Nantes was another young woman who had

come from Auray with similar aspirations to lead a life of extreme poverty amongst Muslims. Anne Cadoret too had been prevented from joining a religious congregation because of ill health. Without declaring his reasons for doing so, Father Baeteman had brought the two women together and once Madeleine's departure became an imminent reality he directed Anne to follow her and Madeleine to take Anne as her companion. Madeleine agreed to do so, without, it should be said, being fully aware of the fact that Anne had health problems. The last weeks before their departure for Algeria were spent in busy preparation. Every spare moment was devoted to studying Arabic. In Aix-en-Provence Madeleine had met a young Muslim girl who gave her classes in Arabic in exchange for coaching in arithmetic.

For Madame Hutin who had never wanted to go to North Africa even with her husband, it was not an easy step to take. She was torn between her personal reservations and her reluctance to let the daughter, for whose sake she used regularly to walk the full length of the market to ensure that she did not have to eat stringy beans, set off alone with only a young companion. Indeed, she remained undecided until the very last minute. Madeleine had opted first to go via Spain to reduce the length of the sea-crossing about which her mother was particularly apprehensive, but at that very juncture civil war broke out in Spain. Madame Hutin caught a chill. Madeleine resigned herself to leaving her mother behind, but when it came to the day of departure there were three passengers ready to board the ship to Algeria. On 6 October 1936, with very little notion of what lay ahead but almost beside herself with joy, together with her first companion and the elderly mother who was pleased at least to be still at her daughter's side, Madeleine Hutin set sail for Algiers and the 'land of Islam'.

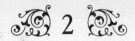

2

The Mystery of the Infant Jesus

THE SOIL OF AFRICA and of Islam – Madeleine Hutin's first step on to the crowded quay in the busy port of Algiers was a double source of joy. The three women were immediately accosted by a chattering, jostling host of small Arab children vying with each other to carry the new arrivals' luggage. To Madeleine their smiling faces were abundantly lovable yet around her, on the faces of her fellow passengers, she could see the traces of suspicion. Later she would write of how their hostile expressions instantly became a painful reminder of the reality of racial division. Physically she was in an even worse condition on arriving in Algiers than on leaving France. The Superior of the Daughters of Charity in Algiers surveyed her three guests with pity and incredulity when they informed her that their intention was to go into the Sahara. Otherwise their plans were quite undefined. The prophetic nature of the Abbé Chancerelle's directions were soon to be confirmed, however. Almost immediately and in a way which Madeleine Hutin saw as providential they did indeed meet a priest who was glad of their assistance. The Abbé Declercq, a very dynamic Frenchman serving at the time as priest in charge of Boghar and Boghari, small mountain settlements nestling in the Upper Plateaux at the northern edge of the desert about 150 kilometers from the Algerian capital, had heard of their arrival and came to ask for their help. Boghari had four hundred Christians and four hundred Jews amongst its population but the plan was to set up a work centre right in the heart of the much more substantial Muslim quarter. It was not the Sahara proper but it was at least to be a life of extreme poverty amongst the people of Islam. Within twenty-four hours everything had been decided. On 15 October, satisfied at last that she was following in the footsteps of Charles de Foucauld, together with her elderly mother and Anne, Madeleine moved into a very poor house occupied by several Muslim families.

22

Three days a week were devoted to providing medical aid in a dispensary, working with the local women and providing soup for the poor. Three more were spent going out to pay visits further afield. In an attempt to establish and maintain contact with the local nomads they covered long distances on foot, over difficult terrain. For all the frailty of her early years, Madeleine enjoyed physical exercise to the point of feeling deprived if she found herself too confined. She learned to ride and eventually managed to purchase a white mare from the local market. On the whole animals responded well to Madeleine's obvious affection for them, but in the course of one riding lesson she was obliged to throw herself off her mount as it galloped, out of control, towards a deep ravine. Having rolled for several metres and hit her head against a sharp rock in the process, Madeleine managed to get back on her feet, surprised to be still alive and laughing. She recorded the incident in her diary with the humour that crept into many similar accounts, but for her mother the incident was the last straw.

Madame Hutin did not share her daughter's attraction to the Sahara and its environs. She was used to a certain comfort and the stifling heat and rigours of the life Madeleine had chosen to lead were too much to take for an elderly woman who dreamed only of ending her days in peace. Madame Hutin had to be placed in the care of the Sisters of St Vincent de Paul in Algiers. Separation from her mother for the first time since the wartime tragedies which had decimated her family was, Madeleine maintained, the first great sacrifice Africa had claimed of her. The choice between her mother and the work she felt she was being called to do was by no means an easy one. Had she known that her mother would be unable to remain in Boghari, she insisted, she would never have had the courage to leave Aix.

Madeleine remained in Boghari, however. The work became overwhelming and all absorbing, so much so that there was little time for prayer or reflection. By day people invaded the house. At night the two French women were called out to deliver babies and tend to the sick. The queues for the dispensary grew ever longer. Soup had to be provided regularly for in the region of seventy people. The only relative peace the two women found was during the sorties they made into the mountains to places as yet unvisited by any Europeans or into the open desert to spend time beneath the nomad tents. Madeleine had wanted, not a cloistered religious life but at least, following the example of Charles de Foucauld, a contemplative life in the very midst of the Muslim world. The work she and Anne were undertaking in Boghari and its environs failed to satisfy what one of her closest companions would many years later describe as 'the absolute desire for God which was present in her from the beginning and which was not oriented towards activity'. Yet the need amongst the people for food and for medical care was so great. From a material point of view the venture was flourishing. After a period of extreme poverty during which they had known what it was to nourish themselves on only what was left in the bottom of the saucepan of soup they dispensed to the poor, the government of Algeria was even promising them the funds to construct a shelter for old people who had been abandoned. They could not simply forsake the project they had started and the people they had grown to love.

It was to reflect upon this problem and to seek a way forward that in March 1938 they made their way to El Golea, the oasis in the Sahara to which in 1927 the body of Charles de Foucauld, first buried further south in Tamanrasset, had been moved. They had learned from a newspaper article that there on 19 March the Church of Saint Joseph, constructed next to his tomb, was to be consecrated. The women had no money for the journey and the Abbé Declercq was away and could not be informed of their proposed absence but for Madeleine the occasion was an irresistible opportunity to pray at the tomb of the one to whom she turned constantly for inspiration. It was also to prove significant in that it brought her for the first time into contact with Father Voillaume, founder and Prior General of a male congregation already established on the basis of the spiritual legacy of Charles de Foucauld. A companion of Madeleine Hutin and Anne Cadoret for part of their journey to El Golea was to share Father Voillaume's lodgings at Saint Joseph's. On his arrival he spoke of his travelling companions to Father Voillaume who had arrived at the oasis after twelve days of travelling by camel across the desert. Father Voillaume, who had already some time previously received a letter from Madeleine Hutin telling him of her desire to follow in the footsteps of Charles de Foucauld, expressed an interest in meeting them. René Voillaume was ostensibly a rather withdrawn man whose natural shyness was concealed by an authoritative intellect and a sometimes forbidding manner. Yet beyond the apparent differences between his temperament, which was essentially that of a man of reason and prudence, and that of the apparently much more impulsive Madeleine Hutin, there lay deeper points of union and understanding.

Born in Versailles in 1905, by the age of seventeen René Voillaume had experienced a call to be both a missionary and a priest. 'I was thinking of becoming a missionary,' he explained in his historical account of the origins of the Little Brothers of Jesus. 'What attracted me was (1) the evangelisation of simple souls and (2) the suffering and resemblance of the missionary life to that of Jesus Christ and the apostles, and a secret desire for martyrdom.' He also wrote of an experience he underwent during his late teens. It was an experience which defied rational comprehension and which he took to be a 'direct intervention of Christ who wanted me to consecrate myself to him and to his Eucharist'. It occurred after the young man had just received communion. The monstrance containing the Blessed Sacrament had been placed under a baldachin above the tabernacle. As he knelt, head bowed in prayer, he felt himself transported in what he could only describe as a very powerful inner vision towards the monstrance where he penetrated the Host in a manner which defied both words and explanation: 'It was as if I was merging with the Blessed Sacrament.' At the same time he felt overwhelmed by a powerful sense of grace which brought about an immediate inner change in him, a fact which Father Voillaume would later claim made more of an impression on him than the vision itself. The effect of the experience was to centre his spiritual life upon the Eucharist and the Sacred Heart.

When, like Madeleine Hutin, he read René Bazin's biography of Charles de Foucauld shortly after its publication, he too was fired with enthusiasm for the example it offered, so much so that he would remember many years later the exact place where he first read the book: in the living room of his family's flat in Paris. The book came as a profound shock to him. In the life of Charles de Foucauld he found the response to all his missionary aspirations, his attraction to the monastic life and to adoration of the Blessed Sacrament. In October 1923 he entered the seminary of Saint-Sulpice at Issy-les-Moulineaux and in 1925 boarded a ship from Marseille to Algeria to join the White Fathers, the society of Missionaries of Africa founded in Algeria in 1868, whose members made up of priests and brothers were bound by solemn oath to lifelong work in the African mission. Ill health soon obliged him to return to France, however, and it was during a second period at the seminary at Issy that he found among the four hundred seminarists a group who shared his special interest in the life and spiritual writings of Charles de Foucauld. Gradually the desire he had been harbouring for some time to embark upon an apostolate similar to that of Charles de Foucauld began to seem more realisable. It was at this point that the Rule written down by de Foucauld in 1899 and conceived in Nazareth fell into the hands of the group of men aspiring to form a congregation in his spirit. They were captivated by the ideal expressed in its pages, but perhaps even more so by the spirit of humility, brotherly love, and gospel simplicity which emerged from the Rule.

By the time René Voillaume met Madeleine Hutin for the first time on a garden path outside the cell he was occupying at El Golea, the Little Brothers of the Sacred Heart, as Charles de Foucauld had wanted to call his fraternity of Brothers and as the society founded by Father Voillaume was accordingly first known, were well established. On 3 February 1936 a Decree from the Congregation of Propaganda Fide in Rome had formally recognised them as a diocesan congregation. Since 1933 the Little Brothers had been leading an essentially monastic life at El Abiodh Sidi Cheikh, a small village in the Southern Oranais in northern Algeria, which had grown up on the banks of a wadi which when in flood formed a sizeable river and thus a suitable watering point for numerous nomads on their journey between the High Plateaux and the Sahara. At that time the inhabitants of the tiny cluster of baked clay houses forming an oasis in the desert sand consisted almost exclusively of the family of the local caid, the Algerian administrator who formed part of the French administration, and their servants. The area had also been the home of Sidi Cheikh, a sixteenth-century Sufi of whom it was said that he could work miracles. Not far from the domed white monument which marked Sidi Cheikh's tomb, the Little Brothers were occupying a large building with extensive grounds which had originally belonged to the French military authorities, had subsequently passed into the hands of the local caid and finally been bought by Father Voillaume for his by then quite large community. The Little Brothers' sizeable chapel was built in the style of the local *koubbas* but initially all the work they undertook was within the confines of the high walls which surrounded their vegetable gardens and livestock; and their life was essentially that of cloistered contemplatives living in community in the desert. Their days and their nights were punctuated with the traditional monastic offices and they kept grand silence.

Certain differences existed between Little Sister Magdeleine and Father Voillaume in their understanding of the appropriate means of according with the intentions of Charles de Foucauld. Madeleine Hutin had come to Algeria as a result of a largely personal missionary vocation and not with any idea of founding a congregation. For her the realisation of the ideal she had found rendered concrete in the life of Charles de Foucauld was beginning to crystallise into the idea of sharing the life of the desert people by actually living as they did in a tent. From their earliest days the Little Brothers, on the other hand, had affirmed the importance of the cloistered life set down in Charles de Foucauld's Rule. To Little Sister Magdeleine, however, the fact that Father Voillaume's essentially monastic vision was somewhat at variance with her own did not detract from her deep regard for him as someone who could cast light upon the spirit of the one whom both sought to follow. In the tall, thin, bearded man who had ridden through the shifting desert sands astride a camel, dressed in a white robe of coarse wool, adorned with the heart surmounted with a cross, she identified at once a likeness to Charles de Foucauld.

Throughout the mass in dedication of the Church of St Joseph she noted how he sat in a shadowy corner leaving the attention to be focused on the White Fathers who had initiated the ceremony. Afterwards she asked to speak to him. An extract from her diary published in *He took me by the Hand* records how she told him about everything she wanted to do, especially about the life in a tent to which she felt so strongly attracted. In her account she wrote of how he listened to her with great kindness and agreed to correspond with her, but of how she would have been at pains to say whether or not he approved of her. Father Voillaume, for his part, did not notice anything extraordinary about the woman revealing to him what he would later describe as 'intuitions which she could not keep to herself' except perhaps the rational folly of her plans. Here was a woman virtually alone talking of Sisters living in the desert with the nomads in a tent. Years later he would remember the encounter well but not what he had said to her at the time. He had probably remained silent primarily because he was by nature inclined to silence but also because, as he pointed out, he did not yet know her. He could have no intimation then of the significance and dimensions of what was to follow. He did however arrange for her to come for a retreat at El Abiodh Sidi Cheikh during the following June. The gathering at El Golea also brought Madeleine into direct contact with Mgr Nouet, the Apostolic Prefect of the Sahara from Ghardaia, with whom she had already been corresponding. He told her that her work had won his confidence and that if ever the diocese of Algiers closed its doors to her, she would be welcomed in the Sahara.

On their return to Boghari, the two women went to inform the Abbé Declerq of their journey. In her published diary Madeleine wrote of how the Abbé seemed preoccupied and appeared to be trying to tell them something which he found hard to say. In fact the priest had a rather fiery temperament and was not unduly impressed that they had gone off without saying anything. In their absence it transpired that his sister had been appointed general superior of a congregation of Sisters in Boghar and, knowing that the work at Boghari did not correspond entirely with Madeleine Hutin's vocation, brother and sister had made plans to incorporate the work in Boghari into part of the missionary activity of the Sisters at Boghar. What Madeleine immediately perceived as the answer to the prayers she had offered at the tomb of Charles de Foucauld had come rather sooner than anticipated and it was not without certain regrets that she accepted the idea of abandoning the Arab friends she had grown to love to set off once more into the unknown. Humanly speaking it was folly to abandon work which was so well established in order to pursue an uncertainty but Madeleine saw in the events which had led to such a step once more the hand of God which she could only blindly follow and the fulfilment of the Abbé Chancerelle's prediction that the work undertaken initially in Algeria would not be the 'end'.

In May 1938 Madeleine Hutin and Anne Cadoret went once more to see Mgr Nouet to remind him of his promise at El Golea that the Sahara would be open to them, should they decide that they wished to go there. Madeleine was by then experiencing a need for some form of spiritual renewal after the surfeit of activity in Boghari. She still had no intention of founding a new congregation. She did not want, she had told a friend in France, to be a foundress. The prospect terrified her. What she requested of the Apostolic Prefect, Mgr Nouet, was to spend a few months of silence and reflection as preparation for leading a more authentically religious life. First, however, she and her companion would attend the retreat at El Abiodh as previously arranged with Father Voillaume. Her diary entry for 31 May 1938 recorded the fact that on their arrival the Little Brothers gave them lodgings in what had once been a hospital run by the White Sisters and provided them with meals. The Little Brothers' food was, she commented, really poor. Their water tasted horrible. Such was the extreme poverty of Charles de Foucauld. In the great silence of the

28

desert they spent a week's retreat, Madeleine was struck by the beauty of the Little Brothers' chapel, and by the *Veni Creator* sung in Arabic. Of her time spent with the man who was to become her spiritual confidant and director for many years, her published diary recorded simply: 'During this retreat, I saw Father Voillaume several times'.

After the retreat Madeleine returned briefly to France to visit her mother who was by then living in Aix, unable to tolerate any longer the life in Algeria where, she pronounced, 'everything tasted of mud'. The departure once more for Africa was by no means easy. Friends reproached her for leaving her mother but Madame Hutin, despite the fact that she did not fully understand her daughter's as yet unclearly defined vocation, was nonetheless courageous through her tears and defended her going. In Algiers the White Sisters had agreed to take Madeleine and Anne into the noviciate at Saint Charles-Birmandreis for six months. It was a period of trial during which Madeleine claimed that, like any other novice, she had to pass through the 'arid desert in which the heart is often severely battered but in which the Lord sometimes comes to console'. It was also a period of great joy because, as she pointed out without further explanation in her diaries, the little infant Jesus was the companion of her journey. For her the desert invariably brought with it its particular grace. Years later, not insignificantly, she would write that the grace of the desert was 'solitude, silence, prayer, smallness, poverty, deprivation, simplicity, abandonment of self, charity, gentleness, peace and joy'. 'It is all these things', she explained, 'because it creates in us an immense vacuum which God fills with his presence.'

Madeleine Hutin was a woman firmly rooted in concrete reality, who in expressing her religious beliefs constantly resorted to the tangible and the practical. She believed fundamentally that the mystery of God should be respected rather than deliberately explored and was inclined to be sceptical about purported manifestations of the supernatural. In 1950 during a journey through Lebanon she would visit the tomb of a Maronite saint who had spent many years as a hermit and who, both during his lifetime and after his death, was credited with the capacity to bring about healings and conversions. In her account of her visit, Little Sister Magdeleine reported how his body was said to be miraculously preserved and to give off a sweet odour. 'I seemed to smell it too,' she wrote, then added: 'but as that might well be imagination, I shan't make too much of it . . .' The fear that she might in some way become the victim of illusion or imagination and her rejection of 'extraordinary ways' were to remain with her throughout her life. Nor did she wish to encourage members of the congregation she would found to seek to pursue such ways. It was partly at least for this reason that she did not speak to her Little Sisters until 1974 of what she referred to even then only somewhat obliquely as the 'graces' she had received during her time at Saint Charles. In a letter written to them on 8 December of that year, endeavouring to add a further dimension to what she had been telling them about the infant Jesus for the past thirty-five years, she decided to confide in them, ('and why shouldn't I because now people no longer conceal the graces received'), that at Saint Charles the infant Jesus had asked her to 'bring him into the Fraternity to live there in the heart of each Little Sister'.

In 1991, just over a year after Little Sister Magdeleine's death, Father Voillaume felt it his duty as the 'only one who can witness to the truth and authenticity of these supernatural events' to shed a little more light on the nature of the 'graces' to which she referred. There was in Madeleine Hutin a certain childlike simplicity. She had promised God that she would always be as open with Father Voillaume as a little child, and that she would hide nothing from him. So it was that on 24 January 1939 she had written a letter to him in which she described, with characteristic insistence that she did so only in obedience, an experience she had had at the beginning of the year 1937, probably in January during the liturgical season of the Nativity and not long after she had arrived in Boghari. She knew the cynicism with which such claims were generally received, the accusations of an over-active imagination or excessive sentimentality to which she might render herself liable, and her own human pride and confusion made the disclosure a difficult one. Indeed at the time she had told no one, partly because she had not known whom to tell but primarily because she had put it all down to being a dream, 'though I only half believed that – because from that day on there has been a great change in me'.

The letter she wrote to Father Voillaume during her noviciate, two years after the actual event, described how after experiencing strong temptations against her commitment to chastity she had gone to bed that night in 1937 feeling frightened and upset, weeping inconsolably:

> – and suddenly I found myself in an inner courtyard which, by a strange coincidence, resembled the one in the noviciate. I can still see it as though it all happened only yesterday. Two or

three holy persons, whom I did not know, were walking before me – and at the end of the courtyard on the right, was the Blessed Virgin, holding the infant Jesus in her arms – an infant Jesus such as I could never have imagined in my life, for it surpassed all human vision. I cannot even describe it because I cannot find any other words for it than 'light', 'gentleness' and, above all 'love'. And the Blessed Virgin was preparing to give him to someone. What anguish! I was absolutely sure she would not give him to me, because my heart and soul were not pure enough to receive such a favour; and I stood back, crying more than ever because of my unworthiness. I didn't dare look – and yet, drawn to do so despite myself, I was more and more stupefied to see the first, then the second, then the third person pass in front of the Virgin Mary without noticing anything. They were in such a state of pious recollection but I would have liked to shout at them to look. So, I found myself all alone in front of this vision and . . . it was to me that the Blessed Virgin gave the little child Jesus she was holding. After that I no longer thought about my sins, but only of this joy which I cannot express in human words either. And in the great upsurging of my love, I embraced and clasped the infant Jesus so closely to my heart that he became incorporated into me – (and again this is something I don't know how to explain).

At Saint Charles-Birmandreis the scene became even more powerfully present to her. Despite admonishing herself for being guilty of what, in the language of the day, she referred to as 'spiritual gluttony', despite an endeavour to dwell on the sinfulness of her own nature, she found herself irresistibly driven to ask the Virgin to give her little child to her again. During Advent the desire became even stronger. She was struck by the thought that Jesus had found in Mary a 'paradise of delights' and yearned herself to be such a 'paradise'.

Then it was that I began to hear, very distinctly, words which were not coming from my own self. These words first of all: 'There is too much clutter in your heart and soul. For the baby to be entrusted to you, you must clear it all away.' These words 'clear away', 'clutter', I heard them constantly for ten to fifteen days, every time I turned in on myself or sought to satisfy my own heart. I was almost tired of hearing them.

31

The author of the letter laid claim to a heart that was very troublesome in its tendency to unreserved attachment:

> From the beginning my novice mistress became the object of such an attachment and I was too frequently preoccupied with thought of her, her presence – not in any immoral sense: she was far too holy and spiritual, full of God, to elicit love of a sensual sort; it would almost be sacriligious to think of that – but from the point of view of perfection, there was certainly something in me which was not yet sufficiently mortified and I could not say to Jesus that he was 'my only love'.

On 20 December, after many days of struggling with herself, she felt suddenly enlightened:

> . . . something so blinding that it penetrated to the depth of my soul; it was a cause of real suffering, and at the same time of joy at possessing the light. And it swept everything clean. And I understood so well what it was that was cluttering me up that I would have liked to tell the whole world: 'I have understood.'

Madeleine Hutin had not in any way envisaged the six initial months spent at the noviciate of the White Sisters as preparation for the foundation of a new religious congregation. Mgr Nouet, however, had decided otherwise. Before the first six months had been completed, he asked the White Sisters to keep the two women for a further six in order that they would have completed a full canonical noviciate and thus be able to go into the Sahara as religious. For Madeleine it was the fulfilment of a vocation she had harboured for many years and which hitherto she had been unable to follow. It was accordingly a source of great joy afforded her by the only voice which at the time she saw as entitled to show her the will of God. Her personal inclinations had not had a bearing on the decision. She had only therefore to follow the light she believed to be leading her. Following Mgr Nouet's visit on 27 December it was as if the upsurge of love and joy she experienced at the news he brought of her possible future in some mysterious way swept everything clean:

> And in a very palpable manner, tangible not so much to the external senses as to all the faculties of the heart and soul, the Blessed Virgin gave me her little child Jesus.

Madeleine Hutin was at a loss as to how to explain the experience. To Father Voillaume she protested:

> If another woman were to tell me this, I would treat her as over imaginative and sentimental.

Yet for all her inability to explain or give adequate expression to them, the 'manifestations' were convincingly clear to her:

> For three weeks after that day I lived in the most delightful intimacy with the baby Jesus, passing the time from morning to evening and into part of the night in conversation with my dear little companion, who was changing in appearance and growing – appearing at first so weak and touching, like the little 'bambinos' in Italian pictures. But alongside all the sweetness, what anxieties there were. Once again, each time I identified some imperfection in myself I experienced such fright at having lost his presence, and after begging ardently: 'Baby Jesus, don't leave – Blessed Virgin don't take him away from me', I would hear very clearly the words I was so thrilled to hear: 'I am here'.

On the eve of the following Epiphany when she arrived in chapel Madeleine was saddened to find that her novice mistress was not there. Her health had always given cause for worry and Madeleine began to think of how grieved she would be if the novice mistress had to leave. She tried to turn and check whether she had arrived but something irresistible seemed to prevent her:

> As though someone were holding my head still, and I heard the baby Jesus' voice so full of pain and love that it still upsets me terribly: 'You love her more than me'. This was the miraculous healing of everything in my love for her that was still too natural, and I have never again since then had to reproach myself for a fault of this kind.

Madeleine confided in Father Voillaume the manner in which the conversations continued and her own love of humility, obedience and purity of intention increased. She wrote to him of how she relived all the 'shameful failures' of her past life to a point where she wanted only to throw herself on her knees and ask forgiveness. One day, however, the voice she heard gave her to understand that she had been granted such an experience precisely because of her weakness, because she would have been unable to work the necessary transformation in herself alone.

> And with a love that moved me even more profoundly, the infant Jesus asked me to be so generous as to 'permit' him to leave so that I might embrace for love of him a more austere path: that of suffering and the cross – having no other devotion and no other love than those of the Crucifix . . . And so all the sweetness disappeared – but I found a new joy in love of suffering and of the cross and I asked God to permit me to suffer much. Besides, I do not know the meaning of what I now see before my eyes where once I used to see the infant Jesus: a very austere, very bare cross, planted within a heart – Does it mean I should mortify my heart more – or does it mean that a very difficult trial awaits me?

The January letter concluded with a reassertion of the writer's doubts about what her reaction would have been to other people experiencing such 'crazy things'. She professed to be tormented by the urge to write down in a notebook all the 'insights of her heart' and simultaneously by the desire to dismiss the impulse, but to every objection to the idea of a notebook, even to the fear that in the long run it would cause her to focus inwards on herself and feed her pride, she found an answer and when, finally, she started to write it was as if the first page were being dictated to her. In it she was to humble herself, acknowledge her iniquitous nature and her incapacity to attain of her own accord the insights which were entirely gratuitous gifts of God. If all this and other experiences of a similar nature came from her imagination she expressed her regret to Father Voillaume for wasting his time; if on the other hand they came from God there would be even more grounds for humility. Of one thing Madeleine was sure: she emerged from them with a greater desire for generosity and love. The least infidelity to the rule became a source of deep sorrow and she wanted to become small before God, the last amongst humankind.

The novice mistress to whom Madeleine had felt so particularly drawn was to leave Saint Charles-Birmandreis for a while. Her departure, and the loss of the 'intimacy of soul' it occasioned, intensified Madeleine's sense of solitude, which was already highlighted by the fact that Anne, the companion of her earliest days in Algeria, was experiencing doubts about her vocation. As far as Madeleine was concerned there were two clear elements in her own calling: one was that she had a vocation to the religious life. She had some time previously taken a vow of lifelong chastity but she yearned also to be bound by vows of poverty and obedience in their most rigorous form, insisting that for her any other way could only result in unhappiness. The second point about which she had no doubts was that she was to live in the spirit of Charles de Foucauld. Since her arrival in Algeria several congregations had in fact asked her to affiliate to them but Madeleine Hutin could not even consider the possibility. She had searched before for other congregations that corresponded to her vocation. Her mother could not really understand why, given the number of religious communities there were already in existence, nothing seemed quite to suit, but it was exclusively the vision Charles de Foucauld had offered which called to her. Recognising that Madeleine's vocation was unlikely to find its fulfilment in any existing religious order, Mgr Nouet called upon her to write down her plans and even the constitutions for a new congregation, at a time when she was experiencing a profound sense of solitude. She had moreover to commit her ideas to paper without being exempted from any of the other requirements of her noviciate life and with little experience on which to draw other than the months she had spent in Boghari. The plans for the congregation of which she was to become the foundress were laid in painful isolation.

By 7 June 1939 Mgr Nouet, who had sent Madeleine to the White Sisters to test the authenticity of her calling, had expressed his confidence in her. He had been to Rome and spoken to the Pope about the two women. Pius XII had shown a great interest in their vocation, stressing the importance of religious congregations being open to vocations from the indigenous population, and sending them his special blessing. On his return to Algeria Mgr Nouet resolved to pass on to an expert on canon law everything that Madeleine had written to date to ensure its canonical correctness. Madeleine herself wanted everything to be checked not only from such a standpoint but also from the point of view of its spirituality. She wrote to Father Voillaume,

> If everything were to be condemned, I would still be at peace, it would be God who wanted it that way. And I would have full assurance about whatever might be approved – since for several months I have suffered so much from the isolation of working out all these plans alone – no one here wanted to take any responsibility for advising me – and Mgr Nouet himself told

me that he would do no more than go along with me, since it was up to me to follow the insights that came to me from the Holy Spirit.

In what was a particularly difficult time for her the infant Jesus became once more a source of consolation in what she described as simultaneously 'much less and much more than a vision because it is a continual presence, the effect of which penetrates the whole soul – and at the same time, it does have some kind of shape'. In fact she identified two distinct baby Jesuses. One was in some sense which she did not fully understand a replacement for the novice mistress who had left her. This new novice master, whom since her novice mistress's departure she had sensed constantly at her side, left her no rest until she had done even the tiniest and apparently most insignificant things as perfectly as it was possible to do them – 'and with the same love with which I would approach martyrdom – for despite their insignificance they are steps along the path of obedience and humility'. The presence of the second baby Jesus who replaced this one seemed to Madeleine to coincide with those times when she turned in upon herself or when her thoughts dwelt too much upon her novice mistress. At such times the baby Jesus who appeared to her seemed to invoke pity and remorse. He was the abandoned baby whose expression of desolation invited her repeated reassurances that it was he whom she loved more than her novice mistress. Only when he had received such assurances would the 'novice master' return.

> Only two things bother me: the fact that this new novice master, so exacting when I am alone and no one sees me, lets me make the most stupid and humiliating blunders when everyone else is looking. True this provides me with excellent opportunities to practice humility, but I also have to try not to set a bad example to my companions. What's more, he's never displeased at the same time as my novice mistress – the more she scolds me and puts me down (if only you could see how good-heartedly she does it) the happier he is – Yet if she reproaches me for something, isn't it because I deserve it and she has the grace to see clearly?

There were other trials and humiliations which she was apparently required to undergo, not least of them the fact that for several months she found herself unable to attend community offices in chapel without dissolving into floods of tears so that it was difficult for her to make the responses to the rosary or join in other prayers. The thought of her present wretchedness, her past transgression, the overwhelming love of God of which she felt she would always be unworthy, her loneliness and uncertainty about the work that lay ahead, reprimands which she felt keenly because she feared the displeasure of God – the reasons for this surfeit of emotion were confused and manifold. As the uncontrollable attacks of weeping persisted, she confided in her confessor at the convent, telling him that her failure to respond to the prayers was due to laziness and disobedience to the Rule. The priest, however, questioned her closely and then assured her that there were no grounds for worry even if she did find herself unable to make the responses, assuring her that her tears could have a partly physical cause or that they could otherwise be a grace granted her by God. The worst that could happen would be that she would be made conspicuous. Initially this consideration did not concern her unduly but then, as if to compound her torment, she was required to change her seat in chapel to a place where she was right on the end, in front of a whole row of senior sisters. There the flow of tears which she was still quite unable to control was the cause of numerous reproaches. Madeleine felt deeply the humiliation of what she herself regarded as her ridiculous state, and all the more so because the mental and spiritual anguish was intermingled with physical suffering.

To her mother she wrote letters of reassurance, lamenting her own ineptitude when first she had been required to assist in the kitchens and the fact that human beings were less tolerant than God in judging actions by their results rather than according to the heart that had been put into them, but insisting that she was being well looked after. In fact Saint Charles-Birmendreis was by the sea and subject to precisely the kind of climatic conditions which Madeleine had been advised to avoid. The lack of physical exercise in the convent made her crave the arduous twenty-kilometre treks into the mountains of Boghari or even a forty-kilometre ride on horseback. Instead she spent dreadful nights crippled with violent cramps which forced her to get up. Walking around brought her relief from the cramps but not from the other pains which wracked her body from head to toe. She thought of Charles de Foucauld, whose sacristy, she knew, had also been too small, and she tried not to complain, but there were days when she felt that only a miracle would see her through the novitiate, or even through the day. Yet she was happy to suffer, she told Father Voillaume:

> Pray hard for me. I want to love Jesus infinitely, and my heart is too small for that. I have such a longing to go to Paradise in order to be at last united with him forever.

The last manifestation of the infant Jesus mentioned by Madeleine took place on 12 August 1939:

> During the Thanksgiving mass, the baby Jesus is there on the right, standing, standing on the bench. I don't see him, but he is there, so affectionate, all smiles – He puts his little arms around my neck, leans his head against mine – Is it really him? This contact is a purification of my whole being, such a profound renewal, such a desire to become as little as possible so that I may be a source of delight to him. I would like to hug him back. I don't dare.

For the first time, on this occasion she had a negative reaction to the presence:

> I became frightened because it was the first time that he was so affectionate. So, in the name of God and of the Blessed Virgin, I reviled him, ordering him to leave if he had come from the devil to weaken my resolve. He smiled even more, became even more delightful – and he stayed – How I beg him to forgive me for having treated him that way.

On 8 August 1939, Mgr Nouet gave his approval to the first constitutions of the new congregations and one month later the two women made their profession as religious. In the chapel of the White Sisters and in the presence of Mgr Nouet's representative, they formally put behind them their lay existence and their family names and became Little Sister Magdeleine of Jesus and Little Sister Anne of Jesus. It was, by Little Sister Magdeleine's own account, a very moving occasion during which she was profoundly aware that an initial stage was over and being superseded by another crucially important one. To her it was not insignificant that 8 September, the date of her vows, was the date which commemorated the birth of the Virgin Mary. It was also to be the date regarded as the foundation of the new congregation of the Little Sisters of Jesus.

Four days previously she had noted in her small neat handwriting in a notebook, which was most probably the one she had mentioned feeling inspired to write in her letter of 24 January 1939, the brief but all-important comment:

Only Jesus
'Mary kept all these things in her heart.'
'And Jesus was silent and answered nothing.'

When after her death some of the experiences about which Little Sister Magdeleine had chosen to keep silent came to light, they would come as a revelation even to many of the Little Sisters of Jesus who had lived in close proximity to her. For many it was precisely the ordinariness and the humanity of a woman who had herself been drawn to follow God through the human example set by Jesus, the humble carpenter in Nazareth, that were her most evident and her most appealing qualities. In the course of her life it would become apparent to most that for Little Sister Magdeleine spirituality was not a question of thinking, reasoning and logic but of transcending rational thought. She was manifestly not one who came to know God through clear images and careful argument, nor with the eyes of the body, but with an intuitive inner eye. To those around her she gave expression to these 'intuitions' for the most part only in terms of impulses which came to her as spontaneous convictions and which she did not endeavour to explain but sought rather to turn into concrete reality.

Little Sister Magdeleine does not appear to have explored the complex avenues of the unconscious rendered conscious, the paranormal elements of religious faith, nor even those maxims of scholastic philosophy which, in examining the manner in which supernatural truth is revealed to the individual, suggest that *Quicquid recipitur, per modum recipientis recipitur* – whatever is received is received in the manner of the receiver. Her experience of intimate union with the Christ-child was a means of preparation and a source of revelation. It centred her spiritual life on a particular aspect of the life of Jesus and pointed the way to the special focus of the congregation she was to found. In the light of it much of what she subsequently set out to do could be regarded as symbolic in that it exemplified the truth she believed to have been given to her by God in order that she might pass it on to her sisters, but she never used the claim to a privileged mystical experience to lend significance, grandeur or weight either to herself or to what she sought to express. Instead, on feeling herself impelled to make the mystery of the Nativity one of the centres of the spiritual life of her congregation, she sifted through the writings of Charles de Foucauld to establish whether it would conform with his spirituality and found a small section entitled 'Christmas' published in 1938.

Throughout her life Little Sister Magdeleine searched for an artist capable of reproducing in the form of a statue of 'Our Lady of the Whole World' the double gesture of Mary offering her child and of the infant Jesus holding out his arms, as though he himself were trying to escape from her hands in order to give himself to the world. 'No one understands this gesture – forever deeply engraved as it is in my mind's eye, in my heart; I can't change it, Mary herself showed it to me,' she would write in her notebook in 1944. It was an image that was full of movement and awkward to balance and Little Sister Magdeleine was never quite satisfied with numerous successive attempts by different artists to capture it. The precision of her requirements, which appeared at times to verge on the obsessive, would have been more readily comprehensible to some had they known of the powerful experience which lay at the roots of her exigencies, but for Little Sister Magdeleine it was not the experience itself which was of paramount importance but the spirit which it had communicated to her. Like Father Voillaume, in relation to his experience of 'fusion' with the Blessed Sacrament, she stressed the importance of the transformation brought about. Similarly the details of the statue were important only in so far as they conveyed a spiritual message, the same spirit which she sought to pass on to her new congregation. 'People can't manage to understand that it is through the eyes that this devotion will enter into the heart,' Little Sister Magdeleine wrote to Father Voillaume in October 1950 of her frustration at the failed attempts to convey a gesture which was central to the spirituality of the congregation. When in later years she looked at the statue of the baby Jesus she kept on her table it was not a statue that she saw but 'him, the real Jesus.'

Little Sister Magdeleine regarded the infant Jesus as the real founder of the Little Sisters of Jesus. Among the rare and indirect references to the supernatural inspiration of the congregation are words she wrote to her sisters in a letter dated 1 September 1949, on the tenth anniversary of the Little Sisters of Jesus. 'It is all his work. In its beginnings, it was not the work of any human being. You already know, and you will know even more one day, what the solitude of the beginning was . . .' 'Always remain', she directed them, 'little Sisters of no account, and when you are tempted to forget that, look at the crib of Bethlehem and the tiny child Jesus who was the true founder of the Little Sisters of Jesus.' 'A special light has come to us from the manger of Bethlehem,' state the Constitutions of the Little Sisters of Jesus, who are to maintain the 'tiny newborn baby of Bethlehem' at the source of their spirituality.

The infant Jesus which Little Sister Magdeleine felt to have been so mysteriously 'incorporated' into her had taught her that true holiness lay in becoming very little and very recollected, although not with the kind of recollection which focused inwards to the point of failing, like the 'holy people' of her vision, to see the proffered child. Jesus the novice master had taught her the nature of true humility learned through weakness, failures and faults, especially those made externally visible. She had learned that it was not vital to do great and spectacular things from a baby who carried with him a message of vulnerability, gentleness and weakness and who in turn would call forth tenderness and concern in others, but she never lost sight of the fact that this tiny child full of external helplessness was nonetheless God with his infinite power and intelligence. If at times her language could appear sentimental to a different generation, she knew the challenge of conveying the message of Bethlehem in a sophisticated age and even referred to the fact that the imparting of such a message with all its potential for appearing infantile would be a real test of her sisters' humility. Her own devotion to the child of the manger was neither sentimental nor precious. The baby Jesus, she would insist, was not something saccharine or spineless to her, but a source of strength.

On 3 September 1939 news had reached Saint Charles-Birmandreis of the outbreak of the Second World War. Two days later Mgr Nouet had arrived in a state of considerable anxiety wanting to know whether, in view of the desperate conditions the war was likely to occasion in the Sahara, the prospective Little Sisters of Jesus were still intent upon going there. The response was unhesitating. If as a consequence of the war they were destined to a life of extreme poverty, they would be following all the more faithfully in the footsteps of Charles de Foucauld. In the face of such conviction Mgr Nouet offered them a choice between three possible locations: Ghardaia, Ouargla and Touggourt which was a centre for the nomads. Little Sister Magdeleine's initial reaction was to opt for Ghardaia where the Apostolic Prefect himself resided. She was conscious of the radical nature of the life she and Little Sister Anne intended leading, devoid of the traditional separation between religious and the world surrounding them. She would have preferred to begin such a life where Mgr Nouet could see it for himself rather than be dependent on potentially uncomprehending reports of two European women living initially alone in a Muslim world. On 14 September the two women left the White Sisters and after a brief return to Boghari completed a 'prospecting' tour of the three proposed places. Ghardaia had a very dry climate but at the same time had numerous gardens surrounded by rocks and mountains. Touggourt, on the other hand, was situated at sea level and even below it. It was set in the real desert, completely flat but for seemingly endless undulating expanses of sand-dunes. Little Sister Magdeleine was still taking into account the possibility of her mother rejoining her in Algeria. In either place Madame Hutin would be able to live during the cooler winter months between 1 November and 1 May but Touggourt had the advantage of a railway station. Touggourt was also manifestly Mgr Nouet's first choice for them. It was a place where the French administrative presence was still in evidence. It was also a place where there was little work and little water but a centre upon which the people of the desert converged, some of them settling in small huts built out of palm fronds. Little Sister Magdeleine's vision of the congregation was still of a very small community of sisters who would spend part of the year living in a tent and sharing the lives of the nomads, but for the remainder of the time they would need more substantial accommodation.

A short distance from Touggourt, in a small village called Sidi Boujnan nestling on a sand-dune overlooking the vastness of the desert, the Little Sisters found a house once built for workmen employed to sink an artesian well there. The supply had proved insufficient to warrant their continued labours and the house had stood empty for a while during which the sandstorms of the Sahara had gradually begun to reclaim it. By the time it had been requisitioned by the French army it was half-buried in sand. The well, however, still remained with a limited supply of essential water. Nearby stood a small building erected in honour of a Muslim venerated for his outstanding spiritual qualities and known as a *marabou*, a name also given to the building to which the faithful came on pilgrimage. It was here that on 10 November 1939, amongst the nomad tents and the *zriba* huts of those who sought now to survive by a more settled existence, Little Sister Magdeleine and Anne came to found what, despite the more usual masculine associations of the word, they would call a 'fraternity'. The Arabs had referred to Charles de Foucauld's modest dwelling as a 'fraternity'. In this, the first of many such fraternities, Little Sister Magdeleine wished to continue the associated ideas of 'brotherly' love for all human beings, of gentleness towards even those who appeared the most arrogant or unjust, of kindness to all those who were in need.

On 10 November 1939 the two Little Sisters of Jesus officially took possession of the house at Sidi Boujnan which the soldiers had agreed to vacate. One week previously they had been brought an almost life-size plaster representation of the baby Jesus with two broken arms. They repaired its broken limbs with bandages and installed in on an old tea chest covered with a piece of red cloth at Sidi Boujnan.

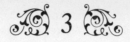

3

Human Before Religious

CHRISTMAS IN THE SAHARA: 'It is so moving to experience it here amidst the destitution of these poor nomads who suffer so greatly at this time of war,' wrote Little Sister Magdeleine in her diary entry for 26 December 1939. 'That is why we wanted the baby of the manger to be a source of joy to all around us.' That morning she and Little Sister Anne had set out beneath a cluster of palm trees an array of small toys, cakes, oranges and sweets, and the children had come quietly to pick out what they wanted. There in a setting of sand-dunes which extended as far as the eye could see, where people knew the meaning of real need, there was a conspicuous absence of jostling and pushing, and when the children had received their gifts, it was time to load up two mules with bread and dates and ensure that the occupants of the nomad tents ate their fill at least that day. That evening the deafening celebratory sounds of trumpets, rattles and drums resounded late into the silence of the desert darkness.

Little Sister Magdeleine had become architect, mason, labourer and joiner all rolled into one. Sleeping at night in lodgings nearby, by day she and her companion laboured tirelessly. The neglected house stood in nearly a hectare of land. The building itself must be cleared of the all-intrusive sand, the military lavatories must be removed from the centre of the courtyard and the accommodation extended to suit the requirements of the 'fraternity'. Like Charles de Foucauld before her, she laid out the outline for the walls of her proposed new inner courtyards with pebbles in the sand. The construction was to be made out of clay and very basic, but there were to be a number of large courtyards: one for the chapel, one for any Arabs in need of hospitality, one for the Little Sisters and one for the animals. Inside the house there was to be no furniture, only cupboards and niches hollowed out of the walls. The chapel was to be beautiful in its poverty, a 'real call to prayer in the midst of the desert', and outside, on the highest point

44

of the dune, she made plans for a *koubba*, a small religious shrine consisting of a cupola resting either on walls or pillars to accommodate a statue of 'Our Lady of the Sahara'.

The construction provided some of the local people with the work they so desperately needed. In their tents the women spun or wove. The men made belts, slippers or ropes out of camel hair or palm fibre, but the Little Sisters' building work provided them with a much needed additional source of income. The children too came to work on the site, the older ones keeping the masons supplied with small stones which the younger ones prised out of the sand. Every morning the children would come begging for the work which they knew would at least guarantee them their evening meal. The tents surrounding the fraternity gradually increased in number until the Little Sisters were obliged to sell their mule to provide the workmen's wages. For them the labour was exhausting and sometimes disheartening when the wind blew and the sand which had been so laboriously transported away was redeposited where the new foundations had not as yet been begun. Yet the construction work gradually progressed. Around the as yet uninhabitable fraternity they planted thirty date palms. In February their first postulant arrived, full of enthusiasm, from France, but she was a woman in her fifties and the life of hard labour and deprivation she found in Sidi Boujnan was a far cry from what she had anticipated. One morning in April, as the sisters were walking to the site with their tools over their shoulders and their buckets in their hands, having had nothing to eat for breakfast but raw onions and very little water in which to wash, Marie threw down her bucket in desperation. Such conditions were too harsh for her. She decided to leave. A second postulant who had arrived in March went a few days afterwards.

By the time they left, however, the *koubba* of Our Lady of the Sahara had been completed in defiance of the opinions of the pundits who had announced the task impossible in such a location. In this as in many other instances for Little Sister Magdeleine the word 'impossible' was merely a stimulus to more concerted effort. If the local masons regarded the task as impossible the Little Sisters would do it themselves. Work also began swiftly on a small *koubba* of the Sacred Heart in the central courtyard of the fraternity. Little Sister Magdeleine was absent for a few days transporting medicines, clothing and animal feed by mule to the nomads of Taibet who were, if anything, even poorer than those in the immediate vicinity of Touggourt. On her return she found the cupola complete. Athman, a mason who together with his younger brother, Tahar, would labour with extraordinary dedication and devotion on the construction of the fraternity, had struggled to erect it before her return. The fact that the cupola was not precisely square on its axis did not fail to attract the instant attention of Little Sister Magdeleine's exacting eye but she was touched by his attempt to surprise her and he took the unspoken criticism in her initial reaction in good part and subsequently rectified the error.

Little Sister Magdeleine's concern for the plight of the poor, the provision of medical care, food and work, the fact that the sisters were prepared to work alongside the labourers and once a week to sit and drink tea with them – all these factors touched the hearts of the local Arab people. Above all, however, at a time when the prevailing attitudes of French colonialism made such an approach rare, it was her trust in them and respect for each and every individual which made its mark. The local French administrator wanted to provide her with a guard but she declined it. She spoke little Arabic but she had a gift of communication which did not require many words. It was a gift of which she was aware: 'I love them', she once wrote, 'and my eyes tell them so.' Because of this love she could go off into the desert confident of her safety, knowing that the local people had already begun to see her as one of them and that even in her absence the process of construction would continue. It did not matter that she was Christian and they were Muslims. She wanted to live among Muslims as a witness of Christ's love for all, but this did not detract in any way from her sincere regard for their commitment to their own religion. Like Charles de Foucauld and indeed her own father before her, she was stirred by the rhythm of the Muslim devotions, by the resonance of the call to prayer and the manner in which even in the emptiness of the desert people knew instinctively when it was time to pray, stopped what they were doing and, facing East, performed the rituals of their faith. She was uncompromising in her personal belief but profoundly respectful of theirs. She kept Sunday as her day of rest and particular devotion but gave them time on Fridays for worship in accordance with their Muslim faith. As one of them would remark many years later: 'She remained herself. She had her religion and we had ours. That was how it was.'

By 5 June 1940 the supply of funds was exhausted. Hitherto the means to pay the workmen on Friday had been found, often in quite unexpected ways and even when on the previous Monday the prospect had seemed hopeless, but now, finally, Little Sister Magdeleine was left with no alternative but to return to France to raise the money necessary to continue. In the meantime Athman would continue with the work. He would keep his own record of the days he had laboured and as soon as she had managed to acquire further funds she would send them to him. It was with heavy hearts that on 16 June the Little Sisters left Touggourt and the people to whom Little Sister Magdeleine would invariably refer as 'our friends' and the relationship of mutual trust and affection which she would value to the end of her days.

Berths aboard ships between Algiers and France in wartime were by no means readily available. Little Sister Magdeleine was obliged to wait in Algiers until the end of August, during which time she was dealt another harsh personal blow. Mgr Nouet, concerned that there should be no outside influence on the founding spirit of the Little Sisters of Jesus, asked her to initiate her new congregation without the assistance of Father Voillaume, the man who had become the sole confidant of her experiences of intimacy with the infant Jesus and in whose judgement she already placed considerable trust. The requirement was a great trial to her but obedience was for her of crucial importance. Obedience was fundamental to the mystery of Nazareth which had been so central to the spirituality of Charles de Foucauld. St Luke's Gospel described Jesus' relationship to his earthly parents in Nazareth after they had found him conversing with learned men in the temple in Jerusalem: 'And he went down with them to Nazareth, and was subject unto them' (2: 51). For Little Sister Magdeleine the obedience of the adolescent Jesus to his human parents, who in their failure to understand came to take him away from his heavenly Father's house, contained the key to a relationship of the heart in which reason had no role to play. The Gospel understanding of obedience implied a total gift of self in an irrational love. The total gift of the self to God could not be made other than through the way of 'blind' obedience. Impelled as she felt herself to be by inner lights and rationally inexplicable intuitions, obedience also represented for Little Sister Magdeleine a form of safeguard against the fear which she harboured of being subject to illusions. The Church's confirmation of her ideas and activities through its representatives brought her reassurance. Obedience was the guarantee that the work was God's work and not her own. So it was that she bowed to Mgr Nouet's direction, and continued to work on the foundation and the Constitutions in the isolation which she found most difficult to endure.

It was during this period of waiting also that the idea came to her of assembling various photographs she had taken in Touggourt to make a short film entitled *Under the care of Our Lady and her Son, Jesus, a corner of the desert will bloom*. Unless the work was brought to the attention of more people the prospects of more postulants was remote. A letter to the port commander, informing him that the two Little Sisters' need to leave for France was so urgent that they would accept any form of transport whatsoever (even a submarine) eventually produced results. When finally she set foot in wartime France she set off at once on a lecture tour, taking with her the short film which she would show at least six hundred times between 1940 and 1945. It was a very unassuming piece of film. It showed Little Sister Magdeleine and Little Sister Anne in the Sahara, sitting on the ground with the nomads in their tents. It showed the interior of the house furnished with old packing cases, and interwoven with these simple scenes were Gospel texts: quotations from the beatitudes, 'love one another as I have loved you', 'greater love hath no man than that he lay down his life for his friends'. Somehow its simplicity and its message of hope would touch the hearts of a divided, war-torn France.

By September 1940 another issue had become a burning one for Little Sister Magdeleine. Even before she settled in Touggourt Mgr Nouet had impressed upon her the importance of having a noviciate outside the Sahara in the north of Algeria, because of the climate and also because of considerations of accessibility. Little Sister Magdeleine had responded that she felt such a noviciate should actually be in Provence. In a letter to her mother dated 14 October 1939 she had described her requirements in characteristic detail. It was not important that the building should be in a large city; only that it should be close to a church where mass was celebrated. The house itself must be large but poor. It would have to have enough land with it for the cultivation of fruit and vegetables. She also envisaged a small corner of it for her elderly mother. By the time Little Sister Magdeleine had returned to France and Aix-en-Provence where her mother was still living, the experience of the first two postulants at Sidi Boujnan had vindicated her view that others could not be brought directly into the desert without proper religious formation and that someone must be found to provide that formation. Her own commitment to speaking about Charles de Foucauld, making the Fraternity known and finding funds for the fraternity at Sidi Boujnan, would not, she recognised, allow her adequately to fulfil the role of novice mistress. In any case, her intention was to return to Sidi Boujnan to prepare everything for the arrival of the first Little Sisters.

Her talks, combined with the showing of her unpretentious little film, were beginning to attract potential candidates, among them the future Little Sister Marguerite, who would later spend many years in the Orient, and Little Sister Jeanne who succeeded Little Sister Magdeleine as Superior General or what the congregation called its 'General Responsible' for more than twenty years. The uncertainties and insecurities that were all that Little Sister Magdeleine could at that stage offer prospective members of her as yet unestablished congregation were not designed to convince parents of the validity of their daughters' claimed vocations. In many instances the seeds of such vocations were sown by only the briefest of personal encounters with Little Sister Magdeleine herself, frequently characterised by the exchange of few words. Among the accounts of the many that would follow are frequent references rather to a certain look of which she was capable. The dark eyes that could communicate love to her Arab friends without resorting to words appeared also to be endowed with a capacity for penetration, even when her attention was diverted only fleetingly to an individual from a multitude of practical concerns. Memories of even those who were closest to her were imprecise as to the actual colour of her eyes – 'neither blue nor brown, hazel perhaps with green tints'. More memorable was the way in which they were transparent with goodness and with energy and when she smiled it was 'as if they were lit by some inner light'. There was great depth in her look and it could, according to the circumstances, reflect joy, sorrow or concern, both hers and other people's. The woman who spoke with fervour of the message of Charles de Foucauld and of her beloved Algerian friends manifestly had charisma. She had, it seemed also, in many instances the capacity to convince potentially critical parents that they could entrust their daughters to her care. On 10 December 1940 she opened the first noviciate of the Little Sisters of Jesus courtesy of the Marie Reparatrice Sisters in Ste Foy-les-Lyon whose novice mistress was to take charge of the first five novices. Little Sister Marguerite came from a devoutly Catholic family. Her mother, in particular, had been quickly converted to Little Sister Magdeleine's vision. At the inauguration of the noviciate to which the parents of the novices were invited, her father found himself lighting the fire in the large room, half of which was to serve as a refectory and community room, the other half as a dormitory. The mothers were duly invited to confirm for themselves that their children would be sleeping on proper mattresses.

Christmas 1940 brought the present for which Little Sister Magdeleine had been yearning. Three kilometres outside Aix-en-Provence stood a large house with a dozen rooms, a chapel and outbuildings, set in an estate of over seven hectares with a substantial kitchen garden. The property had been given to the archdiocese of Aix by a Monsieur Boulanger whose widow had the usufruct of it for the duration of her life but who particularly wanted it to become a place of adoration of the Blessed Sacrament and the Sacred Heart. On receiving the news that Mgr de la Villerabel, the Archbishop of Aix-en-Provence, and Mgr Monnier, his vicar general, were making this property available to her, Little Sister Magdeleine wrote with uncontained excitement to her novices at Ste Foy-les-Lyon of how two to three hectares of the land were pine forest which would provide wood for heating. Three more were vineyards, two were meadowland. She waded ankle-deep through the snow to inspect the place to which she was already referring as 'our house' and pronounced it to be the answer to all her prayers. There were plenty of beautiful little spots for meditation, and even a pool overhung by a cave. The house itself was in good condition. Madame Boulanger would continue to live there in three of its rooms but there was still accommodation for at least fifteen to twenty people. The wood and the vineyards would provide a means of meeting the rates and taxes. The sisters could move in in six to eighteen months' time. Little Sister Magdeleine was overjoyed.

In the meantime it was clear to her not only that the Little Sisters to be must be adequately prepared, but also that the fraternity in Sidi Boujnan must be properly established before she could take a community there to lead a regular, structured life. Leaving Little Sister Anne with the novices at Ste Foy-les-Lyon, she set sail once more for Algeria together with her mother and a woman companion to keep Madame Hutin company in Touggourt while her daughter continued the construction work nearby. 'I shall be alone,' she predicted, 'without a daughter when I long so much for a community life . . . alone without a Superior when I dream so much of obedience.' In fact it was amongst the 'friends' of Sidi Boujnan who greeted her return with such overwhelming warmth that she found the companionship she craved. In her loneliness she discovered the true expansiveness of Muslim hospitality. She ate as the poor people about her did. She slept as they did on the floor. In her long white habit, she worked alongside them through sandstorms and adversity. She showed them the film she had used to raise money for the work and she shared with them her future plans. It was to Athman, the foreman of the workers, that she turned in moments of doubt and between this devout Muslim and the French Christian woman, with her extraordinary vision and exacting practical requirements, a deep and lasting understanding was established.

It was a time of great hunger in the tents. The war had brought with it a shortage of the corn supplies which were essential to the nomads' survival. Little Sister Magdeleine interceded on their behalf and managed to obtain provisions for them to buy. She did her best to create work even for the small children who came begging, setting them to pick up camel droppings to use as manure. To the young novices in Ste Foy-les-Lyon she wrote of the hardship of the life. Fearful that when their turn came to venture into the Sahara they might find the conditions too rigorous or that they might be idealising the vision offered to them by Charles de Foucauld, she asked them to look deep inside themselves and not to continue their noviciate unless they were prepared to suffer in every conceivable way and give up everything without complaint. What she needed was Little Sisters who were tough, women who were prepared, in accordance with the stipulations of Charles de Foucauld's spiritual writings, to be 'no more concerned with their health and lives than a tree is with a falling leaf'. Her own health, extraordinarily, was not an obstacle to all that she was undertaking. She suffered badly from sea-sickness during the crossings between France and Africa. There were times when the bitter cold of Sidi Boujnan was a great trial to her. There were also times when she was stricken with fever, a liver infection, jaundice. She fell not infrequently from the horses, mules or ponies that were so often her means of transport. On one occasion she was stung by a scorpion of which the local Arabs were terrified because of the severity of its poison, but was back working alongside the masons within a matter of hours. When she was a small child her father had been obliged to tell the dentist that he was hurting her because she herself would give no indication, but in later life she would admit to being afraid of physical pain, and in general the adult Little Sister Magdeleine spoke freely of her discomforts and hurt in part at least because she wanted her Little Sisters, not deliberately to seek suffering, but to be ready to accept it if necessary.

The crippling arthritis which had first been the means of her coming to Africa appears no longer to have been a consideration. In a letter dated 8 September 1941 to the Archbishop of Aix-en-Provence she referred to the manner in which the extreme symptoms from which she was suffering on her departure from France disappeared in Algeria:

> I left with my arm in a sling, anchylosed, with my muscles atrophied and my shoulder deformed: on my arrival it had all vanished, and since then, with my supposedly diseased lung and heart, for five years I have been leading the most unlikely life of fatigue and physical effort which would suggest to anyone that I have the constitution of an ox.

To her it was nothing short of miraculous but humility and discretion required that she make little direct reference to the unusual nature of her healing, and about this as about many other things she kept silent.

At the end of May 1941 she returned once more to France partly because she had still not adjusted to the extreme heat of the Algerian summer, partly because she needed to raise more funds for the continuing construction work at Sidi Boujnan, but above all because there were young novices awaiting her at Sainte Foy. By then the Marie Reparatrice Sisters were feeling unable to keep the prospective Little Sisters of Jesus. Already it was becoming clear that the life the young novices were destined to lead, a life in profound spiritual union with Jesus and not separated from the humanity which he had chosen to take upon himself, was too singular and too far removed from their own experience of the religious vocation. In a Dominican, Mother Henri-Dominique, whom she had met some five years previously, Little Sister Magdeleine felt she had discerned one capable of understanding what she was envisaging for the new congregation. In August her five novices were duly transferred by train to the Dominicans in Tourelles as a temporary measure until later in the month the noviciate was opened at Le Tubet, the property outside Aix. Although at this stage the aspiring Little Sisters wore no formal habit except a veil and a cross, the sheer fact of their carrying their few possessions in rucksacks was enough to create a sensation during the journey at a time when religious status was associated with more dignified luggage.

Once Le Tubet was properly opened the Dominicans lent the Little Sisters a Mother Superior and a novice mistress to take charge in Little Sister Magdeleine's absence. Little Sister Magdeleine was convinced of the rightness of Mother Hyacinthe for such a future role when she showed her willingness to travel across Aix in a horse and cart with an enormous green parasol as protection against the torrential rain. Her unconventional reasoning proved to be well-founded. The two women won the admiration of their novices by not seeking to impose upon them the viewpoints of their own extensive and well-established Dominican formation and by turning their hands to the kind of manual work to which their own Order had scarcely accustomed them.

On 2 October 1941 the first five novices formally received their white habits at Le Tubet. The war in France meant that conditions in the large property which they shared at first with a group of Oblate Fathers were far from easy. There was no electricity. Food and candles were often in short supply. Little Sister Magdeleine struggled to keep her young novices supplied with the basic necessities of life without resorting to the black market to which the poor, whose lot they sought to share, would not have access. The talks she was required to give necessitated frequent absences, as did the necessity to supervise developments in Sidi Boujnan. In November 1941 she returned to Algeria. By then Mgr Nouet had been obliged by ill health to retire as Apostolic Prefect of the Sahara. Little Sister Magdeleine's first meeting that month with his successor, Mgr Georges Mercier, was an opportunity for her to submit her plans to his judgement as a representative of the Church. Writing of this to her sisters in France, she begged those who would continue after her to retain this love for the representatives of the Church. Without it, she insisted, they would not be in the vein of Charles de Foucauld. That same year she saw Mgr Mercier again on several occasions, once at Sidi Boujnan itself. The outcome of his tour of inspection and subsequent meeting was completely contrary to Little Sister Magdeleine's own intentions but welcome nonetheless. Mgr Mercier wanted her to move some Little Sisters into the house at Sidi Boujnan at once, to try and live in practice the new form of community life she was still endeavouring to commit to paper in the form of the Constitutions. Their author was delighted to undertake in obedience what she would not have had the temerity to do of her own accord. God, she maintained, was once more taking her by the hand. She had but to close her eyes and obey. A telegram was despatched to France asking Little Sister Anne and one of the novices, Little Sister Francine, to come and join her as soon as possible.

The arrival of the newcomers at Sidi Boujnan was met with an enthusiastic reception. Little Sisters Anne and Francine made the final three kilometres of the journey, from Touggourt to Sidi Boujnan, on mules, full of the joy of the novelty of the experience. For her own part Little Sister Magdeleine heaved a heartfelt sigh of relief at the opportunity to accompany them on foot. For her the attractions of riding mules were wearing thin. The people of the tents and the *zribas* were warm in their welcome and delighted that the sisters were to spend their first night actually in the fraternity amongst them, assuring them of their safety. Seated on a packing case, by the light of a paraffin lamp, Little Sister Magdeleine wrote to the novices in Le Tubet of the magnificent clarity of the desert sky that night. Rolled up in a blanket, she would soon fall asleep on one of the wooden coffers built on to the wall of the slowly developing building, to the sound of dogs barking at the moon. Here at last was the life she had craved for so long. 'Doesn't it make you want to come?' she enquired of her young followers in France.

As it transpired, when next she managed to visit Le Tubet in June 1942, the small number of novices had been further reduced. Southern France had suffered severe restrictions. The Little Sisters had endured a daily diet of gourds, Jerusalem artichokes or beetroot varied only with salads made out of wild herbs. Two of them had fallen so ill that they had to be admitted to hospital. Two others had left. All Little Sister Magdeleine's plans seemed on the point of collapse. Even the prospect of giving more talks seemed slight in a stricken country in which travel itself was difficult, but as always in apparently indomitable circumstances, she held on to the thought that God was master of the impossible. The need to resurrect Le Tubet and maintain Sidi Boujnan spurred her on. In 1942 the future Little Sister Jeanne who had first met Little Sister Magdeleine in October 1940, finally came as a postulant to Le Tubet. Her father had been strongly opposed to the idea, but at the age of twenty-three she braved his anger to start life with the handful of others who were still sustained by Little Sister Magdeleine's dynamism.

Years later they would remember how their foundress appeared at intervals to tell them with infectious enthusiasm of the Sahara, Touggourt and her Arab friends. In the sizeable kitchen at Le Tubet, huddled around a stove, they would listen enthralled as she described to them the warmth and piety she had encountered amongst the simple souls of Sidi Boujnan. Charles de Foucauld in his spiritual writings had emphasised the importance of hospitality: 'With what love, respect, joy . . . what tender eagerness we should receive whoever presents himself to us, every human being whoever he may be – everyone, everyone, everyone. . . . In receiving them we are receiving Jesus.' The Arabs of the desert understood the importance of hospitality. People who frequently had so little nonetheless gave everything they had. The Little Sisters must do the same. She talked to them too of the infant Jesus, freely acknowledging that this was her 'favourite subject'. Convinced as she was that the message had been entrusted to her to pass on to her Little Sisters, she wanted to give him to them in all his smallness, simplicity and joy. On such subjects she could speak straight from the heart and at great length. On others she was less forthcoming.

Recognising perhaps that a venture that was to be in many respects something radically new should be firmly rooted in a knowledge of the Gospels and the teaching of the Church, she was from the beginning concerned about their theological training. Her very first draft of the Constitutions had envisaged that at least one year of their formation would be devoted to theological study. During the earliest years of the Fraternity a French Jesuit by the name of Prosper Monier gave her assistance and support in communicating to her Little Sisters an understanding of the Gospels. Father Monier had refused the offer of a university Chair in Holy Scriptures in order to avoid the risk of 'turning Christianity into a religion for teachers' and had become instead a kind of travelling preacher. Little Sister Magdeleine recognised him as belonging to the line of Charles de Foucauld, and he spoke to her young postulants of Jesus, the Gospels and of love, with infectious conviction. She herself communicated to the first generation of Little Sisters her deep knowledge of the Scriptures and of Jesus the person, but it was more by a process of osmosis, through what she was actually living than by intellectual debate. She was not one to indulge in involved or abstract discussions about theology or indeed about the individual vocations of her young novices. Little Sister Jeanne began her noviciate in January when Little Sister Magdeleine was free to give a retreat at Le Tubet. They spoke briefly together by the light of a small lamp but there was no profound verbal exchange. The encounter set the tenor for this and most of Little Sister Magdeleine's other personal relationships. Even with the first to join her she was not given to intimate conversations. Rather she got on with the process of living side by side with them and providing for their needs. In order to get them eggs, potatoes and cheese she would literally climb mountains.

At the age of twenty-one Little Sister Marguerite had already found herself being told to go and take part in an exhibition about missionary work in Marseille. As in the case of so many others who would follow, Little Sister Magdeleine put her trust in the young woman, throwing her in at the deep end, and Little Sister Marguerite rose to the challenge. She had never so much as set foot in Africa but she struggled to do her bit to make known the work of the embryo congregation of the Little Sisters of Jesus. Little Sister Magdeleine loved her Little Sisters with a maternal tenderness but she was not demonstrative in her affection and she was rigorous in her requirements of them, admonishing them when they fell short of the ideal of which Jesus was, she constantly reminded them, the unique model. In doing so, however, she told them always to remember that her reproaches were probably directed more at herself than at them. She asked nothing of her aspiring Little Sisters that she was not prepared to do herself. Her response if they did come to her with their difficulties was inclined to be the direction not to focus on themselves but outwards. They should forget themselves and just keep going. Yet the young women of whom she asked so much loved her and would remember how when she came to Le Tubet it was as if she brought with her 'a wind of the wide open spaces which blew over all our little community problems'.

By mid-August 1942 Little Sister Magdeleine was making characteristically detailed plans for a celebration to mark the occasion of her final vows. She herself could appreciate good food. Even in her old age she would not accept preferential treatment from the point of view of the food or water she consumed, but she could enjoy dishes that were well prepared. Precisely because it was a time of food shortages, she wanted to give her invited guests a special treat: a chocolate cream dessert. By the time she returned to Le Tubet from one of her lecture tours, only one week before the ceremony was due to take place, some one hundred people had accepted invitations to the celebration but there were no signs of the means with which to feed them. On 7 September, however, the day before Little Sister Magdeleine's final profession, a friend from Toulouse who had previously attended one of her talks opened before the stupefied eyes of the Little Sisters a case full of ducks and chickens and a box containing three dozen eggs and half a kilo of chocolate – exactly what they needed for the planned dessert. By then there were thirteen Little Sisters. They and one hundred people sat down next day to a meal following a mass held in the open air. A rustic altar made out of a plank resting on two enormous pine trunks had been set up beneath an awning of branches. In this simple setting and in the presence of Mgr de la Villerabel, the Archbishop of Aix-en-Provence, Little Sister Magdeleine made her final profession:

> I, Sister Magdeleine of Jesus, undertake to observe unto death the vows of Obedience, Poverty, Chastity according to the Constitutions of the Little Sisters of Jesus and the Spirit of Father de Foucauld, in order to consecrate myself to the most forsaken people of Islam in immolation for the redemption of Islam and in order, O good and merciful Father, that this oblation may be the more acceptable I offer it in union with the immolation of Jesus, Victim of Love.

For Little Sister Magdeleine her final profession as a 'Little Sister of Jesus' was a much craved token of the recognition of the Church. Hitherto Madame Hutin had been inclined to believe that her daughter's failure to commit herself to any existing congregation might be an assertion of her personal will but now, as she sat in the front row of the assembled congregation, the occasion seemed at last to confirm that God was at work in her daughter's vocation.

At Christmas 1942, at the suggestion of Mgr de la Villerabel, Madame Hutin came to stay at Le Tubet for a trial period to establish whether she would like to move in on a more permanent basis. She had been living alone in Aix. The Little Sisters visited her regularly but she still felt the separation from the daughter of whom she acknowledged she was proud and who she nicknamed her 'shooting star' because of the rapidity and frequency with which she came and went. 'The separation of a mother and her daughters is too hard,' wrote Little Sister Magdeleine to the novices she regarded as her own daughters in the course of one of her lecture tours to spread the message of Charles de Foucauld and raise funds for the extensions to Le Tubet necessitated by the growing noviciate.

Lourdes, the Upper Loire, Le Lot, Le Puy-de-Dome, Bouches-du-Rhone, Isère, the Haute-Garonne, the Atlantic Pyrenees, the Upper Pyrenees: these were just a few of the many locations to which Little

Sister Magdeleine struggled across war-torn France to give her talks, in defiance of all rational objections. 'Whatever you do, don't become reasonable or the Lord will leave you,' advised one priest friend whose spiritual qualities she revered, but there were times when she felt discouraged and wondered whether the Little Sisters themselves really understood the reasons for her frequent absences or the urgent need for her to keep on talking. Sometimes she gave as many as five talks in one day. The little film was worn out and had to be patched together and she was frequently exhausted. Alone, through the shelling of a blacked-out Paris or the dark isolation of country lanes, weighed down by her projector and her rucksack and a large case containing cards, pictures, and camels made out of palm fibre by the people of Sidi Boujnan, she would struggle through the snow and ice, often on foot or hitch-hiking, to reach her destinations. It was small wonder that at times she sat down at the side of the road and wept. Yet in the midst of this physical and mental anguish she would write to her Little Sisters to tell them that there was something missing at Le Tubet. Why were there no flowers in the chapel? She wanted flowers at the foot of the altar when the Blessed Sacrament was exposed. Without being over-lavish, they were to grow flowers in the garden. If possible she would like the altar of the Virgin Mary to be covered with flowers for the next ceremony, to bring a smile to the hearts of the Little Sisters but, above all, to the hearts of their parents, 'a small smile that will be the outer expression of the joy of their offering'.

There were encouraging signs. At the end of a retreat which Little Sister Magdeleine attended in June 1943 with several Little Sisters who were shortly to take their vows, Father Monier strongly encouraged her to be herself and not to turn to other religious congregations to form her young sisters. In September that year Mgr de la Villerabel confirmed this opinion that the Fraternity should now 'spread its own wings'. This meant the painful step of saying farewell to Mother Henri-Dominique who had helped the Little Sisters with such dedication and devotion. In future Little Sisters Jeanne and Marguerite would stand in for Little Sister Magdeleine during her absences. As the situation in the vicinity of Aix deteriorated, however, Mgr de la Villerabel's attachment to the congregation turned into concern that it should not be wiped out in the bombing. The Little Sisters were divided up. Five professed Sisters were studying Arabic in Paris. Two were left at Le Tubet together with a priest and Madame Boulanger who remained there throughout the war. The rest were sent at very short notice together with Madame Hutin to a convent in Lyon. Little Sister Magdeleine herself divided her time and her energy between the three groups and still, in a context of despair, arrests, shootings and torture, the talks must go on. As far as she was concerned it was precisely in such a context that the Christian message of 'love thine enemy' became particularly pertinent.

On the night of 18 August 1944 a loud banging was heard at the door of the house at Le Tubet. A voice was heard to shout: 'Open up at once. It's the German army.' The sisters were hesitant but the blows increased in intensity until, fearing that the door would be broken down, they mustered enough courage to open it. When they did so, three German soldiers burst into the entrance hall pointing their sub-machine-guns at the two Little Sisters nearest the door and demanding to know where the explosions they could hear were coming from. In her diary entry for that day, Little Sister Magdeleine recorded how at this point she found herself in her night attire, clearly lit at the top of the stairs. Mustering all her strength to shout in a loud voice, 'We are religious. You have no business here,' she rushed downstairs at the intruders. Whereupon, overcome by the sight of her in a long white robe, which she acknowledged must have made her look like an apparition, the soldiers beat a hasty retreat out of the door and along the railway line which ran not far from the house. Next night the hill on the other side of Aix was alight and word was abroad that the nearby port of Marseille had been destroyed. Suddenly, however, around midnight on 20 August the sound of artillery and bombardment gave way to an extraordinary calm. The allied troops were at the gates of Aix. Next day brought all the joy and celebration of liberation but that in its turn swiftly gave way to cruel acts of vengeance. 'I suffer so greatly from all that is going on,' wrote Little Sister Magdeleine in her diary.

It seemed that the Little Sisters at Le Tubet were safe at last but those in Lyon were reportedly still under threat. Unable to rest while the youngest of her sisters were still in danger, Little Sister Magdeleine appealed to Mgr de la Villerabel for authority to join them in Lyon. Despite the danger involved, the Archbishop saw her proposed action as a duty and actively encouraged her to go. Before doing so, however, she resolved to check first on the welfare of the sisters' families in Marseille. Marseille was reported to have been liberated. Little Sister Magdeleine hoped to be able to take good news of their parents' safety to the young novices in Lyon but the announcement of the port's liberation proved to have been premature. Taking with her one other Little Sister, Little Sister Magdeleine hitched a lift with a military jeep only to find the streets still occupied by tanks, armoured vehicles and heavily armed soldiers, and the people of Marseille still sheltering in their cellars. With difficulty, they found the Little Sisters' families safe and sheltering together. Not far away, however, was a convent of the Sacred Heart. Resolved to take news of them to the Sacred Heart convent in Lyon, Little Sister Magdeleine and her companion made their way through a wood lined with trenches in which, unbeknown to them, soldiers were waiting in battle positions.

No sooner had they entered the Sacred Heart convent than an assault began on the surrounded house. Only later would the sisters discover that the attack was due to the deaths of two French soldiers whom their comrades believed to have been killed by bullets fired from the windows or roof of the house. In fact the shots had been fired by their fellow soldiers on the other side of the building who were also erroneously convinced that they were attacking the enemy. For an hour and a half the occupants of the building were subjected to a terrifying onslaught of gunfire from both sides, unable even to approach the windows with a white flag. Finally one of the Sacred Heart Sisters managed at last to do so, just as tanks and armoured vehicles were standing by to break into the building which had been designated a hide-out for German troops.

For Little Sisters Magdeleine and her companion, however, the danger was not yet over. Their furtive movements through the streets of Marseille had made them objects of suspicion amongst their compatriots. Only the intervention of a priest, previously condemned to death by the Gestapo, secured them their freedom. He escorted them to the home of Little Sister Magdeleine's mother, giving them firm directions not to move from there until Marseille had actually been liberated. Defiant while the lives of the Little Sisters in Lyon were still in danger, Little Sister Magdeleine disregarded his instructions. She wrote a letter to French General Headquarters begging them to get her and her companion out of Marseille and, dressed in 'civilian' clothes, with her precious letter in an elegant handbag, she slipped out once more into the streets and handed her request to the first French soldier she encountered.

On 26 August a military chaplain escorted the two women as far as Aubagne where he directed a soldier to find them a vehicle going to Aix. After a day of preparation at Le Tubet, on the morning of 28th, Little Sister Magdeleine set off alone to hitch-hike to Lyon. Half the journey was made without undue difficulty courtesy of a small convoy of American military vehicles, and by the time she reached Grenoble she was delighted with her unexpectedly good progress. Some time previously, however, she had replaced her worn-out sandals with a pair of men's shoes she had been given. She had also removed the cape she usually wore and her blue veil, having been advised that they made her look too much like a nurse attached to the army of occupation. In her white habit she walked through the streets, oblivious to the hostile looks, the whispering and the half-opened windows and doors that greeted her passage. She did not know that on the previous day German soldiers had been in the area disguised as nuns. Nor was she conscious of the effect created by her men's shoes. Suddenly, however, a short blast on a whistle and a curt command to halt brought her face to face with a member of the French resistance forces, threatening her with a machine-gun. The production of her papers and an identity card issued in the Sahara did nothing to allay his suspicions.

Taken for a spy, she was marched away between two lines of hostile onlookers, and finally made to stand up against a presbytery wall with four guns pointing at her. She had yearned for martyrdom, as the ultimate expression of her love for God, but at that moment something in her protested that she did not want it to be like this. 'You have to have been through it to understand the bitterness of such a fate,' she wrote in her diary afterwards.

> To be shot because you have served your country in time of war, is glorious! But to be struck down in the street by your brothers whom you can't manage to make recognise you, and who take you for a spy, a traitor to your country, is a veritable torture! It would have been even more distressing, if I had not had the certainty to sustain me that I had undertaken this perilous journey in obedience!

As it was, she struggled to evoke the way of Calvary and the abjection which Charles de Foucauld had held so dear, but at the same time found herself crying out: 'To think that I am from Lorraine, that my grandmother was massacred and my two brothers killed during the 1914 war and now you want to shoot me as a spy. I am not afraid of death, but this sort of death is too hard.' No sooner had she spoken these words than she reproached herself for them. Nothing should have seemed too hard to a faithful disciple of Brother Charles of Jesus following Christ along the way of Calvary to the point of abjection on the cross. Something in her voice, however, moved one of her guards to lower his gun and draw a little closer. Speaking more calmly, she did her best to explain the anomalies in her identity card and the way she was dressed. She spoke of Charles de Foucauld and appealed to the crowd of onlookers. Only two years previously she had given one of her talks in this very town. Finally she was recognised. The four guards, confused and ashamed, did everything they could to redeem themselves by helping her on her way.

Next day, faced with the prospect of endeavouring to cross the German line, she admitted to being terrified, but the words of Charles de Foucauld were ever exacting: 'When you set out saying that you are going to do something, you must not come back without doing it.' Charles de Foucauld had maintained that fear was a sure sign that a course of action was the right one. Fearful but resolute she continued to make for Lyon and, as it transpired, was given the opportunity of a lift aboard a Red Cross vehicle. On 30 August she arrived at her destination, without having encountered a single German soldier or bullet, announcing to her stupified mother and Little Sisters who thought she had dropped out of the sky the imminent arrival of the French and allied forces. A terrible battle took place in Lyon over the next few days, during which Little Sister Magdeleine found herself once again caught up in the explosions and gunfire which destroyed the city's bridges and ricocheted through its streets.

By 8 September and the fifth anniversary of the foundation, however, the war in France was effectively over. In the relative calm that followed Little Sister Magdeleine announced her intention of returning to North Africa. She wanted to see Mgr Mercier in Algiers and then go on to Touggourt to be with her Arab friends and check the progress of the building work. On the way back she would call in at Tunis to look into the possibility of having a fraternity there for the Little Sisters to study Arabic. The idea had also come to her of going to Rome to speak to the Pope about her new congregation and express her desire to him that one day this 'Fraternity' might have a general house in Rome.

Her narrow escape from the firing squad in Grenoble, terrifying as it had been at the time, was to prove not unfruitful. On 12 September 1944 Little Sister Magdeleine, hoping to avoid any further similar experiences, went to the General Headquarters of the liberating forces in Lyon to request a pass to return to Aix before leaving for the Sahara. Just as she was relating what had happened on her journey there, an officer in the FFI who had witnessed her narrow escape entered the room. In reparation she was allowed to choose whatever form of compensation she wished. In response to her request to be allowed to travel to the Sahara and to Rome, the colonel immediately made out an order which would allow her to make use of any form of military transport and to travel without any other authorisation.

With the fighting over, Little Sister Magdeleine left for Tunis that very same month, full of joy at the prospect of renewing old friendships in Sidi Boujnan. The war had left its mark nonetheless, most obviously in highlighting the need she had already felt to break down the barricades which existed between people. Not for the first time but perhaps on a larger scale than hitherto she had witnessed suffering, division and the full spectrum of human emotions occasioned by the conflict and the separations it brought in its train. She had experienced at first hand mortal fear, the bitterness of injustice and the need for forgiveness, and all this had brought home to her in a particularly poignant way the need to hate the sin but not the sinner and the requirement, above all else, to grow in love. The letters which Little Sister Magdeleine wrote to her sisters sometimes as frequently as four times a week during the early years and which she would continue to write throughout her life, were invariably rooted in concrete and specific situations from which the wider vision sprang. She told them that their horizons should be as expansive as those of the desert, that they should always see things from a very large, high, broad perspective. Love could transform the smallest things into something much more significant. Early on in the war, she had watched the seemingly endless march past of the invading German troops and written to her Little Sisters expressing her heartfelt desire that in the Fraternity everything should be love and gentleness. There was to be no harshness in their opinions but only the love, indulgence and forgiveness of Jesus, their model. Notwithstanding the succession of personal tragedies inflicted on her by the First World War she had urged her sisters to pray for those about to die on both sides. Surrounded by all the tragedy of war, she directed them to raise their sights to focus on that place where Germans, Americans, British, French, Italians and Russians would be united in the same love, to the place where Carthusians, Dominicans, Franciscans, Jesuits, Trappists would be fused in the same harmony, in which each would have his or her own note, not the same note, because that would scarcely be harmony, but his or her own.

Little Sister Magdeleine had talked in hospitals, theological colleges, sanatoria, and even on one occasion in a concentration camp, to people of all kinds, backgrounds and convictions. Her travels throughout France had made her the frequent guest of other religious congregations. At one sanatorium, following her talk, she had sat down to eat at the communal table with the patients, until the Sister Superior had her place setting removed to a small table at which she could eat alone. The Superior, Little Sister Magdeleine was swift to point out, had thought she was doing the right thing. It was usual to expect such a separation between religious and the laity. She could not know that her guest's deepest aspiration was that there should be no barriers between herself and her fellow human beings. Nevertheless the feelings of rejection her fellow diners may have experienced weighed heavily on Little Sister Magdeleine. Elsewhere, in convivial company following many hours spent travelling alone, she came to appreciate in a very personal way the importance of a warm welcome. Even intrusions upon their prayer time, she told her Little Sisters, were not to be resented. Times of retreat were intended to be opportunities in which to grow in love. If therefore people disturbed them at such times they were to be greeted with a loving smile. Jesus himself had derived pleasure from relaxing amongst friends in Bethany after his long journeys. He had allowed himself to draw comfort from them in a very human way. Little Sister Magdeleine saw her Little Sisters' role as one which did not deny the importance of what was good and holy in humanity itself. They were to be human as divinely as possible and religious as humanly as possible.

The emotional needs of her own mother, and those manifested by the parents of her Little Sisters, the experience of a friend who was a nun whose Superior had denied her the right to visit a mother who had asked to see her on her deathbed – these and other instances of the subordination of humanity to the supposed requirements of holiness pointed her towards the need to incorporate into the religious life of her new congregation the message of a God who had assumed the human form of a tiny baby born in a manger in Bethlehem. Her Little Sisters were to be Christian and human before being religious. They were also be be 'fraternal', a family, a fraternity, open to all human beings who were their brothers and sisters.

Traipsing eight kilometres on foot, alone, after one of her innumerable talks, the thought had come to her that if ever one day she were to write down everything that she had in her heart, she would like to bequeath to her Little Sisters her great ideal of a human holiness. She wanted them to fix their eyes and their hearts on the simple life of Jesus, to remove from them for ever any taste for the extraordinary except for the extraordinarily simple. Then, on to that humanity must be grafted a love that was divine . . . an immeasurable love . . . a love devoid of self-interest and gratification, a love that was a gift of self in which all personal interest was forgotten.

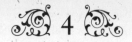

4

The Way of the Cross

THE MEETING WITH MGR MERCIER exceeded even Little Sister
Magdeleine's expectations. The Apostolic Prefect of the Sahara
approved what Little Sister Magdeleine was envisaging essentially as
a form of contemplative life amongst the nomads, even giving his
blessing to the idea of his members of the new congregation moving
about the desert as the nomads did. He also asked Little Sister
Magdeleine and a companion to come to El Abiodh at the end of
October 1944 to attend a retreat conducted by Father Voillaume. Mgr
Mercier had been struck by the manner in which the independent
paths pursued by Little Sister Magdeleine and the founder of the
Little Brothers of the Sacred Heart, at the request of Mgr Nouet,
were in fact drawing them closer together in the spirit of Charles de
Foucauld. He saw no reason therefore to maintain his predecessor's
direction that in order to allow the founding spirit to express itself
freely, there should be no close association between Little Sister
Magdeleine and Father Voillaume. From November 1944 onwards
Little Sister Magdeleine began to keep Father Voillaume intimately
and regularly informed of the difficulties and sufferings of her spiritual
journey.

The retreat at El Abiodh, during which Mgr Mercier had been so
encouraging, in fact paved the way for a considerable sacrifice. At the
end of it the Apostolic Prefect informed Little Sister Magdeleine that
he felt it best that the Little Sisters did not return to Touggourt
before September of the following year so that the building work
could be completed before they did so. In the chapel of the Little
Brothers at El Abiodh Little Sister Magdeleine wept. It was a harsh
disappointment for all those eagerly preparing to begin life in Algeria.
By letter she informed her Little Sisters that they were entitled to
their grief, but not to any recriminations or regrets and that, if they
were to be true Little Sisters of Charles de Foucauld, they were to

find even amongst their tears the joy of blind obedience. The year of waiting was a period of her life during which, in her own words, 'one cross succeeded another'. In December 1944, with the aid of a military plane and thanks once more very largely to the endeavours of the FFI resistance forces to compensate her for the way they had treated her in Grenoble, Little Sister Magdeleine arrived in Rome in defiance of all reasonable expectations. Since the war, travel had been fraught with apparently insurmountable difficulties, but a series of encounters which she saw as providential finally brought her the opportunity to kneel at the feet of Pope Pius XII. Like Charles de Foucauld before her, she was deeply respectful of the 'authority of Christ present in his Church'. Jesus, she would remind her Little Sisters, had said to those whom he had charged with representing him on earth, 'Whoever listens to you, listens to me' (Luke 10:16). She directed them to have for the Pope and for the hierarchy of the Church a love 'like that of a child for his father'. Charles de Foucauld had loved Rome as a city where, in poverty and surrender, martyrs had suffered for their faith. Little Sister Magdeleine shared that vision. She loved Rome, she asserted, because the blood of so many martyrs had been spilled upon its earth, because of what it represented in terms of the mystical body of Christ, because it was the heart of Christianity and because it was the seat of the Father of the Church. In her notebook (again, probably the one to which she had referred in her letters to Father Voillaume concerning the 'manifestations' of the infant Jesus) she wrote on 16 December 1944 with eager anticipation of how she would offer the Pope the gift of her 'little religious family'.

In the same notebook she wrote of how she came to present herself to the Holy Father and 'to all the great episcopal and pontifical authorities' as a 'Little Sister of no account' to dispel for ever any ideas they might have of treating her as a 'Reverend Mother' and a 'Foundress'. The phrase 'of no account' had come to her as she and another Little Sister huddled together in the bitter cold on the back of a lorry surrounded by oil and petrol cans, and she loved it because the 'smaller one is, the more audacity one has'. She wanted her sisters to be the kind of Little Sisters who were of so little account that they could be anywhere without shocking anyone; in the holds of ships, in military trucks, tents, hovels; who could go anywhere without anyone thinking of offering them comfortable chairs or placing them in offices but who would be equally at ease in a luxurious aeroplane or drawing room 'because they are so small that no one will even look at them':

Small, as tiny as the little Christmas Bambino, like the humble workman of Nazareth – so small that even disdain and the experience of being overlooked no longer touches them.

It was in such terms that she introduced herself to the Pope in a long letter she wrote to him prior to the requested audience. It was, she maintained, precisely for this reason that she was being used by God to found a new congregation consecrated in its prayer, immolation and apostolate exclusively to the world of Islam, a congregation which she wanted to call the 'Little Sisters of Jesus (of Father de Foucauld)' under the patronage of the 'great hermit of the desert'.

She asked for the Pope's blessing on her small family which did not yet have any canonical status but which did have, she was pleased to inform him, the support and paternal affection of the Archbishop of Aix and the Apostolic Prefect of the Sahara. She also expressed the desire to lay before him, not as yet the finished Constitutions, but at least an indication of the spirit and intention of the proposed congregation. That intention was to be in the midst of people of all milieux the leaven lost in the dough to make it rise. The Little Sisters were to become 'Arabs amongst the Arabs' – 'nomads amongst the nomads'. They were to adopt the language, customs and even the mentality of the people amongst whom they would spend their lives. They were to give charity precedence over all other rules, and they were to open wide the doors to vocations from amongst the local people with the idea of placing themselves at their service, respecting their race, and giving their own lives joyfully for the redemption of their Islamic brothers and sisters. Charles de Foucauld had been her inspiration, she informed the Pope. He had also bequeathed to her his love for the Holy Father and his blind obedience to the least of the Pope's directions. That was why she asked humbly that he receive her and her companion to speak to him of the apostolate of which she dreamed.

The audience with Pius XII was postponed but changed at the Pope's personal request from a special audience, which would have meant her being received in the company of others, to a private one. 'If you only knew what I felt when I saw him', she wrote to her Little Sisters at Le Tubet immediately afterwards. She told them of how tiny she had felt beside him, not because of his person because he was so humble, but because of the holiness he had radiated. 'How we must love the Holy Father and maintain this characteristic of our fraternity!' she urged them. She also sent them a copy of the notes she had used as the basis of what she had said during the audience and which she had afterwards submitted to him. Under the heading of 'Our dearest wishes' she had outlined not only the desire to be the leaven in the dough amongst the Arab people and offer the life of the Little Sisters for the redemption of their Islamic brothers and sisters, but also the aspiration that their congregation be above all human and Christian, devoid of the rigid barriers which might separate them from the world and at the same time based on a profound inner life. In particular she wanted her congregation to remain always a fraternity of Little Sisters who could, without shocking anyone and without being reproached for their lack of dignity, live, be lodged and travel as the least of their brothers and sisters . . . 'like Jesus who lost none of his divine dignity by assuming the humanity of a poor craftsman'. The Little Sisters sought the right to be really like the poor, as Jesus had been, earning their living with their hands without the dowries and income from capital which constituted the more usual source of security for religious congregations. They did not want, Little Sister Magdeleine insisted, to leave to lay people the privilege of depriving themselves if they so wished in order to follow the poor Christ; nor did they wish to take a vow of poverty only to find themselves obliged to secure their future and ensure that they wanted for nothing.

It was a plea for the privilege of following the example of the Christ born in poverty in a manger who went on to work as a humble carpenter in Nazareth. Yet this ideal of Christlike poverty had already provoked criticism, especially in ecclesiastical and religious circles where paradoxically it was rejected as 'unworthy of a religious'. Little Sister Magdeleine did not fail to mention this fact and the suffering it caused her as she addressed Pope Pius XII. As she spoke the Pope smiled and looked at her with eyes which, she afterwards reported, made her feel at once accepted and understood. On that occasion she did not give him a copy of the Constitutions as they existed to date because she had been told by a priest prior to the audience that the Pope had 'other things to do than read them'. Afterwards, however, she regretted the omission. She was fond of photographs. Throughout her life she derived pleasure from keeping carefully ordered albums full of them. In Rome she set about illustrating the best copy she had of the Constitutions with photographs and gave it to Mgr Montini, then Under-Secretary of State but subsequently Pope Paul VI, to pass on to the Pope. Mgr Montini showed himself to have great understanding and sympathy for their cause. It was he who drew Little Sister Magdeleine's attention to the fact that the Holy Father himself had changed the audience to a private one. He added with reference to her outlined intentions, as she would afterwards record, 'the sign of God is there'. Little Sister Magdeleine was quick to point out that she had received nothing but kindness and encouragement from the official Church authorities in Rome. Nor did she wish to imply a judgement of other congregations whose lives were structured differently. If they did not share the same rule of poverty it was because they had 'other aspects of the life of Christ to personify'. The struggle for the ideal of poverty which was so close to her heart, however, was to be a long and complex one, and would render her liable to criticism in quarters where she might have hoped for a different reaction when the burden of difficulties confronting her was almost intolerable.

In December 1944 Mgr de la Villerabel, who had supported her wholeheartedly and with great understanding in what she was endeavouring to undertake at Le Tubet, was obliged to resign. At a time when the wartime allegiances of the French people were divided, Mgr de la Villerabel had found himself classified as a supporter of the Vichy government, a fact which made his position in the episcopate untenable once liberation came. The fraternity at Le Tubet with all its problems was thus left under the temporary jurisdiction of the Vicar General, Mgr Hyppolite Monnier. The provisional nature of this arrangement, coupled with the fact that because of the locations of the other fraternities Little Sister Magdeleine was also answerable to the Apostolic Prefect for the Sahara, the Archbishop of Lyon and, a short while later, the Archbishop of Tunis, was a source of deep concern to her. The fraternities' problems were also sometimes aggravated by the fact that they had as yet no canonical status. The question arose therefore as to which of the three or four diocesan bishops was the appropriate person to establish the Fraternity as a pious union, the first step towards official recognition as a religious congregation of diocesan right. For a while Mgr Mercier assumed not only the role of bishop responsible for the fraternity at Sidi Boujnan but also that of spiritual director to Little Sister Magdeleine. It was difficult in her case to separate her personal spiritual life from her undertakings as foundress. There was a case, therefore, for the overall spiritual direction of both the new congregation and its foundress being borne by one person. Increasingly, however, she felt the need for that person to be someone other than one of the bishops in whose individual diocese the fraternities were located.

The uncertainty of this position highlighted the sense of isolation to which Little Sister Magdeleine was subject throughout the founding years. Precisely because of the radical nature of what she felt called to initiate, and in some respects was already living, she wanted the guidance and control of the Church to which she felt deeply attached. She was the first to admit that she was not capable of ensuring the adequate preparation of her Little Sisters, the first to crave obedience to someone placed by the Church in authority over her both in the direction of the Fraternity and at a very profound personal level. In her growing spiritual isolation she confided in Father Voillaume. She was, she acknowledged, physically, desperately tired. The incessant travelling, the talks, the need to explain what it was she felt so power-fully impelled to do, to guarantee the well-being of her Little Sisters and to raise money, were taking a heavy toll. She became so prone to accidents that even one who fought shy of the 'extraordinary' began to see them as something unusual: near asphyxiation as a result of a gas tap left open, a sharp jolt of a train carriage which injured her head and face – 'I assure you, Father,' she wrote to René Voillaume, 'that these successive accidents are not normal.' She was, she pro-tested, ready for anything, but physically she had reached her limit. 'Physically,' she wrote to him from Lyon on 19 March 1945, 'I haven't an ounce of strength left, having problems with my lungs since my return to France, and not being able to stop to rest.' Next day Little Sister Anne, her very first companion, came to see her in Lyon to inform her that she was leaving the Fraternity and returning to North Africa. She could not accept Mgr Mercier's direction not to return to Touggourt before September and in Little Sister Magdeleine's absence had asked for authority to quit the Little Sisters. She left with her few possessions wrapped up in a newspaper in a state of poverty which Little Sister Magdeleine described as 'either heroic or mad', to go and live alone in Kabylie amongst the people she loved so dearly. There she would fall seriously ill and die in Algiers only three years later. The Fraternity would always regard her as a Little Sister. She had so generously shared the rigours of the very first years of the foundation, but her departure left Little Sister Magdeleine heartbroken.

Feeling she could take no more, in desperation she turned to the various confessors in the towns through which she passed, but they were at variance in their advice. One told her that she must never miss her offices, with the result that for the next three days she found herself unable to attend a single one. The next priest to whom she resorted told her that her responsibilities to others came first, that her duty was to give herself and that that would be the best expression of her faith. 'All I can do is what I believe best in the eyes of God and for me, that is charity,' she concluded. At the deepest point of her anguish and her pain was a growth of her love of God. Her physical difficulties, however, were to increase. They were accompanied at times by a deep peace and an ineffable joy but they tested her to the limits of her endurance. Never before had she known such suffering and yet somehow she found the necessary energy to continue the work and the capacity to conceal her pain.

It took an act of supreme will-power but she managed it so successfully that people expressed their admiration for the robustness of her constitution and for the energy she displayed in all her undertakings. Her efforts were manifestly fruitful in that they attracted a growing influx of vocations but they also drew shocked reactions and jealousies. The fact that in Algeria Little Sister Magdeleine wore the *haik*, the large white woollen square in which the Arab women enveloped themselves, provoked criticism amongst those with more traditional ideas of the religious habit. It was a time when sisters did not usually leave the convent other than in pairs and when they did so it was with 'suitable transport'. Even some years later the Bishop of Dublin, taken aback by the Little Sisters' practice of walking to work, would insist that if he saw a sister in the street he would give her a lift. In the forties Little Sisters travelling with rucksacks on their backs on lorries laden with baskets of vegetables or cans of petrol, or seen to be resting, sitting on a staircase in a convent in Paris, ill befitted, in the eyes of some, the dignity of the religious life. To Little Sister Magdeleine hitch-hiking was part of her commitment to poverty. It was also an opportunity to make contact with people and a means of holding out her hand to God and allowing Divine Providence to shape and direct her journey. Others saw it either, yet again, as a degradation of religious status or as an abuse of relgious privilege because people would feel obliged to offer lifts. There were those who, not knowing quite how she managed it, envied her the apparent freedom of her movement when others were constrained by wartime restrictions. They criticised her apparent liking for travel and her absences from Le Tubet, even alleging that she was shaping the life of her congregation amongst the nomads to suit her own natural predilection for physical activity and movement. They speculated about her access to the Vatican, claiming that it was by intrigue that she managed to go where others could not. They were also critical of the manner in which she talked publicly and, as they saw it, excessively. The latter tendency was one which she recognised in herself. It was a characteristic of the new persona which, on her sister's death, had supplemented the more taciturn 'mummy' of her childhood years, to talk and act very directly and spontaneously.

Even Father Voillaume had difficulty at first in believing that the rush of activity in which she was constantly involved in fact ran counter to her nature and that the talkativeness which seemed to come so readily to her – at least in relation to the work – was in reality over-compensation for a retiring and sensitive Lorraine personality. Yet this was how Little Sister Magdeleine herself explained it and Father Voillaume, whose own family came from Lorraine, but who handled his shyness rather differently, would eventually recognise the validity of her claim. It was not without a certain satisfaction that she discovered, contrary to her original belief, that Charles de Foucauld had himself on occasions given talks. Such confirmation gave her confidence but in any case she also maintained that, when faced with a duty, it was wrong to take too much notice of others' opinions. She knew that if she talked less people would judge her less harshly but her commitment to what she was doing was absolute and not to be tempered by the possible criticisms it might incur. 'When I go to heaven,' she wrote to Father Voillaume, 'you will see, that everything will quieten down and before I die I shall have left organised foundations, at the expense not only of all my strength but also of the opinion people have of me.' Nevertheless the criticisms did hurt her. The price she was having to pay for her successes was high, but it was one which she would not relinquish. In her letters to Father Voillaume her protestations of love for the Lord Jesus grew in intensity and frequency.

With the prospect of returning to Sidi Boujnan finally in sight and with the number of prospective Little Sisters growing faster than the building at Le Tubet, between 10 September and 4 October 1945 Little Sister Magdeleine committed to paper her thoughts on what a vocation to join the fraternity entailed. Addressing herself to all those drawn to the fraternity of the Little Sisters of Jesus because of Charles de Foucauld, in what would later become known as the 'green booklet', she invited them to come and see for themselves, as Christ had said to his own followers 'come and see'. She enquired of them whether they had given sufficient consideration to the requirements of such a vocation. The 'love of the heart of Jesus' was so great that it took in the whole world. A Little Sister must be prepared to go to the far corners of the earth to carry the love of Jesus to the poorest and the most forgotten, to those people whom others would overlook because there were only a few of them scattered over a large area or because they were otherwise inaccessible. She must reach out to such people, the poorest and most forgotten, from preference because if she did not then they might never learn of Jesus' love for them, of his suffering and death for their salvation. Like the good shepherd before her, a Little Sister of Jesus must be prepared to leave everything for the sake of a single lost sheep. She must be prepared to 'cry the gospel', not by her words but by her entire life, and in order to do so she must be ready to abandon her family, friends, country, language, customs – everything that she loved and to which she was attached. In preparation for this mission she must be ready to spend long years studying the language, customs, religion and thought of the people to whom God was calling her. She must accept that she would not always be understood, that she would encounter hostility, that the voice of reason would always be there to tell her that it was a waste of time travelling the world in search of one lost sheep while there were huge numbers of people waiting for her elsewhere. Had she really taken into account, the booklet enquired, the physical suffering the change of climate, food and customs could cause; the psychological suffering the renunciation of everything that she loved could bring about; the spiritual suffering occasioned by the renunciation of everything, even the satisfaction of seeing the fruits of her labours? Like Charles de Foucauld before her, she might never see a single soul come to Christ because of her.

The vocation of a Little Sister would involve total obedience to the authority of Christ as expressed through his Church. 'Think hard', directed Little Sister Magdeleine, 'before you embark upon a way in which there can be no compromise or reservation for you.' A religious vocation meant placing oneself in the hands of the Lord in a state of total dependence. A Little Sister's vocation would require going to the extreme limits of this dependence in the footsteps of Charles de Foucauld for whom obedience had been 'the most perfect expression of abandonment to love.' 'I offer you my life for the Touaregs,' Charles de Foucauld had written in his diary on 17 May 1914. He had wanted, Little Sister Magdeleine asserted, to be a 'universal Little

Brother' but he had chosen his Muslim brothers from preference, offered his life for them and eventually died amongst them. For this reason a Little Sister would be required to offer her life in self-sacrifice united with Jesus on the cross, for the sake of the people of Islam. Living as the poor amongst the poor, they must seek to be the least considered and treasure the lowest place, becoming poor in spirit and holding nothing as their own. They must be ready to give their lives in 'immolation', in sacrifice in deep union with Jesus. They must desire 'in total submission to the Will of God, the highest of graces, martyrdom, so that like Jesus you may give the greatest proof of love'. More than all else they would be asked to die to themselves in sacrifice day after day, hour after hour, as they carried out their duties of their everyday life, which was 'the hidden immolation everyone can attain'.

The 'green booklet' was a frank statement of the hardships an aspiring Little Sister would be required to accept. It was also a profound expression by Little Sister Magdeleine of the spiritual legacy of the man to whom at that time she referred as Father de Foucauld but whom she would later call Little Brother Charles of Jesus and finally Brother Charles of Jesus. Here it was Charles de Foucauld whom she presented to her prospective Little Sisters as the Father and the true founder of the congregation she was struggling to have erected. Her own role she described as simply that of endeavouring to transmit his thinking and spiritual message after having researched as faithfully as possible what could be gleaned from his life and his death. She had indeed made a comprehensive study of his spiritual writings and what was known at the time of his life. It was arguable and some did argue that she had found in her reading of René Bazin's biography essentially the confirmation of her own ideal and that she was selective in the image she chose to pass on. From the texts of Charles de Foucauld, some suggested, she chose to emphasise the boldest, the most extreme statements, using them to transmit what was to some extent her own vision and creating a static model for the Little Sisters which did not fully correspond with the global human reality of Charles de Foucauld whose life had been strongly characterised by spiritual growth and evolution. Exceptionally, when it came to Charles de Foucauld's life, Little Sister Magdeleine paid scant attention to details which did not accord with her own strong intuition. It was possible to claim that the evolution of his character and his spiritual journey found a broad reflection in the signatures he chose to use at various stages: Viscount de Foucauld; Lieutenant de Foucauld; after a period he spent at the Trappist monastery Brother Alberic, Brother Charles, Brother Charles of Jesus at Beni Abbes; towards the end of his life Brother Charles de Foucauld; and finally simply Charles de Foucauld. The two appellations he never actually applied to himself were Father de Foucauld and Little Brother Charles. Unusually, for one who tried herself to be meticulous in the choice of words to convey exactly the meaning she intended, for a substantial part of her life Little Sister Magdeleine chose to overlook such considerations. But then, for all her capacity to focus on details, she was not by temperament one to allow herself to be trapped in the letter of the law, and it was, above all, the message of Charles de Foucauld's heart that she sought to transmit. As in the case of the supernatural graces afforded her before and while she wrote the first Constitutions of her new congregation, so in Charles de Foucauld's endeavour to live a life in accordance with the gospel message, it was the truth as revealed in Jesus that had so captivated Little Sister Magdeleine. So it was that elsewhere she could write without inconsistency of how the infant Jesus was the true founder of the Fraternity and so it was that it was the continued expression of her perception of this truth to which she gave priority.

The Little Sisters of Jesus were not the first or only congregation for women to be inspired by Charles de Foucauld. The Little Sisters of the Sacred Heart had begun in Montpellier, France, in 1933 and, by the time Little Sister Magdeleine wrote the green booklet, were on the brink of initiating their first fraternity in a Muslim country, in Tunis. For them, however, fidelity to the ideal of Charles de Foucauld found its expression, at least initially, in terms of a more traditionally structured cloistered religious life along similar lines to that first led by the Little Brothers founded by Father Voillaume. Like the Little Brothers they had been strongly influenced by the Rule which Charles de Foucauld had set down in writing but never actually lived. In explaining her own position, Little Sister Magdeleine insisted on the message of the practice rather than the untested theory. Charles de Foucauld might have talked of a strictly cloistered life but his own cloister had been for the most part the vastness of the desert. In his Rule he had left the plan for an enclosed convent from which the Little Sisters were not to go out other than to be transferred from one fraternity to another, but he himself had been a nomad, travelling the desert from tent to tent and setting an example of being totally available to others and of the most expansive and fraternal hospitality.

The man whose motto had been 'Jesus-caritas – Jesus-love' had opened his heart to all and this was the message which Little Sister Magdeleine, at the risk of showing herself to be at variance with others who were equally committed to the inspiration of Charles de Foucauld, was eager to pass on.

For some aspects of the new congregation she knew she must accept total responsibility. If the first half of the green booklet was attributed by her entirely to the inspiration of Charles de Foucauld, to it she appended a section commencing, 'This is my will and testament' into which she poured her heart and soul. In it she outlined, without any intended criticism to other forms of religious life, which 'for centuries have produced saints in the Church', her conception of a 'religious life which is trying to answer the needs of our times'. Not without considerable personal reluctance, Little Sister Magdeleine had discerned the need to construct something new. 'You'll never believe it,' one friend remembered her having confided as if it were just one of a multitude of daily problems, 'I'm going to have to found an order and it's very tiresome.' A little more profoundly she would write some time later, in July 1948, to Father Voillaume:

> This morning I'm thinking about it more than ever. We must build anew. Out of the new that is in the ancient, out of the authentic Christianity of the first disciples of Christ. We must take up the Gospels again word for word.

Charles de Foucauld before her had turned for inspiration, not to contemporary models of the religious life, but to the life of the first communities who had lived in close proximity to the Gospel source. Now Little Sister Magdeleine called upon her Little Sisters to look to Jesus as their one and only model; and when Little Sister Magdeleine spoke of Jesus, she saw him before her in a very concrete, human way: Jesus, son of Mary and foster son of the carpenter Joseph; Jesus in Bethlehem, Jesus the workman in Nazareth, Jesus going about Palestine, Jesus during his Passion, accepting out of love to die on a cross before a crowd that mocked him with jeers and insults. The foundations she set down were for a vocation lived as a poor person following the example of Jesus at the very heart of humanity. Like Jesus who came to serve and not to be served, the Little Sisters were to give themselves completely to people and to become 'one with them'. Their vocation, encapsulated in the image of the leaven in the dough, gave precedence to charity above all other rules as the prime commandment of Jesus, the perfect model of human life, and stressed the importance of cultivating not only the religious virtues but human virtues also.

The Little Sisters of Jesus were to be human in order better to glorify the Father in his creation and bear witness to the humanity of his son Jesus. The more perfectly and completely they were human, the more perfectly and completely they would be able to be religious. Little Sister Magdeleine wrote of how her Little Sisters must be prepared to defend such a viewpoint because it could well make them a sign of contradiction. They would be accused, as Christ had been accused, of eating with publicans and sinners, but what did that matter? She wrote of the importance of believing with a faith that could move mountains in a God who was master of the impossible. They were to do their utmost to develop the human qualities of daring, courage and vigour and do away with the defects of timidity and fear. They were also to root out the 'feminine defects of being too sensitive and too imaginative' but not in the process to destroy the feminine qualities of gentleness, of dedication, of knowing how to give themselves in complete self-forgetfulness. Their formation was to take into account good common sense, sound judgement, prudence and fairness. Practising these qualities would help to avoid the 'illusions' of charity.

Little Sister Magdeleine's own 'good common sense' did not fail to creep in here as elsewhere even when discussing the transcendental elements of the Christian life. 'Be careful not to be mean and petty,' she wrote. 'Do not be too easily scandalised over unimportant things. Above all, avoid being stiff or formal and acting like a Pharisee. Never be narrow-minded for this can ruin true love.' She wanted her Little Sisters to smile and never show indifference in their eyes. They were also to guard against the subtle danger of passive resignation, against the illusion of too easy a submission to Providence which was in reality the abdication of human will. At the same time they were to remind themselves constantly that what might appear folly in the eyes of human beings was frequently divine wisdom. The balancing of the impulse towards 'blind' faith in an all-powerful God with the rejection of 'illusion' in its multifarious forms and an appropriate respect for what was human and reasonable was the direct fruit of her personal experience. In her own life there was evidence of a struggle for an appropriate equilibrium. The brief and intermittent entries she made in her private notebook bespoke a constant and intense inner life with the infant Jesus and with her Lord to whom she turned repeatedly in the suffering caused her by the incomprehensions she encountered, especially amongst other members of the Church. Predictably her suffering frequently found its expression in the image of the cross. The lack of understanding from those who were dear to God was:

> the cross in all its nudity because it is the only cross one would not have chosen, the inglorious cross, the cross intermingled with anguish because one can no longer see clearly, because owing to us – there is amongst your dearest friends a lack of indulgence and love.

At the same time she was caught up in a whirl of activity, of practical commitment in a way which appeared to leave no room for doubt or compromise.

On 21 October 1945, despite her extreme fatigue, Little Sister Magdeleine set sail at last with a small group of Little Sisters for Touggourt and the faithful affection of the friends at Sidi Boujnan. Throughout the three-year closure because of the war, the garden, the palm trees and the house had been carefully maintained and even extended, for under the team of Arab workmen the building work had continued in Little Sister Magdeleine's absence. Some of them brought their first-born babies for her to meet. The small boys who had first worked alongside her, helping her to shift the sand in readiness for the foundations, were just a little taller, a little older now. Life in the tents had never been more difficult. The nomads were cold and desperately hungry but the bonds of friendship remained unchanged. For Little Sister Magdeleine, as she hastily drew the Sacred Heart of Charles de Foucauld beneath the cupola of its now completed *koubba*, Sidi Boujnan was like the 'vestibule to heaven'. Already she was envisaging the Little Sisters she had brought with her going on to Tunis at the end of April to continue their study of Arabic. All the Little Sisters, she had decided, must have direct contact with the Sahara, before making their final vows in Rome. Yet the reopening of Sidi Boujnan had once more raised the issue of spiritual direction not just for Little Sister Magdeleine but also for her sisters. Increasingly Little Sister Magdeleine felt the need to 'entrust her soul' to Father Voillaume, and to live in close union with the fraternity of Little Brothers. Her letters to their founder contained oblique references to the fact that at that time, in relation to the White Fathers and White Sisters, she did not feel entirely part of a family or fully trusted. The sense of spiritual isolation had not left her and nor had the physical suffering. In November her foot was badly crushed by a trailer pulled by a bicycle. Some nomad friends, in their eagerness to help, had pushed the wheel over her foot, causing a deep wound. She made light of the incident for their sake. For them and for her sisters she found strength and a ready smile. The diary entries she would later publish, so comprehensive in their details of the practical events which made up the daily life of the fraternity, made little or no reference to her personal struggle. The practical work went on, and to the first friends and supporters of the congregation in France, to whom at intervals she wrote a progress report, she spoke of the many joys in which they could share and appealed to them to send the wool, materials, sugar and sweets she required to pass on to the nomads.

To Father Voillaume, however, she wrote in the language of intuition, of presentiments which at times she did not fully understand herself, and of suffering. On 21 November she informed him that Mgr Mercier felt unable to continue his role as her spiritual director. By then she had been passed so much from one person to the next that her reaction was a strong desire to remain without a director for a while. She was, she told Father Voillaume, tired, physically, morally and spiritually and yet she had never felt closer to God. Less than a fortnight later she told him how she felt she could take no more, but then as she herself acknowledged she had been saying that for some time. Some months previously doctors had advised her to take a period of complete bed-rest far away from Le Tubet where the debts incurred as a result of the extension were increasing. The work had prevented her from doing so and in any case rest appeared to do little to alleviate her fatigue. Another letter written on 8 December repeated what she admitted was becoming a refrain: 'I can't take any more. I am suffering so much.' Her lungs had been X-rayed. There was no sign of any bacillus but there were shadows. She could not understand it. She had even prayed for her temperature to rise as a sign that she had the right to a rest, but there was no fever. Still she felt dreadfully ill. Every morning after mass she had to be helped out of the chapel to go and lie down. On several occasions she actually lost consciousness but then, as soon as she began to work, she felt very much better. 'Don't worry', she reassured Father Voillaume, 'I shall hold on until there is someone to take my place, but it is terribly hard.'

Some alleviation of Little Sister Magdeleine's anxieties concerning the spiritual direction of the Fraternity and the question of who should steer it towards canonical recognition would come in January 1946 with the appointment of a new Archbishop of Aix-en-Provence. Little Sister Magdeleine was in Sidi Boujnan at the time, interceding with the local administrator on behalf of the nomads who were being driven away by the police. She gave the administrator her personal guarantee of their good conduct, offering if necessary to go to prison in their stead. To the nomads she gave pink cards on which were inscribed simply their names and the words 'Friend of Oukhti Majdalia'. With the consent of the administrator the production of these cards, a token of her confidence, would entitle her nomad friends to remain with their tents and their animals and their children in the vicinity of Sidi Boujnan. Living amongst the people of the Algerian desert, Little Sister Magdeleine knew the gentleness that lay behind their rough exterior, but as she joined in spirit with the Little Sisters of Le Tubet who attended the ceremony of enthronement of the new archbishop in France she could not help wondering what he would think of the new congregation committed to being 'one with them'.

As it transpired Mgr de Provenchères was a man of extreme simplicity and humility. As a bishop his great fidelity to the Church expressed itself in obedience to all the requirements of Canon Law but he sought also to be very open to the action of the Holy Spirit even when it seemed to be leading in new and unaccountable directions. From the time that they first began to correspond, a vital relationship of extraordinary understanding and trust was swiftly established between Little Sister Magdeleine and Mgr de Provenchères. By February of that year, before having actually met him, she wrote to the new archbishop explaining that although the congregation had been blessed by the Pope, because of the resignation of Mgr de la Villerabel it had not as yet been officially recognised by Rome, and asking him to be the founding bishop. There were still numerous decisions to be made, however, with regard to developments not only at Le Tubet but also in Touggourt, Tunis and Algiers where a plan for a foundation was initiated because Little Sister Anne was in hospital there; and Little Sister Magdeleine was receiving different directives from different quarters.

As the Fraternity began to show signs of expansion, more than ever she felt the need for confirmation that what she was undertaking was in fact the will of God. The very highest authorities in Rome had told her that she had a duty to defend the work, that she should never give in if something seemed to her to be the divine will, but how was she to be certain that the lights that seemed to be guiding her were not the product of an over-active imagination? For one as firmly rooted as she was in the realities of the everyday the possibility was a source of acute anxiety. She told Father Voillaume that she had the presentiment that 1946 was to be a year of inconsolable suffering for her and that she yearned to come with her new group of Little Sisters to spend a few months at El Abiodh. They would work alongside the Little Brothers, assisting particularly with the women in need of care, but it would also be a period of retreat for them, and an opportunity to draw closer in spirit to the congregation of brothers from whom Little Sister Magdeleine felt they could learn. 'I am thirsty for rest in the presence of the Lord,' she explained to Father Voillaume, 'before hurling myself into the great affray, because I can see that it is all going to go faster than I would wish and that the creation of foundations is going to have to be accelerated.'

On 30 March 1946 came the painful trial which she had in some way anticipated. Mgr Mercier was resolved that the Little Sisters should start a fraternity at El Abiodh where they could live in close collaboration with the Little Brothers and Father Voillaume. The Apostolic Prefect refused to take responsibility for Little Sister Magdeleine's work in the Sahara unless she took her young sisters to El Abiodh to benefit both spiritually and apostolically from the experience of the Little Brothers. Gradually the structure for a noviciate involving a first year spent at Le Tubet, a second at El Abiodh and a third at a study fraternity in Tunis, was emerging. A fraternity at El Abiodh was something which Little Sister Magdeleine had long wanted. She had always envisaged the formation of her Little Sisters there rather than at Sidi Boujnan but the price of seeing this deep-rooted aspiration fulfilled was high. In order to initiate the El Abiodh fraternity Little Sister Magdeleine would have to close Sidi Boujnan for several years and abandon the people to whom she had come to mean so much. Sidi Boujnan was a place that had become vibrant with life, a centre to which so many nomad hearts had been drawn. Above all, in Little Sister Magdeleine's eyes, it was a tabernacle from which Jesus in the form of the Reserved Sacrament was present to the small village nearby and the hundred or so tents that had clustered around it. She was heartbroken at the prospect of closing the fraternity there even temporarily. Seeking to console her, in the meeting he had with her at Laghouat, Mgr Mercier was imprudent enough to suggest that at

El Abiodh she would find other Arabs. It was like suggesting to a mother, she afterwards recorded, that she leave her children to go and find some others. 'At Sidi Boujnan', she informed him, 'the Arabs each have a name: Ali, Aich, Tahar, Athman . . . and they trust us.'

Through Mgr Mercier's insistence she discovered how painful the obedience she had craved could be. Years later she would come to a better understanding of the vital importance of a foundation in close proximity to Father Voillaume but at the time she could think only of the suffering of those she was being required to abandon. She left the house of the White Fathers where she had her meeting with the Apostolic Prefect 'like an automaton' and went to break down in the chapel. She had not the courage to tell her Little Sisters the news at once. 'All that night,' she recorded in her diary. 'I thought my heart would burst, so much so that the Little Sisters, very worried, went to fetch the nursing sister who could never have suspected what had caused me to be in such a state.' Obedience, Little Sister Magdeleine had told her sisters, should be 'liberating' otherwise religious obedience had not been properly understood. By her own account, she was also discovering that obedience could be 'heroic'. In her notebook, which she opened in May after nearly a year in which she had no time 'to think of me', she wrote of the experience of Laghouat:

> That was pain in all its profundity – first the bare Cross – and then the Cross with you, Jesus!
>
> You know that I only want your Will, the Will of the Father – but, with You, like You in your agony may I not say: 'Let this cup be taken from me . . . if it be Thy will.'
>
> Sidi Boujnan after Boghari – afterwards . . . all that was my cross as a pioneer made greater by all that You have given me of depth of love to love – with a human heart – like Yours – all those who entered into my life.
>
> Ali – Hatman – Fatima – Aich – Amoua Ali – Bouka – Aicha – Maamar – all the great – all the small – all those amongst whom I wanted to give my life . . . so one day I must abandon them.
>
> Lord, with my eyes closed and with my hand in Yours – with all my growing love for You, I repeat once more: 'Thy Will be done.'

By the time, in 1992, Father Voillaume felt it right to make known the content of some of the correspondence appertaining to Little

Sister Magdeleine's spiritual life, he could not recall precisely when it was that, after a period of reflection, she asked him to assume the role of her spiritual director. It seemed most likely to him that it was during the month of April 1946 but the first letter addressed to him in that official capacity was undated. It expressed a desire for the new union between them to be one of total trust, in which everything, even the most painful issues, were to be open and straightforward between them. That month, during a few days spent with him in Algiers, he had given her his writings on the spirit of the fraternities to read, and she had recognised the total accord which existed between them at the very deepest level. Later she would write to him of the graces she had perceived in him that had dispelled any nervousness which his theologian's intellect might otherwise have occasioned. Jesus was to be the link which bound them. When she thought of Father Voillaume she saw him holding Jesus in his hands as he did at the consecration during mass. 'And because of Jesus whom you will give to me, I shall lean very hard upon you.'

Their relationship was indeed to be one of profound union but in human terms not always one of spontaneous harmony. Even the project of bringing the Little Sisters to live and work in close proximity to the Little Brothers in the midst of the desert was one about which Father Voillaume, who was by nature more cautious in his reasoning, had initial reservations. Little Sister Magdeleine was envisaging relations between the brothers and sisters in characteristically simple terms, but a life of such extreme closeness for young men and women who were new to the religious life once again ran counter to more traditional views about the necessary reserve and separation that should exist between monks and nuns. Father Voillaume took advice from the Little Brother who was serving as novice master in El Abiodh at the time. The response came back that the combined presence of Little Sister Magdeleine and Father Voillaume was highly desirable and would help to develop and perfect the spirit and life of both congregations. After consultation with others Father Voillaume wrote to Little Sister Magdeleine, telling her that despite his previous reservations, he would welcome her and her ten novices at El Abiodh with all his heart. He could see now, he told her, that it was the will of Jesus. The preliminaries to this harmonious outcome were characteristic of the relationship that would exist between them for the remainder of Little Sister Magdeleine's life. Nor was it uncharacteristic that their eventual agreement based upon the shared recognition of the will of

God was in defiance of potential criticisms based on sound reason. Priests in France for whom Father Voillaume had considerable respect considered the proposal most ill advised.

In April 1946, before returning to France and the controversy the Fraternity was occasioning in certain religious circles there, Little Sister Magdeleine called in at Tunis where the way was being paved for a fraternity in which the Little Sisters could make a more formal study of Arabic. Together with Little Sister Jeanne and three other Little Sisters who had come from Sidi Boujnan to begin the fraternity, Little Sister Magdeleine went to see the Bishop of Tunis. She showed Mgr Gounod their religious habit: a veil like the *bernouk* worn by the Arab women, a hooded cape and long robe. After his initial shock the bishop appealed to his vicar-general to help him make a judgement. The latter pronounced that the general effect was too poor for Tunis. Tunis with its noise and bustle, its cars and trams and the curious stares aroused by the simply dressed Little Sisters provoked feelings of panic in Little Sister Magdeleine, but she wrote afterwards of the warmth of the reception she had received from the religious authorities and their generosity of spirit. Even their reading of her 'testament', the 'leaven in the dough', had not apparently diminished their affection.

Elsewhere her 'testament' was proving to be more controversial. The 'green booklet' and in particular the section of it prefixed 'My will and testament' had been written exclusively for the Little Sisters and those considering a vocation to the Fraternity. Without Little Sister Magdeleine's consent, however, it had been published out of context in a religious publication entitled *La vie spirituelle* and was beginning to provoke conflicting reactions in ecclesiastical circles. To Father Devillard, a Jesuit in Algeria, who had actively encouraged Little Sister Magdeleine in her calling since her earliest days in Boghari and with whom she would continue to correspond until her death, she wrote at that point of how difficult it was for her to be alive while human passions were being stirred up around her conception of a religious life lived as the leaven in the dough. Mgr de Provenchères had wholly approved of it. Indeed, it had found considerable support in certain quarters, but some potentially supportive elements were not of a kind that Little Sister Magdeleine could welcome. The Vicar-General and the Cardinal of Lyon were fearful that the 'leaven in the dough' might be used by certain liberal young priests and religious as a licence to remove their cassocks or habits, to frequent disreputable places, and otherwise conduct themselves in a fashion which Little Sister Magdeleine herself would have found unacceptable. In her 'green booklet' she had appended a section on humility and the contemplative life. The director of *La vie spirituelle* had omitted this section and the modifying thoughts it contained. Provided God was not offended, Little Sister Magdeleine professed not to be concerned about any attacks directed against her, but she spoke simultaneously of the cross carried by foundresses 'who must be ground into their foundations like minced meat'. Once more she was being made a sign of contradiction and she did not feel that she had the physical stamina to cope with such a role.

On her return to France in May 1946, she felt an increasing desire to withdraw and shut herself away in solitude with God. The energy with which she had hitherto struggled round her native country, giving her innumerable talks, seemed finally to abandon her. She declined to give any more and expressed instead a growing desire to disappear from the world. This did not prevent her from laying plans for a fraternity in France which would be strongly devoted to craft and manual work. Charles de Foucauld had esteemed manual work highly, 'in union with Jesus the Divine Workman, Son of Mary and adoptive son of Joseph the carpenter'. The example of the carpenter of Nazareth was ever before her, as was the recognition that there was beauty in work well done, and in the dignity that even a poor man could derive from the lowliest of work undertaken to earn his daily bread. Of the ten Little Sisters of which this new fraternity would be comprised, she stipulated, three would be engaged in needlework within the fraternity, two in a pottery, two in a bindery and two at a printers. By then both the Little Brothers and the Little Sisters of Jesus were moving towards the idea of 'worker fraternities', from which the brothers and sisters would go out to undertake salaried work. Despite a carefully cultivated vegetable garden, their own bakery, carpentry and goats, it was proving difficult for the growing number of Little Brothers in El Abiodh to be self-sufficient. The financial situation for the Little Sisters in France was sometimes so desperate that it threatened to jeopardise Little Sister Magdeleine's case for having no dowries or income from capital. It was a time when the worker priest movement was gaining strength. The possibility of having working fraternities was likely to satisfy not only an economic requirement but, more significantly, the need to draw closer to the world of the poorer workers, which in France in particular had become increasingly alienated from the Church and from the gospel message. It was a new direction for the Roman Catholic Church to which both the Little Sisters and the Little Brothers felt drawn without either being able to say which congregation was taking the lead.

It was out of Little Sister Magdeleine's intense personal desire for 'Bethany', however, out of her craving for a period of time spent in retreat from the world, at the feet of Jesus, that the idea for what she saw as the 'most marvellous project of all' was born. The longing to spend time alone with Jesus as Mary had done had become a 'real obsession', so intense during the Easter of 1946 which she had spent in Tunis that, on her arrival back in France, she had told one of her Little Sisters that one day she would go away without leaving them any address, only a note saying 'Gone to Bethany'. In the middle of a street in Marseille the Little Sister accompanying her had responded: 'And what about us? Can't we do the same and have our Bethany?' Instantly the plan for a 'fraternity of adoration', a fraternity very specifically devoted to prayer and contemplation, was formulated. The idea brought relief from an inner desire which had been so intense that Little Sister Magdeleine had expressed it in terms of an actual pain.

The nostalgia for heaven grew. Believing that she was on the brink of what she called her 'beautiful departure', on 1 June 1946 she wrote a letter to Father Voillaume which she entitled her 'new testament' and in which she entrusted to him her new foundation. In his directives to the Little Sisters she urged him never to forget that they were women and not men. To treat the Little Sisters in the same way that he treated the Little Brothers would be in some way to distort the service and the love that they, as women, must give to God. She asked him to retain as far as possible the heart and soul of Father de Foucauld and his sayings, even if they were not always in full accordance with Father Voillaume's own temperament. She entrusted to him the realisation of her statue, for he alone knew why her heart was so set upon communicating the gesture of the Virgin giving her child to the world. She also asked him to safeguard what she saw as the 'trademark' of the Little Sisters: the simplicity of small children around the Jesus of the manger.

Confronted with her extreme fatigue, Father Voillaume had directed her to take a week of rest. During that week she wrote a few lines in her notebook about the yearning for solitude which had accompanied her even amongst the crowds she had encountered during her lectures, which meant that this week alone with Jesus was precisely what she had wanted:

Oh, how well hidden it was, Jesus, the secret between the two of us. Even Father Voillaume was able to think that it would be hard for me to take a week's rest. I wanted it too much to accept it unless obedience imposed it on me. That was what I was waiting for – not so that I could have a rest but so that I could be with You, Lord, with You, completely alone, as Mary was in Bethany.

This more retiring personality was in fact, Little Sister Magdeleine insisted, a reversion to her true temperament. The greatest miracle God had ever wrought in her was in managing to make her speak out. Yet for all her professed desire for 'disappearance', for heaven, to 'spill her blood', the creative thrust continued. Her language continued to reflect the apparent contradictions in her: the feeling of being out of step with the mentality of many combined with a sense of profound union with all people; the love of creation juxtaposed with the yearning for paradise; the desire even for martyrdom offset against her obvious zest for life; the human protestations that she could endure no more alongside an avowed love of suffering. They found their mysterious unity in the love of God. If she longed for death it was as the ultimate expression of that love. At the same time, because God had become man in the form of a tiny baby in Bethlehem, the love of God could not be separated from the love of humanity. Suffering and ultimately death were an expression of love and the desire for intimacy with Christ. They were also part of the great redemptive process. Little Sister Magdeleine chose as the emblem of her congregation 'the Heart of Jesus and his Cross united', symbolising the Little Sisters' mission of love and self-offering. To have joyfully and generously accepted Jesus meant to have entered into his work of salvation. It meant being ready to accept suffering, understanding the meaning with which it was imbued by the crucifixion and thus even, little by little, growing to love it. Like Charles de Foucauld before her she had taken deeply to heart the words of Jesus: 'Greater love hath no man than that he lay down his life for his friends.' She wrote often to Father Voillaume of her suffering in terms of a price that she felt must be paid for the founding of each new fraternity, and beyond her assertion lay all the richness of meaning inherent in the image of the leaven lost in the dough of humanity in order that it might rise and of the Christ who died on the cross and rose that others might live. Suffering, she told her Little Sisters, was not to be deliberately sought but if it came, it was to be accepted, as part of their life of self-surrender in union with Jesus.

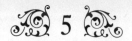

5

Unity in Love

'ON 26 JULY 1946, at Ste Baume, the certitude came to me – as if imposed on me by a great inner light – that the Fraternity was to spread throughout the world and become "universal".' This brief entry in the historical account of the fraternity Little Sister Magdeleine later published, and in the collection of letters and documents she assembled for the benefit of her sisters, in fact represented a momentous step for the Fraternity and one which ran counter to everything that Little Sister Magdeleine had envisaged to date. Until this sudden revelation by an 'inner light' the Fraternity had been uniquely and strictly consecrated to the Islamic peoples of the Arab world with a special preference for the nomads. The Constitutions were being written with this specific orientation in mind and Little Sister Magdeleine had made a point of emphasising repeatedly an aspect which distinguished the Little Sisters of Jesus both from the Little Brothers and from the Little Sisters of the Sacred Heart. Referring to the Fraternity's consecration to the world of Islam, Little Sister Magdeleine had written only three months previously to Father Voillaume: 'I assure you, Father, that it is an inspiration against which I cannot struggle' and even later: 'There is a difference in thinking which explains many things. You envisage fraternities with very different orientations. For you there will be the Arabs, the workers, the Chinese . . . For us there is solely Islam, hence the necessity to unify everything in a shared spirit.'

It was precisely the fact that it involved the sacrifice of an idea that was personally so dear to her that convinced Little Sister Magdeleine that the opening out of the Fraternity to encompass non-Muslim countries was the will of God. The sudden and unexpected inspiration came to her not in the grotto at Ste Baume but simply as an overwhelming certainty which overtook her somewhere on a road. At the time she told the Little Sister accompanying her in the simplest terms and afterwards relayed her conviction to the small group of Little Sisters waiting to start a study fraternity in Tunis, again in terms so unspectacular that they did not think to question her further about the nature of the experience. On a piece of paper that day in Ste Baume, however, she had drawn up on a diagram of a heart united with a cross and under the heading 'Universality' her new vision of the structure of the Fraternity showing the Little Sisters after their final profession in Rome being directed out not only to Islamic peoples, but also to 'China, India, Japan, the black African countries, America, Oceania, Russia, France etc.'. From there they would all rejoin each other in paradise. The diagram also outlined the new formula for the Little Sisters' final vows which would enable them to orientate themselves to the people to whom they felt specially called: 'to consecrate myself to the Muslim or Chinese or Russian . . . peoples and offer my life in total self-surrender for the whole world and in particular for the redemption of the people of Islam . . . or China or India'. Little Sister Magdeleine's meticulous handwriting also recorded the fact that she was embarking on this new plan with her hand in the hand of Jesus 'who is making me sacrifice what is most dear to me: exclusivity to Islam'. She signed it: 'Sister Magdeleine of Jesus, Little Sister of Father de Foucauld, the Universal Little Brother.'

The change of orientation was to involve complexities other than the requirement to alter the Constitutions of the Fraternity. In some quarters it confirmed a criticism that the Little Sisters were abandoning the world of Islam, already latent as a consequence of the opening of the fraternity devoted to manual labour in Aix-en-Provence and a fraternity of adoration also in France. The removal of the specific commitment to the people of Islam also served to highlight the differences between the respective understandings of Charles de Foucauld's inspiration among those who sought to pass on his legacy. Some maintained that the interpretation Little Sister Magdeleine placed upon the word 'universal' which she applied increasingly to 'Little Brother Charles' was not the meaning with which he himself would have imbued it.

Charles de Foucauld had wanted his brothers to be 'universal little brothers' in that in humility they were to learn to respect all human beings. Little Sister Magdeleine, however, was giving that ideal of universal respect a concrete application which would scarcely have entered into the head of one immersed in the nomadic life of the

Sahara. By the end of July 1946 she was envisaging a fraternity in which two Little Sisters would go out to earn their living through manual work in a factory. Such a means of identification with the working class world was a far cry from anything Charles de Foucauld had conceived. Yet at a time when colonial pride and the disdain of the white man for his colonial conquests were rife, his call to universal respect had been equally radical. Furthermore the impulse to broaden the direction of the Fraternity in many respects seemed to Little Sister Magdeleine to come clearly from God. Her conviction was confirmed by a growth in the number of aspiring Little Sisters who felt called to pursue their vocation as Little Sisters in varying directions. It also passed the acid test to which Little Sister Magdeleine submitted all the 'lights' which seemed to her to be guiding her, namely the approbation of God's representatives on earth. Mgr de Provenchères, among others, was quick to approve the 'universality' of the Fraternity. For Father Voillaume it was merely the fulfilment of something he had been expecting for some time. Far from having to promote the new thrust of the Fraternity by a deliberate assertion of her own will, for Little Sister Magdeleine it now became a question of restraining a potentially too rapid expansion of the congregation. 'You will help me, Monseigneur,' she appealed to Mgr de Provenchères, 'to resist the requests that are too pressing.' Privately, she was still experiencing a yearning to escape 'all the evil, the Pharisaism, the lack of love' amongst which she was obliged to live in the world. She yearned for 'paradise' from where, she maintained, she would be able to work far more effectively for her Little Sisters.

On Sunday 13 October 1946 Little Sister Magdeleine arrived in El Abiodh with Little Sister Jeanne. Not far from the Little Brothers' fraternity with its high walls and chapel, built to Father Voillaume's design in the style of a domed mosque, a large disused barrack-style building, erected at the end of the nineteenth century to serve as a hospital, had been placed at the disposal of the Little Sisters by the French administrator in Geryville. It was there that the Little Sisters would lodge until such time as they could build their own fraternity. A group of about a dozen would follow shortly afterwards to receive spiritual direction and formation from Father Voillaume. The content of the series of talks he gave that year would afterwards be amalgamated in a book entitled *Au coeur des masses (Seeds of the Desert)* which would attract numerous vocations to the Little Brothers and the Little Sisters. This 'session' held at El Abiodh would also prove to be the first of many he conducted there annually until 1955. Thereafter, because of the Algerian war of independence, these yearly sessions would have to be held elsewhere. For the Little Sisters in 1946 the stay at El Abiodh was also to be an opportunity to make several sorties into the Sahara to experience for themselves the 'graces' of the desert, to make contact with the nomads, learn at first hand something of their lifestyle and prepare to initiate the first 'tent fraternity'. For Little Sister Magdeleine herself it was the first time she would have the opportunity to live in the Sahara amongst an Arab population that was almost entirely nomadic and far away from any presence of the French military authorities. It was also the realisation of a longstanding desire to spend an extended period of time close to Father Voillaume.

'Allow me this joy', she wrote to him the day after her arrival, 'of having a superior for these four months, of being through him in the hands of Jesus.' They saw each other almost daily but that did not prevent her from needing to communicate frequently with him by letter. Wanting nothing about her life to remain secret from him, and still fearful lest she was the victim of what she referred to as 'a woman's imagination', she told him of her experiences of temptation:

> For years, it has been frightful. Onslaughts of every possible
> temptation. Against purity, they were the ones that troubled me
> the least, despite one painful period – above all against faith
> and that's when I realised that it didn't come from me,
> especially when the worst blasphemous thoughts were
> accompanied by a very clear sensation of odious derisive
> laughter. That's what I don't like to tell you about and I am
> having to take my courage in both hands to write to you about
> it, because it could well be considered the product of a woman's
> imagination. What does it matter, true or untrue, or rather
> real or imagined, I suffer just as much as a result of it. It was
> worst at the moment of communion when the derisive laughter
> would sometimes follow me – but not any more. I didn't dare
> tell anyone, even less than about my life with the baby Jesus.
> And all the more so since I sensed a lack of understanding
> around me.

Others to whom Little Sister Magdeleine had turned for spiritual direction on less sensitive matters had been nervous of the 'inner lights', the authenticity of which she sought constantly to have confirmed. She had no fear, however, that Father Voillaume for all his reasonable caution would not understand the terrible extremes between which she was torn: 'the love of God which draws me ever more strongly towards the most marvellous heights and these dreadful temptations which disgust me, especially when they find in me the complicity of original sin'. To him she confided how one morning she had been working in the Little Brothers' chapel behind the grille which separated the brothers' choir from the part of the chapel accessible to people from outside. She had been reflecting upon some notes on the subject of adoration and praise when suddenly

> a veritable blast of rage beat down upon me from outside myself – in the same way that what I believe to be the devil invariably presents itself, with this very clear sense of something I call derisive laughter – a rictus which is not perceived with my senses but which is even more real. And this rage prompted me – of all unlikely things – to break the grille. When it is ridiculous things like that, afterwards I only laugh – but it isn't always like that. Sometimes it is a rage against the crucifix – and then temptations of hatred, murderous temptations, I who would never have the heart so much as to kill an animal. That's why I think that it comes from the devil. I couldn't come up with ideas like that.

Little Sister Magdeleine was confident that the devil whose presence she felt in such a concrete way would be dispelled and broken by the deep love she had for God. For this reason, she maintained, her experiences were not a source of excessive worry to her. Nor was she prepared to satisfy the devil by dwelling unduly on his activities. The assaults remained nonetheless a source of suffering to her. By November 1946 even her love of God itself was expressing itself in terms of the desire to suffer. How, she found herself protesting, when 'one lives with someone one loves with passion (I would like to find another word but I can't) and who is suffering', could she not beg to suffer with him? She was already suffering physically, mentally and spiritually but that was not enough.

Years later Father Voillaume would write of how he realised only imperfectly to what extent Little Sister Magdeleine 'was led as if despite herself by a supernatural force'. There were times when he was taken aback by her predictions. One day at El Abiodh, when first she asked him to undertake the formation of her sisters during the sessions, he expressed grave reservations. Given the nature of the

Little Brothers' vocation at the time, a vocation to enclosure, silence and solitude, the prospect seemed to him impossible. His reticence, however, was met with a sudden forceful outburst by the foundress of the Little Sisters of Jesus: 'You'll see. One day you'll travel the world, you will preach to many priests and you will talk to the brothers and sisters together!' The fullness of time would reveal the accuracy of her prediction but at the time Father Voillaume attributed little importance to it. It seemed so totally unlikely and he put the outburst down to the whim of her obviously enterprising personality. In his old age he believed that there had been many similar instances but at the time he had not considered them significant enough to record and he was not the kind of man to make claims based upon the vagaries of memory alone. Nor was he without personal experience of that which transcended rational explanation, however. His own account of the experiences leading to his vocation bore witness to this. Above all he believed in the authenticity of Little Sister Magdeleine's mission. In response to her expressed desire to suffer with the object of her extraordinary love, he gave her the kind of counsel which she offered her Little Sisters: not to seek suffering but only surrender to the will of God.

In many respects what was to follow was an experience which she herself would treat with extreme caution. In 1943 she had visited the stigmatic Marthe Robin at Chateauneuf-de-Galaure. Marthe Robin had been paralysed since 11 November 1918 and had had the stigmata since 1925. Nourishing herself on the Eucharist alone, during the last three days of each week she suffered with Christ all the torments of his Passion. Encouraged by priests and religious to go to Chateauneuf to ask for the stigmatic's prayers for the Fraternity, Little Sister Magdeleine had expressed her reluctance to do so out of curiosity or even as an act of her own will. She would go only if given an obvious sign that it was the will of God. 'You know', she told her Little Sisters, 'how little extraordinary ways attract me, as long as the Church has not made its pronouncement . . .' A series of circumstances had contrived in February 1943, however, to convince her of the appropriateness of such a visit, when the opportunity arose to go in the company of Canon Zimmerman, the priest who had won her confidence in her youth at Montigny-les-Metz.

Significantly, what Little Sister Magdeleine chose to note about the woman whose bishop credited her with rare second sight and an extraordinary capacity to read souls, was that there was nothing obviously extraordinary about her, that the visit passed off very simply and that Marthe Robin had encouraged her in her way of littleness. Little Sister Magdeleine placed great emphasis on the fact that ever since Jesus had taken a little child by the hand, and put him in the midst of grown men arguing over who would have the first place and dreaming of an earthly kingdom, telling them, 'If you do not become like little children, you will never enter into the kingdom of heaven' (Matt. 18:3), spiritual childhood had become an obligation for those seeking entry to heaven. In his great love, the Son of God had chosen to pass through a little infant's helplessness, the only state in which a person was totally given over into the hands of another. In her life of total surrender and in her simplicity, Marthe Robin endorsed Little Sister Magdeleine's aspiration to become 'like a little child'.

In a letter to her Little Sisters at Le Tubet their foundress referred to how Marthe Robin was all smiles despite the fact that only a few hours after her visitors' departure she was to suffer the entire Passion of Christ. A rapport was instantly struck between the two women. Almost every year until 1959 and at more irregular intervals thereafter because of Little Sister Magdeleine's wide-ranging travels, she took to Marthe Robin the problems of her growing Fraternity. She saw the foundress of the 'Foyers de Charité' as 'one of those privileged souls chosen by God', and claimed to draw from her much strength to face the criticisms and obstructions she encountered in pursuing what she herself referred to as her 'acts of madness'. Yet it remained a relationship of extreme simplicity, about which she spoke little. With Canon Zimmerman Marthe Robin talked theology in a manner which Little Sister Magdeleine reported to have stupefied him. To the foundress of the Little Sisters of Jesus on the occasion of her first visit she said nothing extraordinary 'but we talked endlessly of the Love of the Lord'. 'Above all it does one good', wrote Little Sister Magdeleine, following a subsequent encounter, 'to see something extraordinary which has remained simple and humble, altogether childlike in spirit.' What was more, if she valued Marthe Robin for her spiritual qualities, she wrote with equal enthusiasm of her 'incredible good sense'.

During the winter months which Little Sister Magdeleine spent at El Abiodh at the end of 1946 and the beginning of 1947 the mental and spiritual suffering she experienced as a result of what Father Voillaume would later describe as 'her constant union with Jesus and her encounter with sin and evil' became a source of ever-increasing physical pain, a pain which had no obvious external causes. The desire to be in union with the Jesus for whom she felt such an overwhelming love became so intense that by day she felt obliged to make a conscious effort to banish his presence. By night, however, in the privacy of the chapel and in the company of Little Sister Jeanne, whose support had become vital to her in concealing what she was experiencing from the remainder of her Little Sisters, she could no longer resist the desire to abandon herself to the Jesus who was not now the tiny child of Bethlehem but the adult in his Passion.

Throughout her life Little Sister Magdeleine maintained the importance of constant reference to the infant Jesus in the manger because there was to be found the truth of the whole life of Christ, the God made man in all his vulnerability and surrender. 'Perhaps you did not really stop to look at the crib, or maybe you just looked at it rather disdainfully, as an adult who thinks that the crib is for children and that it has no meaning other than at Christmastime,' she wrote to her sisters in 1952. 'You looked longer at the cross. There you found something bigger and more satisfying for your adult years.' She went on to point out the error of such a misapprehension: 'This crib is something so beautiful and great because it contains the whole Christ, God and man together. And in the extension of this cradle there is the workshop of Nazareth, the passion and cross, and all the glory of the resurrection and of heaven itself.' In 1947 in the Christ of the Passion, she saw still the baby she had previously held in her arms and it was precisely because she identified in the adult Jesus so intensely present to her now, the infant she had loved so deeply, scourged, crowned with thorns, bearing his cross and finally nailed with arms outstretched in total surrender, that she found herself telling him, despite herself, that she wanted all his suffering.

The fear that she was subject to illusion or the effects of hysteria was still with her, as was her frequently articulated horror of what she referred to as 'anything which is not normal, which oversteps the ordinary'. She was tormented by incomprehension and the need for reassurance, and the thirst for obedience was, if anything, growing. In a series of letters written during January 1947 she confided in Father Voillaume, sometimes with the assistance of Little Sister Jeanne because Little Sister Magdeleine herself was too exhausted by what she was experiencing or because the mere thought of Jesus was sufficient for her to become totally overwhelmed by his presence and unable to do anything except remain with him. The letters record her desire to submit to the authority of a priest, even the intensity of her yearning to express her love by sharing in the suffering of Jesus. Father Voillaume finally granted her his permission if indeed this was what was being asked of her by God. In the middle of January 1947 she wrote to him of how during the previous night she and Little Sister Jeanne had remained in the chapel from midnight until five o'clock the next morning:

> I asked Him to let me share in the smallest details, from the agony to the crucifixion and then the flagellation, the crowning with a crown of thorns, the cross, Father, confirm now that this is really Jesus.
>
> I don't know whether there will be other similar days and nights. I can well believe that my poor human heart will not be able to withstand it, but I want everything if Jesus wants it. How reassuring it is to have you. How many times during these days I have had to say to myself to reassure myself: 'Father has forbidden me to be frightened.' It is terribly hard to undergo all this Passion, not on my own account but on His. I don't know how to tell you about it. Above all I would like to talk to you about Jesus. I don't know how to do that either but you will guess. I would like Little Sister Jeanne to explain everything to you. Everything would be difficult because I believe that during those five hours, for half an hour I hardly stopped talking to Jesus who was so present, or giving an account of everything I was experiencing of his Passion, the details of which were present to me as the infant Jesus was, in a way that was perceptible not to the eyes of the body, but inwardly and so real – I don't know how to explain – every form of suffering had its reverberation, especially the scourging and the crucifixion. At times it was so dreadful that my whole body trembled. I was so frightened of upsetting Sister Jeanne too much and that it might be bad for her soul – but on the contrary, it was at the same time so peaceful, so simple; I was living with Jesus that was all.

In accordance with Father Voillaume's directions, Little Sister Jeanne kept him informed of all that Little Sister Magdeleine was undergoing. The letters of both sisters record how there were many subsequent experiences of intimate participation in the Passion of Christ, both in the dreadful physical suffering and in the mental anguish of his betrayal and rejection. For Little Sister Magdeleine the primary source of anguish seemed to be the suffering which she could see but was unable to relieve even by an identification so close that she felt its consequences in her own flesh.

In January and February 1947 she took her Little Sisters on several sorties into the open desert to prepare them for the foundation of the first nomad fraternity. Privately she was desperately afraid of the physical fatigue such journeys would entail and of the bitter cold which pervaded the desert once the sun had set. There were times she could scarcely walk for exhaustion. Yet this, combined with the effects of the extraordinary presence of the suffering Jesus by night, did not prevent her from carrying out the tasks of the day, whether it was amongst the nomads in the desert or amongst the Little Sisters at El Abiodh. She had asked Little Sister Jeanne to speak to no one other than Father Voillaume while she was alive of the 'graces' she had received. It was a cause of considerable concern to her when another sister noticed when at mass one day she was overtaken by what she herself described as 'such abnormal physical suffering' that she was unable to move. The Little Sister in question passed her a note on which she had written: 'Mother, tell us what is overburdening you, what is causing you so much suffering.' Otherwise, it seems, Little Sister Magdeleine managed to keep her suffering a closely guarded secret and continued to work with her customary energy and resolution.

The people of El Abiodh and the nomads in its environs were suffering dreadfully as a consequence of many years of drought. It was a time of great hunger when, as one woman would recall some forty-five years later, people smeared their mouths with a little grease in order that others might think that they had eaten but often they had had no food for several days. The brothers and sisters did what they could to alleviate the consequences of the famine. They distributed bulgar wheat sent as aid from the United States. They set up a soup kitchen and they ran a medical dispensary. Typhus fever was running rife. Trachoma was a common cause of blindness. 'Father Voillaume, Little Sister Magdeleine, the Sisters – they opened many people's eyes': more than forty-four years after Little Sister Magdeleine stayed at El Abiodh for the Little Sisters' first session, a chance encounter with one whose family had for generations guarded the tomb of Sidi Cheikh triggered the immediate memory of the many eye operations Father Voillaume had performed and of Little Sister

Magdeleine's very practical concern for the suffering nomads. At Christmas 1946 she wrote to the early friends of the Fraternity: 'At the crib in El Abiodh, seeing the great poverty of the nomads, starving and sick because of the drought that has ruined their flocks, we have come to understand better the suffering infant Jesus.'

Beside such suffering her own must not be allowed to become a source of self-preoccupation or introspection. When in 1954 she went to see Mother Teresa who had just been given the pilgrims' rest home attached to the Kali Temple in Calcutta for use as her first home for dying destitutes, she wrote to her Little Sisters of the care that was being given to the fifty men and women whom hunger and neglect had brought to the brink of death: 'This is where one must come to measure real suffering when one believes oneself the victim of imaginary illness.' At El Abiodh Little Sister Magdeleine divided her time between prayer, the dispensary, visits to the local people and forays into the desert. The relationships she built up with the nomads would become crucial for the preparation of her Little Sisters for the nomadic existence some of them were to live in the planned tent fraternity. In the early days at Le Tubet the Little Sisters sat on mats on the floor and ate from low tables in preparation for their life in Algeria but television and the ready availability of flights had not yet opened up the world. The European sisters had little idea of what really lay ahead of them. It was from the nomads themselves that they must learn the rhythm of a life shaped by the search for pasture. In winter, livestock and people settled in sheltered valleys out of the cold of the High Plateaux. In spring when the cold was less bitter the flocks could graze in the more exposed *hamadas*. Then there was an abundance of milk and butter in the tents. In summer animals and humans alike gathered around the rare waterholes and when the season was particularly dry they moved northwards. The Little Sisters must learn how to maintain their flocks. They must learn how to make the longs strips or *flij*, meaning literally 'gap-toothed person', which were woven horizontally on the ground from wool provided by the herds of goats and camels, sewn together, and then supported on wooden branches to create a tent. They must learn how to cook couscous over a fire made out of twigs laboriously salvaged from a landscape where wood was often a rare commodity. They must learn the nuances of Arab courtesy and hospitality. The Little Brothers and Sisters were called upon by the local people to teach them how to do certain things: how to plant out gardens, how to make use of water power, how to generate electricity, but the process was reciprocal. The skills that must be acquired in order to survive in the open desert could only really be acquired from those whose very existence depended on them. Little Sister Magdeleine approached the local Caid Cheikh and received from him a warm welcome both for her Little Sisters and for the idea of the tent fraternity.

Even during her travels in the desert which were physically so demanding of her, she was noting down plans for future fraternities in which she detailed the shape and purpose of each one. By then there were a number of Little Sisters spreading news of the Fraternity, its spirituality and its work. A house which Little Sister Marguerite's parents had helped the sisters to find in Marseille and which was used as a base from which they could make their travel arrangements and pause en route between fraternities, was also to be a 'Bethany' where Little Sisters between lecture tours could gather their thoughts before the Blessed Sacrament. She made plans for a working fraternity in Tlemcen. The plans were never brought to fruition but Little Sister Magdeleine's intention at that stage was that it should provide the wherewithal to maintain the Little Sisters of El Abiodh. At Kharoua, the home of a number of poor half-settled nomads not far from El Abiodh, four Little Sisters were to take up residence in a small Arab dwelling made out of clay bricks. They were also to have a tent so that they could join other nomad groups further afield. Her plans were not always realised but Little Sister Magdeleine even went so far as to specify the intervals at which such Little Sisters should be brought back to El Abiodh. She made plans to involve the Little Brothers so that the Little Sisters would be able to attend mass and she specified the principles on which the Fraternity's manual work was to be undertaken, insisting that all the Little Sisters were to live off the proceeds of manual work, be it their own or those of their companions. Charitable gifts were to be used only to initiate new foundations or for the charity work of existing fraternities. It was therefore important, she reasoned, that suitable work should be found to provide for each existing fraternity. Her own practical work went on without interruption, and all her carefully stipulated plans for the future of the Fraternity were made and set down in writing concurrently with her intimate experience of the presence of Jesus.

At the end of one journey into the desert which was to conclude the Little Sisters' first session at El Abiodh, she wrote to Father Voillaume of the crucifixion which, even during her stay in the desert, she had relived 'with my eyes, in my whole being and with Him, as if it were with my eyes but even more real than with my eyes, as if I were hearing it with my ears, but even more real than that'. She described how at the moment of crucifixion the feeling of abjection previously experienced was replaced by love: 'Never before have I understood so well the symbol of those outstretched arms, wide open, completely given to suffering and completely given to love.' To her sisters in Tunis she wrote afterwards from Le Tubet of her plans to reorganise the larger houses such as Le Tubet into several small fraternities in order better to perceive the sense of family spirit, then added something 'more profound' which bespoke, though without personal explanation, a new appreciation of the reality and purpose of suffering:

> All my meetings during this month of March will be centred
> on the Passion and on immolation. Otherwise we shall run
> the risk of a grave omission; the simplicity of small children
> may make us forget the desire for expiation and reparation. . . .
> This year, at El Abiodh, the Lord made me understand better
> the mystery of his suffering for the Redemption of the world.

To those around her Little Sister Magdeleine did not appear morbid, neurotic, or self-absorbed. The process of foundation continued without anyone suspecting what the foundress was going through, other than Little Sister Jeanne who had witnessed her experiences and Father Voillaume to whom she had confided them as a representative of the authority of the Church. Together they could vouch for the calm, the humility of heart, the deep peace that were the consequences of what Father Voillaume would describe in 1992 as the 'graces of identification with Jesus in his suffering, and of the Presence of the Lord'.

The intense interior life, the sense of empathy and identity with the life of Jesus, had undoubtedly brought about an overflow of powerful feelings. Perhaps it was that Little Sister Magdeleine was more than usually sensitive to the rhythms and archetypes of the transcendental in a way that rendered her capable of perceiving a sense of the presence and love of God in vivid images and even physical symptoms. What is sure is that both the message of the Nativity and that of the cross had their place in Little Sister Magdeleine's understanding of 'immolation', the readiness to give her life in sacrifice, in deep union with Jesus. On a cold Christmas Day in 1948 from Khabab where she was in the company of an Egyptian Little Sister who was suffering terribly from neuralgia, she would write a letter to her Little Sisters in France which pointed to the intimate association of the two:

> Today I have asked for you to have, as a Christmas present, the joy of immolation . . . immolation of your body and your heart, of your will and of your whole being, offering itself up to suffering like the newborn baby of the manger who must have found the straw of his crib very hard and the night of his birth very icy, as we are doing here. But the joyful immolation too, of the holy infant who smiled at his mother and the shepherds and the magi, at the great and the small who gathered round his cradle.

Immolation, she wrote then, was not in her view to be something tragic to attract the pity of others. It was not to be cultivated as a means of dispelling egoism. Above all, it was not to be imagined because such immolation would crush instead of bringing with it the grace to be able to 'lift up your heads to try and smile at those who have need of your friendship and your joy because they are perhaps suffering differently and more painfully than you, without letting it be seen . . .' Immolation meant accepting the possibility of martyrdom. It also meant the peaceful, even smiling acceptance of everything the day brought, in solidarity with the suffering of the world and in the belief in its redemptive value.

Certainly also the fruit of Little Sister Magdeleine's experience of the Passion was a growth in love. In 1992 Father Voillaume entitled his record of her letters and experiences during that period: 'Little Sister Magdeleine and the consummation of her love for Jesus'. In it he wrote of how the 'continual presence of Jesus, far from diverting her away from humanity, made her better able to carry out her duties as a foundress and be entirely for her Little Sisters whom she loved with an ever stronger love'. She herself was aware of the change that was being wrought in her: she wrote to Father Voillaume of a transformation that was taking place in her soul, of how the deepening of her love for God was leading to a growth in her love for her Little Sisters and then for all humanity. She looked back on her past life and found that there had been times when she had fallen short of the ideal of love which was being shown her. During the period she spent in charge of the Sacred Heart school in Nantes she had moved between two worlds, that of the working classes and that of the more privileged social groups, and on more than one occasion she had gone as far as to despise those who thought they were above disdain. All her love, she acknowledged, had been directed towards the weak and the vulnerable. She had involved herself with the beginnings of the Young Christian Workers. All that, she reflected at the age of forty-eight, she could have done with a far greater measure of love. Following the deaths of her two brothers killed during the First World War she had felt a dreadful anger towards the Germans. Now she was resolved that before she died she would take all the love she had in her to Germany.

'We never love enough and we can always love a little more,' she insisted. Manifestations of a lack of love became intolerable to her. Words that might give offence, humour that was insensitive to the possible feelings of others, condescension, a lack of respect for anyone, rich or poor, weak or strong, became a source of deep personal sorrow, and she would clamp down on them firmly if she encountered them amongst her Little Sisters. She warned them against the risks of sentimentality but at the same time she directed them increasingly towards the goal of a universal love which could not accept divisions or barriers between people of different classes, milieux, nationalities or creeds. As so often in the case of Little Sister Magdeleine this dynamic found its expression in a very tangible way. If she endeavoured to live the life of Christ without compromise it was still with both feet planted more or less firmly on the ground. For her, she once said, prayer was life. In the gradually unfolding plan for a fraternity committed to her 'dream' of unity at a multitude of levels, by April 1947 she was already envisaging how each Little Sister would be able to follow the particular orientation to which she felt personally called. The spiritual message of smallness, surrender to the will of God, unity through love, must be *lived*. There would be a fraternity amongst the gypsies, a shepherd fraternity in the mountains of France, one among the Eskimos, one in Japan, one in central Africa . . . As far as her Little Sisters and the world was concerned, all Little Sister Magdeleine's energies were absorbed in the shaping and implementation of this new form of religious life. Her metaphysical experiences of intimacy with both the infant and the suffering Jesus were for her inseparable from their fruits. She had been given these graces and the inner 'lights' which continued to guide her to pass on to her Little Sisters that they might bring the message to the world, and she did so in a characteristically concrete manner. Whatever the objective reality of the experiences she kept so closely secret, whatever the potential criticisms to which they might be liable at the level of human suspectibility, many of which she was prepared to direct against herself, what remained significant was that they were an expression of her great love for God. She did not use them as a means to convince others of the rightness of the path she was pursuing but they were a personal confirmation without which she might have lacked the confidence to continue with what the world would frequently regard as madness.

Shortly after the conclusion of the first session at El Abiodh in April 1947, Little Sister Magdeleine began work with three other Little Sisters at a factory in Marseille. Determined that she would not subject her sisters to anything which she had not herself experienced, she spent a month operating with a single monotonous movement a machine which cut out forty thousand pharmaceutical tablets a day. For a while she was able to enjoy a certain anonymity. The experience of not being known as the Mother General of her Fraternity but simply as one of the Little Sisters was one which she savoured until an article about her disclosed her identity as a foundress to her fellow factory workers and thus ended her opportunity to 'disappear'. When she felt ill one day at work her fellow workers had treated her with a kindness which she would long remember. She was struck by the fact that each one of the women at the forty machines on the factory floor had an incomparable value and dignity. As far as she was concerned, sharing their lot, far from debasing the Little Sisters as some critics of the Fraternity were suggesting, was raising them up, especially in a workplace where people really applied themselves to their handiwork. Because of the practical requirements of factory conditions, the Little Sisters had adopted a 'habit' made out of the blue denim from which workers' overalls were frequently made. On their heads they wore a headscarf made out of the same material. When washed the dye ran and Little Sister Magdeleine remarked with amused satisfaction that in their faded denim they really looked the part. She wore her new habit with pride when in June that year she went to Rome for a retreat and the final vows ceremony of Little Sisters Jeanne and Marguerite, and found herself treated with the habitual respect afforded to a foundress, despite her unusual attire. The welcome she received in Rome was important to her. Rome had not criticised the published text on the 'leaven in the dough'. The struggle for the kind of poverty Little Sister Magdeleine believed essential to the Little Sisters' calling to share the plight of the poor and of the workers amongst whom the Little Sisters lived and laboured continued, however. In Tunis it had not been possible to open a study fraternity as planned because the bishop there could not accept the poverty of the Little Sisters' dress or the idea of their going out to work to finance their studies.

On 13 June 1947 Little Sister Magdeleine received a telegram from Mgr de Provenchères in Aix-en-Provence announcing that the Fraternity had been formally erected as a diocesan congregation. With renewed confidence born of the knowledge that the Little Sisters were now officially part of the Church, once more Little Sister Magdeleine went on bended knee to Pius XII to plead the case for living the poverty of Jesus of Nazareth. Her attempt to defy the voices of reason which argued so plausibly the importance of providing for the future of her sisters and of insuring against old age and sickness, was by her own admission somewhat vigorous. When Cardinal Fumasoni-Biondi, Prefect of the Sacred Congregation of Propaganda Fide, the body in Rome to which the Fraternity was initially made responsible because Touggourt came within its jurisdiction, raised such practical issues with her, she retorted swiftly that her Little Sisters' greatest joy would be to go and die as indigents had to in the public ward of a hospital. On the whole, however, she pronounced her reception a warm one. Whilst there in Rome, she overheard theological quarrels between various religious groups. She heard criticisms of particular religious orders. It made her all the more convinced of the importance of 'going beyond all that'. The beauty of God was so much more beautiful.

Of the seat of the Roman Catholic Church she said simply that she closed her eyes to the details that she did not like in order to see only the faith and the love; and she promptly began to consider putting a fraternity of Little Sisters to work in a factory in one of the city's desperately poor suburbs. Invariably she wanted what was new about the religious life of the Fraternity to be open and clearly on view to the Church authorities. She knew that her Little Sisters were subject to close scrutiny. For this reason she kept a particularly tight rein on the first generation, urging them to be disciplined in everything they did. She did not want their laxity to jeopardise the whole vision. A working fraternity in Rome itself would dispel speculation and any criticisms arising out of second-hand reports. After an initial shocked reaction the response from at least some of the Church authorities, among them Mgr Montini, was favourable.

Little Sister Magdeleine's stay in Rome was also the occasion of an encounter with a group of Catholics belonging to the Eastern Rite Church in the Soviet Union who met to pray together. She joined in their worship and afterwards drank tea with them. The sadness of what they had to tell her of their circumstances immediately prompted the idea that one of the Little Sisters should consecrate herself to that country because it was one of the 'most forsaken'. The 'lost sheep', the poorest and the most forgotten, ignored and disregarded minorities, small groups of people situated on the margins of society and of the Church, became the urgent focus for her attention. She wanted, she maintained, to leave a spark of love in all the dark corners of the world and one Little Sister with a heart full of love would be sufficient to light such a spark. From that one Little Sister two or three others would evolve and so the vision expanded. It excluded no one. Little Sister Magdeleine might well feel no particular spontaneous affinity with the world of intellectual or theological debate, but she saw even the study fraternities from which the Little Sisters would go out to places of learning to study theology and Arabic simultaneously as a means of making contact with more academic circles. The fulfilment of the ideal of simplicity for a Little Sister was that she should feel at ease anywhere and everywhere. Above all, however, it was the suffering of the poor who worked long hours and endured harsh living conditions without complaint because no one was there to listen to them, to be a reflection of the love of God amongst them, which touched Little Sister Magdeleine most.

The idea of the worker fraternities was spreading. She took it with her to Switzerland when in November 1947 the debts, incurred as a result of the building that was going on at Le Tubet, obliged her once more to take to the road. Hitch-hiking or struggling on foot through the bitter cold and the snow of the Swiss mountains, she went once more in search of funds and support, but the most significant fruit of her arduous journey was, she afterwards reported, the warmth with which the ideal of the worker fraternities, of Jesus of Nazareth, was received. Instantly she began to lay plans for the location and character of a worker fraternity in Vernayaz.

In April 1948 a fraternity was begun in accommodation attached to the Church of Saint Paul of Belcourt in Algiers. The study fraternity she had hoped to establish in Tunis was moved there but it was also in part to be a worker fraternity. For several weeks Little Sister Magdeleine worked alongside two other Little Sisters who were to earn the living of the fraternity in a metal box factory. At the end of her nine-and-a-half-hour working day on the production line, she wrote to Little Sister Jeanne of how she felt that the Fraternity was entering a new phase in which the dynamism would be even greater but in which they would try to become more stable. She did not believe that their vocation was to personal perfection, or to found well-organised fraternities. Her plan for a Fraternity which would eventually be made up of Little Sisters sharing the life of the neglected throughout the world was, however, becoming more clearly defined. The fraternities would be divided up into regions. Each region would have a 'responsible' who, wherever possible, would actually come from that region. The general house, the heart and soul of the Fraternity, a place of adoration and the family home, was not to be in France but in Rome, a centre of unity for the Little Sisters who would come from all nations and races. Little Sister Magdeleine decided to celebrate her fiftieth birthday as the symbol of a new period of stabilis-ation. Less than a month later, however, she found herself having to remark with amused irony that ever since she had been talking about stabilisation, ideas for fraternities had been springing up all about her. 'One day,' she wrote in her diary entry for 11 May 1948, 'people will realise that there is a whole world in which the Church is non-existent . . . or if it exists, it is on a more exalted plane . . . . And that world expects something different. . . . So may we be allowed to enter it as little ones, on an equal level. . . . I'm sure it will come.'

By the middle of May 1948, in Switzerland the plans for the tiny working fraternity in Vernayaz had come swiftly to fruition. In France later that month Little Sister Magdeleine and several of her sisters took part in the annual Saintes Maries de la Mer pilgrimage made by hundreds of gypsies. Little Sister Magdeleine was beginning to formu-late ideas for a fraternity travelling, living and subsisting as the gypsies did. The gypsies were a despised people, frequently mistrusted simply by virtue of what they were. Yet their annual gathering for a mass and celebrations were full of warmth and spontaneity. Even before actually knowing the Little Sisters, Mgr de Provenchères had felt a special concern for the workers, rural people and gypsies of his dio-cese. He was glad to join the Little Sisters at the annual gypsy pilgrimage. Together with the Archbishop, the sisters cooked their meal among the travelling people, sitting on the ground between the caravans. 'They are gypsies like us,' was the verdict. Word spread that next year the sisters would come in a caravan like the rest of the gypsy community and a place was duly reserved for them. As part of the celebrations Little Sister Magdeleine found herself wading into the sea, drawn along by a companion who would not let go of her arm. The predicament of a people for whom she had felt an affinity since early childhood was one she felt called to explore further. In France administrative attitudes were divided into two camps: the one held that gypsies should be made to settle down in suitable areas; the other maintained that they should be given civil status, a job and a fixed location for the winter but allowed to travel about because that had always been the way of their people. Little Sister Magdeleine, who saw gypsies as the nomads of Europe, subscribed to the latter view and that was what she wanted for her gypsy Little Sisters: a fixed location for a few months and then the opportunity to travel with the people who she hoped would adopt them for the remainder of the year.

A not dissimilar arrangement was envisaged for a group of three Little Sisters who felt called to share the life of the shepherds who tended their flocks in the high mountain pastures of the Alps. Somehow their religious training must be fitted in with the movement of the flocks determined by weather conditions and the availability of grazing land. With a note of triumph Little Sister Magdeleine wrote to Father Voillaume of how she had found a solution which would enable three Little Sisters to live in a hamlet high up on Mount Pelvoux not far from Briançon with a woman whose cows one of the Little Sisters would tend while the other two looked after the sheep with four local shepherds. They would remain there from 25 July until 15 October. Then they would follow the movement of the flocks for a fortnight before returning to Le Tubet and then going on for the session of formation at El Abiodh. In May they would rejoin the flocks and remain with them until their trial period had been completed. Only three months after writing this letter Little Sister Magdeleine herself embarked upon a two-hour climb on foot to visit the Little Sisters living as shepherds some 2,000 metres up in the mountains. They had made their fraternity in a cabin which had once served as a stable and which was also used for maturing cheeses. Three mattresses on the floor served as beds. In the wall was a small niche containing a statue of the Virgin Mary in front of which the Little Sisters gathered each evening after spending their days in the silence of the high mountain pastures. When the flock of six hundred sheep was moved, the Little Sisters slept as the other shepherds did beside their sheep. 'And as this was a little strange for religious,' understated their foundress in her 'Letters', 'they had in their pockets attestations from three bishops,' from Mgr de Provenchères, from the bishop whose diocese they were crossing and from the Bishop of Gap in whose diocese the fraternity was usually located.

Little Sister Magdeleine's conviction that faith without love was useless, and the impulse to express the love which she saw as the ultimate objective of faith in the most concrete terms, was to lead the Fraternity in ever more varied directions. Her long-standing calling to work with lepers, born in 1931 when she visited the leper hospital in Valbonne, was to find confirmation when she encountered a brother who confided in her his secret aspiration to give his life to lepers. Like gypsies, lepers had formed part of the confused adolescent dream she had harboured of her vocation. Now she had ideas of a fraternity in which the sick and the healthy would live together, sharing the tasks of the day according to their respective abilities. Alone she would not have dared to create another fraternity at this particular juncture. She was already struggling for authorisation to implement her radical vision of the religious life on a number of fronts, but the unexpected encounter with someone who shared her dream was enough to convince her that it was right to proceed. 'I am counting on you to get the ball rolling as you are so good at it!' Brother Bernard had told her. 'So I am getting the ball rolling,' she informed Father Voillaume.

By then the Fraternity had extended beyond the diocesan responsibility of Mgr Mercier in the Sahara and of Mgr de Provenchères, who had supported the Little Sisters so wholeheartedly in their extraordinary requests in Aix-en-Provence, to several other dioceses. The struggle for the spirit of the congregation had become an ever more complex one. In July 1948 there were sixty Little Sisters in Algeria, France and Switzerland. Little Sister Magdeleine had recently undertaken a journey to the East which included visits to Cairo, Nazareth, Jerusalem and Amman at a time when travelling conditions were difficult because of the Arab-Israeli war which followed the declaration of the new State of Israel in May 1948. It went without explanation that Little Sister Magdeleine was drawn to the historical locations of the life of Jesus. To walk where once the Christ of Bethlehem and Nazareth had lived and worked touched her to the depths of her being. Her visit was also the consequence of the influence of an Egyptian Little Sister whom she had known even before the foundation of the Fraternity, but in the East also there were Catholics of the Eastern Rite whose Christian worship expressed itself in the language and culture of the Arabs. To Little Sister Magdeleine the attraction of a form of Christian worship which expressed itself in Arabic, the language of the Islamic people to whom she wanted to draw closer in language and in prayer, was irresistible.

During that first visit she discovered a proud affinity with the people of the East, particularly with the Christian Arabs to whom she was able to draw close in worship in a way which had not been possible even with the precious Arab friends of Sidi Boujnan or El Abiodh. The deep vocation she had to give herself completely for the Arab race found a fresh chord of recognition amongst the Arabs of the Orient. She began at once to lay the foundations for the Fraternity to spread there. She would come herself, she resolved, to open a fraternity of adoration in Nazareth, a place of silence, retreat and worship. Little Sister Magdeleine was experiencing a growing conviction that her personal star was leading her in the direction of Russia but she was equally certain that the Fraternity was being called to Cairo, Beirut, Nazareth and a multitude of other places. 'I think', she wrote to her Little Sisters at Le Tubet, 'that we must be prepared to burst forth in all directions, to be sent out into the towns and the villages, two by two.' Preparation, however, involved the initial firm establishment of both the form and the spirit of the Fraternity. It meant the 'stabilisation' for which Little Sister Magdeleine had been calling for some time.

Her visit to Rome in July 1948 was with a view to obtaining permission actually to start the worker fraternity in Rome. Questions were raised, however, as to the appropriateness of foreign sisters taking jobs at a time of widespread local unemployment. Furthermore, almost immediately after Little Sister Magdeleine wrote to the Cardinal-Vicar Marchetti Salvagiani on 8 July 1948, making a formal request for permission to initiate such a fraternity at least for a trial period of one year, she received news that the Congregation for Propaganda Fide required her to rewrite the Fraternity's Constitutions modifying what she had previously said about poverty (the fact that the Fraternity wished to maintain itself without dowries or income from capital), about their proposed life in the midst of the everyday life of humankind and about the worker fraternities. In desperation Little Sister Magdeleine wrote to Mgr Montini asking him to relay to the Pope the vehemence with which she believed in the spirit of poverty she had outlined and how deeply pained she was by the objections that were being raised to it. She asked that the Fraternity be allowed to continue for a trial period of several years on the basis of the existing Constitutions. She compiled a third supplication to Pope Pius XII on the subject of the Fraternity's poverty and she wrote to Father Voillaume of how she was undertaking a desperate struggle to save the spirit of the Fraternity 'and to that end I feel ready to work day and night and run about Rome in all directions'. She did so with an insistence but an evident eagerness to be in perfect agreement with the Church that did not fail to impress some, and once more Mgr Montini showed himself to be sympathetic to the Little Sisters' cause.

Relations with the Congregation for Propaganda Fide, however, were becoming increasingly strained. On 13 July 1948 the position was made very clear to her. The Fraternity had too many houses in France and too few in the mission field to continue to be part of that particular body. By December the Cardinal-Vicar of Rome had once more declined to accept the idea of Little Sisters working in one of the city's factories. The Congregation for Propaganda Fide had also stated unambiguously that it would not take responsibility for the worker fraternities. It had even gone so far as to suggest that the Fraternity should be divided into two: one committed to missionary work; the other made up of worker fraternities. Such a concept could not, however, have been further removed from Little Sister Magdeleine's ideal of unity. As far as the Constitutions were concerned the requested period of respite would be granted if Mgr de Provenchères would assume responsibility for them.

Consoling herself with the recollection that the way of humiliation and abjection she was being obliged to tread by some of the Roman authorities was a necessary part of the Christian way and a way which Charles de Foucauld had chosen before her, Little Sister Magdeleine turned increasingly to another authority in Rome, namely the Congregation for the Oriental Churches. She had already confided in Mgr de Provenchères the fact that if the Congregation for Propaganda Fide continued to reject what she saw as the very essence of the Little Sisters' vocation, the Congregation for the Oriental Churches might be prepared to receive them. Cardinal Tisserant of that Congregation had shown himself ready and willing to give his patronage to the Little Sisters' project for the Orient which was once again somewhat radical

111

in nature. It was part of the intuition of Little Sister Magdeleine that the fraternities in the Orient should form part of the indigenous Church of the Eastern Rite rather than remaining part of the Latin Church as, for example, the Jesuit foundations in that part of the world had done.

The feeling of proximity to the Churches of the Eastern rite was something very fundamental to Little Sister Magdeleine. Some time later, in March 1961, when a number of fraternities had been established in the Orient and organised into a 'region', Little Sister Yva, the Egyptian sister made responsible for that region, would write of this bond of union:

> It is as if there were an affinity between the inner nature of
> Little Sister Magdeleine and the Orient . . . the oriental
> sensitivity . . . the oriental soul . . . like an intimate, essential
> understanding, harmony. . . . To the understanding she brings to
> its problems and suffering but also to its richness and potential
> for life, the Orient will respond with a welcome, an inner and
> an external hospitality that is boundless.

The relationship between the Roman Catholic Church and the Churches of the Eastern Rite was a sensitive one, complicated by an accumulation of misunderstandings and by the sensitivities of a poorer Church with a smaller following in relation to the wide-ranging authority of Rome. Such potential complexities, however, left Little Sister Magdeleine undaunted. If there was a barrier between people it must be spanned. It was part of her vision of unity and an expression of her ideal of universal charity. She was not a diplomat. Her audacity and directness of speech was prone, as she herself knew well, to give rise to criticisms. Nor was she a theologian in the sense of enjoying theological debate or having devoted much time to its formal study, although during her noviciate and during her many years spent at convent schools both as pupil and headmistress she had undoubtedly absorbed a deep understanding of religion. She had nonetheless what Father Voillaume referred to as 'an infallible theological sense'. In all their years together he had never known her to say anything which was theologically unsound. She herself maintained that she had only learned such things from God. When she approached Churchmen it was with directness and lucidity, but it was more by an intuitive understanding than by an intellectual awareness that she found her way spontaneously to the hearts of many who might have presented her with obstacles.

In 1992 Father Voillaume recalled accompanying Little Sister Magdeleine when in 1948 she first approached the Melkite Patriarch Maximos IV with a view to initiating a fraternity in Beirut. He was a bishop in the mould of the oriental bishops of the time, very much a leader of his people, a strong, deeply committed man who was also capable of anger. He had assumed that the Little Sisters wanted, as others before them had done, to start an apostolate, carry out works of evangelisation within his diocese whilst remaining dependent on their Superiors in Rome. This was not, however, what Little Sister Magdeleine wanted and she told the Patriarch so. What she wanted was for her sisters to become part of the Melkite (Greek Catholic) Church and therefore not only to adopt the rite of that Church and thus, as she put it, 'be penetrated by its spirituality' but also to come under its authority. Dependence on the Congregation for the Oriental Churches of the Eastern Rite in Rome was for this reason very important to her. It was a non-intellectual grasp of the situation which won her a warm welcome amongst members of the Eastern Rite Churches and indeed from Cardinal Tisserant in Rome who gave her his wholehearted support.

For Little Sister Magdeleine the experience of forming a friendship was frequently the spur to a more expansive 'dream'. It would not be long before she was seeing the fraternity founded in Beirut as part of the Melkite Church as merely the beginning. As fraternities were founded in various parts of the Orient she found herself 'haunted by the thought' that there should be at least one fraternity in each of the Churches of other Eastern countries: in the Churches of the Armenian, Chaldean, Maronite, Syrian rites. 'It would be so beautiful', she wrote, 'to come together as members of all the different rites, first at El Abiodh, and afterwards in Rome. That would be such a beautiful unity.'

Her early commitment to the people of Islam had meant that in the very beginning, without leaving any room for doubt as to the orthodoxy of her own Roman Catholic commitment, Little Sister Magdeleine had moved beyond the confines of her own particular faith. The process was to prove an ongoing one. Contact with the Churches of the Eastern Rite brought with it quite spontaneously friendly relations with Orthodox Churches. Travels in Arab countries expanded her vision even further and she sensed, in a manner totally consistent with her goal of unity, that she could no more start a fraternity in the Arab part of the Holy Land without simultaneously initiating fraternities in the Jewish sector, than she could have a fraternity in the Christian quarter of Beirut without one in the Muslim sector. In 1941 a young Muslim girl had come to her in Algeria, asking to become a Little Sister. She even had her parents' consent but war had broken out and, when Little Sister Magdeleine returned to Algeria after having had to remain in France for several years, she could find no more trace of the family. The seeds of an idea had been sown, however. Close proximity and links to people of different religions and denominations gave birth to the idea of an ecumenical fraternity made up of women of different Christian and non-Christian faiths committed to being Little Sisters in a life consecrated to God, whilst still remaining members of their respective religions. She would not give official expression to this idea until February 1966 but it was one which she carried around with her from the early 1940s onwards.

In July 1948 she had visited the tiny French village of Taizé where a Swiss Protestant Pastor, Roger Schutz, had begun a community that in time would become widely known for its commitment to reconciliation between the divided peoples of the world, and especially between Christians of different denominations. Of her first visit Little Sister Magdeleine wrote to Father Voillaume:

> Today we visited the community of Protestant brothers at Taizé who live the spirituality of Brother Charles of Jesus and who also want poverty. We spent two good hours together. They are extremely likeable. Their thinking is a little surprising; to restore the Catholic religion by their example in the village.
>
> The Bishop of Autun has given them permission to celebrate their Offices in the Catholic church where there is no longer a priest in charge, but to which they invite Catholic priests to celebrate mass on Sundays.

The Taizé community's attempt to render concrete a vision of peace and reconciliation by living a 'parable of communion' was one which touched upon the deepest aspirations of Little Sister Magdeleine. The relationship with Brother Roger and the Taizé brothers was to prove a long-standing one, for together the two founders shared a similar vision of universal unity to which even the path of ecumenism was subordinated. For Little Sister Magdeleine, irretrievably bound up with considerations of different faiths, rites or denominations were the interests, problems, lives and evolution of nations and peoples of which they were frequently an expression. The goal of ecumenism came after that of universality, and universality involved the initial establishment of fraternities in all races, countries and milieux.

It was with this objective in view that she travelled ever further afield. In October, November and December 1948 she journeyed from Algeria to Morocco, to Aix-en-Provence, the Lebanon, and Syria. The beginning of January saw her in the Holy Land; and so the laying of foundations for the tiny fraternities went on. The travelling in uncomfortable and sometimes dangerous conditions was taking its toll. Little Sister Magdeleine was tired. She felt herself torn apart because she could see that her place was everywhere. Yet there was still a part of her which wanted no more to do with the increasing number of foundations. To her sisters she expressed the desire to withdraw to a quiet place to pray and to die. At one moment she would write of how she could see very clearly before her a 'luminous route' from which she could not deviate, of how the whole plan was unfolding without any intervention on her part. It was this conviction which enabled her to fly in the face of convention, to defend what she knew the Lord had entrusted to her despite the criticism which continued to be levelled at her, and even to battle against the restraining influence of Father Voillaume who was more cautious than she about the expansion of the Fraternity. In the next breath she would speak of how she could no longer tolerate the life she was obliged to lead despite her own inclinations; of her yearning for paradise, for peace, or at least for her withdrawal to a small fraternity somewhere. In November 1948 Little Sister Jeanne had been nominated 'Assistant' and first General Councillor and given responsibility for all the fraternities in France. Little Sister Magdeleine's health was giving such cause for concern that it had been felt necessary to have someone ready to step into her shoes at a moment's notice. Increasingly the foundress began to refer to the necessity for Little Sister Jeanne to be ready to take over as 'General Responsible' of the entire fraternity. She made oblique references to the fact that for years she had been obliged to lead a dual life, that behind the façade of health and happiness she presented to the world, the reality was quite different.

Her fatigue did not prevent her from undertaking, in February and March of 1949, a journey from El Abiodh through the desert to Beni Abbes. Some four hundred kilometres of the six-hundred-kilometre route to the oasis not far from the Moroccan border where Charles de Foucauld had spent his first years in the Sahara, were to be made on foot with a caravan of camels. Only because of pressure of time, the final stages would be made in a lorry. In part the purpose of the journey was to experience at first hand the life that the Little Sisters who were to live amongst the desert nomads would be leading, for by then Little Sister Magdeleine had obtained all the authorisations necessary for the first tent fraternity to begin. In part, she maintained, it was a way of arriving at the place where Charles de Foucauld had conceived the Fraternity in a condition as poor as his own. Her insistence on the importance of his spiritual inspiration was as strong as ever. In September 1948 she had submitted a request to Pope Pius XII for the beatification of the Little Sisters' 'founder and father', the 'universal Little Brother' who had set such a vital example of the total gift of self to his neighbour, of an authentic contemplative life lived in the midst of humanity, a life of poverty, smallness and humility.

The journey Little Sister Magdeleine made in the company of Little Sister Jeanne, three other sisters, an Arab Cheikh ben Bahous who frequently acted as her guide during journeys into the desert, five camels and two camel drivers, was physically demanding, but nonetheless 'magnificent'. They travelled across muddy ground strewn with yellow and mauve flowers, over sand-dunes, through mountainous terrain, across stretches of sharp stones which made the walking difficult and over vast expanses of desert, empty even of sand and punctuated only occasionally with the black and white of a flock of sheep and goats. At night they erected their two tents, joining the other desert travellers around the water holes and the wadis. They built their fire and cooked their *kessra* (bread) as the desert people did and when, on occasions, the anticipated water sources were found to be dry, they discovered what it was to go thirsty like their neighbours. The going was hard. Towards the end of one day Little Sister Magdeleine collapsed unconscious in her tracks. Six hours of walking a day was, she was obliged to acknowledge, her maximum. 'If the desert reveals what one is in the depths of oneself,' she wrote, for even under such conditions she kept up her diary, 'more than anywhere else it will have made us feel our poverty.' But she saw this as appropriate preparation for Beni Abbes. There, in the desert, it came to her that Brother Charles's hermitage which now stood empty and untended must not be allowed to do so any longer. It must become a centre of prayer, adoration and retreat. Next day, in the midst of a sandstorm, a future fraternity at Beni Abbes took shape in all its details. By the

116

time she was finally able to write to her Little Sisters from the actual hermitage, she was envisaging both the Little Sisters and the Little Brothers present at Beni Abbes and making of it what Charles de Foucauld had dreamed of: 'a *zaouïa* [location for Muslim monks] of prayer and hospitality, from which such piety will be radiated that the country will be lit up and warmed by it'. 'He is so present here,' she wrote, 'I would like him to become more and more present, more and more alive to you all.'

Her own sense of the closeness of this presence brought about an intensification of her long-standing emphasis on the importance of his spirituality for the Fraternity and of her insistence that he was their real founder. And with this emphasis on the seeking of the last place, on her own relative insignificance, and the spirit of total abnegation in the spirit of Charles de Foucauld, the idea of handing over her position to Little Sister Jeanne evolved and matured. 'I am giving something careful consideration with the Lord,' she informed Father Voillaume on 17 May 1949: 'Little Sister Jeanne of Jesus, Prioress General, and me . . . the elderly foundress beside her to provide her with a shoulder to lean on. It might be something unique.'

Exhausted to the point of weeping openly in front of some of her sisters, something which her extreme self-containment rarely permitted, she continued the work of foundation nonetheless. Plans for a fraternity among the Eskimos were beginning to take concrete shape. It was not in order to retire and rest that she wanted to resign her position but in order to serve the Fraternity better and also to be available to all the foundations. She spoke of going to live in a tent in silence and solitude at Beni Abbes to work on the Constitutions. She spoke of entering a new phase in which she would be of greater use to the Little Sisters writing and simultaneously being present to the distant fraternities, and at the same time she made plans for a journey behind the Iron Curtain. The conviction that she was following signs from God overrode all personal inclinations because, she maintained, such signs brought with them a strength which exceeded all human weakness. It seemed to her now that the Lord was expecting something of her that was incompatible with responsibility. The transmission of the will of God was a grace which she felt she must renounce.

'The Lord wants me to relinquish my office at Christmas,' she confided to Father Voillaume in June 1949, 'but I am so afraid that it will not be understood, or that it will be understood too late.'

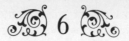

6

Blindly Following

CHRISTMAS: THE SPECIAL FESTIVAL of the Fraternity; the symbol and source of smallness, simplicity and self-surrender; the season of new birth and new beginnings. At 2 o'clock in the morning, after midnight mass on Christmas Eve 1949, in the Grotto at Bethlehem, Mgr de Provenchères celebrated mass assisted by Father Voillaume. During the offertory Little Sister Magdeleine relinquished her role as Prioress General of the Little Sisters of Jesus, which then passed immediately to Little Sister Jeanne. That night, in the very place where the baby Jesus had begun to live and simultaneously to suffer, Little Sister Magdeleine saw herself as giving back to the infant of the manger everything that had been entrusted to her ten years previously, in order that it might now be placed in the hands of Little Sister Jeanne. From that moment onwards, she was at pains to tell her Little Sisters, Little Sister Jeanne was the representative of the Lord for them and for her.

Little Sister Magdeleine's expression of her fears about the incomprehension her decision to resign was likely to meet had been followed almost immediately, although in a different context, by a defiant instruction to Father Voillaume not to tell her that people did not understand. She had experienced criticism before and that had not prevented the Fraternity from growing. Criticism lasted for a short while and then blew over. It would be terrible if fear of it were to be allowed to obstruct the will of God. The practical woman in her ensured that she did everything she could to make the transition a smooth one. In August 1949 Little Sister Magdeleine had been granted a third audience with Pope Pius XII at Castel Gandolfo. She had gone to him once more to appeal for permission to found a worker fraternity in Rome, without which she felt her personal mission would remain incomplete. She had also taken the opportunity of introducing Little Sister Jeanne to him as her Assistant whom she intended also as her successor. 'How old are you?' the ageing Pope inquired of the proposed future Prioress. 'Thirty', came the response from Little Sister Jeanne. 'She is young!' the Pope commented to Little Sister Magdeleine, only to receive the irrefutable answer: 'She will grow older.'

By the time in September 1949 the Little Sisters had gathered together at Le Tubet to celebrate the tenth anniversary of the Fraternity, only seven remained of those who had joined before 1945 but there were over seventy-five Little Sisters altogether and numerous others 'coming to see'. Thirteen fraternities were already established. Another five were in the process of being initiated in Syria, Palestine, France and North Africa. By then Mgr de Provenchères felt that a specimen of each type of fraternity had been created and that the fundamental shape of the congregation was adequately established. In May of that year the gypsy fraternity had begun life in a gypsy caravan at Saintes Maries de la Mer. The caravan which was to become the Little Sisters' home was rather too beautiful for Little Sister Magdeleine's liking, but it was accepted by the troop of other gypsies with whom it would take to the road because it was the 'chapel caravan, the Good Lord's caravan, the baby Jesus's caravan'. It was crucially important to Little Sister Magdeleine that in all the Fraternity's chapels, the Little Sisters had access to the exposed Reserved Sacrament. Faith in the actual presence of Jesus in the Host had been fundamental to the life of Charles de Foucauld. He had spent long hours in prayer before the tabernacle and adoration of the exposed Sacrament had been for him a source of profound joy. In his ideal conception of the religious life, aimed at the imitation of Nazareth, the Sacrament was the primordial, central element around which all else was ranged. The Little Sisters' request for the right to reserve the Sacrament in a caravan had prompted certain queries on the part of the Church authorities, 'How could a habitation which moved about be defined as a convent?' The Fraternity resolved simply to describe it as a house on wheels and on 25 May Mgr de Provenchères had finally celebrated mass in the brightly painted new wooden 'house on wheels'. The extent to which the Little Sisters had been able to enter into the gypsy life had exceeded even Little Sister Magdeleine's expectations. They made baskets like the gypsies, cooked their meals on three stones, carried the special identity cards bearing their fingerprints which gypsies were required to hold at that time, were subject to suspicion and even at times pursued by the police. 'Like us, just like us,' the gypsies had expressed their opinion and gradually accepted them into their midst.

In June the leper hospital in Valbonne had agreed to take two Little Sisters and a Little Brother for a trial period. Plans for a fraternity of Little Sisters who would share the plight of prisoners by actually living, locked up in prison with them, had begun to evolve. They had been initiated with the vague idea that 'the door of one of the fraternities' should be opened to prisoners and that the Little Sisters should live amongst them without any particular role other than to work in some poor fashion alongside them, but had swiftly crystallised into a request by Little Sister Magdeleine actually to spend three or four days as a voluntary prisoner in order better to understand the life she was already envisaging her Little Sisters leading behind bars. A study fraternity was in place at St Maximin in France where the Little Sisters could study theology with a group of Dominicans. A fraternity for language study had also been initiated not, as originally planned, in Tunis but in Beirut. Although the struggle for a worker fraternity in Rome was still going on, a number of worker fraternities had been firmly established elsewhere. The Fraternity had also taken concrete steps towards the opening of the four fraternities of adoration which Little Sister Magdeleine saw as the Eucharistic centres of four regions into which the Fraternity was by then divided. In September 1949 she had founded a fraternity of adoration in Nazareth in a wing of the convent of the Poor Clares in whose chapel Charles de Foucauld had spent long hours in prayer. Simultaneously she had begun a search for a small shop in the village of Nazareth reminiscent of the carpenter's shop where once Jesus had worked, which would enable the Little Sisters to lead a life intermingled with the villagers during the day. The fraternities of Our Lady of Africa in Algiers and Fez were also to be places of the contemplation and adoration which lay at the heart of the active life. So too was Le Tubet. While Little Sister Magdeleine continued to set her sights on Rome as a centre at the heart of the Church which would transcend the barriers of nationalism, Le Tubet remained the 'mother house' with a vital role in the novitiate training of the Little Sisters, the place to which people came to test their vocation, a place of hospitality. It was also, despite the growing number of people coming and going, to be a witness to contemplation. The ground rules of Charles de Foucauld's *zaouïas* of prayer and hospitality had been carefully laid. Those who came as guests must find a place of peace, silence and reflection.

From the point of view of the general organisation of the Fraternity also, she had ensured that the cornerstones were firmly in place. Responsibility was to be increasingly devolved. Regional superiors were to take more responsibility for the fraternities in their own regions. Two general councillors were appointed to assist the 'General Responsible' in the government of the Fraternity. At the time of Little Sister Jeanne's assumption of the role of 'General Responsible' there were not enough fully professed Little Sisters to hold an election by Chapter, but the Constitutions, on which Little Sister Magdeleine had been working constantly even during her wide-ranging travels, did make provision for such an election. Little Sister Jeanne was thus appointed only for an initial three years, at the end of which there would be enough professed sisters to hold a proper election.

For Little Sister Jeanne the assumption of the new task required of her was by no means an easy one. She had joined the Fraternity at the age of twenty-four. She had received her training for the religious life in the early, precarious days of the Fraternity and she had spent some time in close proximity to Little Sister Magdeleine. As far as she was concerned, Little Sister Magdeleine had been granted the grace to found and she had merely followed and at times accompanied her along the way. Her acceptance of the position of General Responsible was an act of faith. If this was what was being asked of her, then ill qualified though she might feel and regardless of the personal cost, it was right for her to accept. She understood what motivated Little Sister Magdeleine. She had shared intimately in some of the experiences which had determined her shaping of the Fraternity and, like many of the early sisters, she had been borne along without asking undue questions. 'Humanly speaking it was often foolish but we felt ourselves profoundly protected,' another of the early sisters would reflect with hindsight. Little Sister Magdeleine's sense of being guided, of being part of a design which came from God, communicated itself to those around her.

Confronted with a role which she approached with extreme humility, Little Sister Jeanne wanted the woman she would always look upon as the foundress imbued with a special grace, to remain as closely at her side as possible: 'I asked her not to leave me all alone to face this new Fraternity.' Little Sister Magdeleine's sights were by this time firmly set on Russia. For a woman to whom barriers of any kind were intolerable the concept of the Iron Curtain was perhaps the ultimate challenge to her goal of unity. The Stalinist regime was currently in power in Russia. Heart-rending reports of what was happening to Christians were issuing from the Soviet Union. At a time when relations with the Eastern bloc countries and the Soviet Union were particularly strained, a less publicised reason for Little Sister Magdeleine's resignation was in order that she might be free to devote her life to the people of the Soviet Union.

Prior to her resignation it had been agreed that Little Sister Magdeleine would retain the title of 'Mother'. Mgr de Provenchères had specifically required her to remain a mother to her sisters. In her capacity as foundress she was also to watch over the spirit of the fraternities, and the maintenance and interpretation of the Constitutions. For a while also she remained at Little Sister Jeanne's side, helping her to familiarise herself with her new role, putting to her what must now be only proposals subject to the General Responsible's approval, and endeavouring to enable her to take precedence in a manner which the younger woman found manifestly difficult. Little Sister Magdeleine's proposals did not diminish in number and they continued to range freely from the spiritual to the practical, between which she seemed to recognise no clear distinction. January 1950 began with the opening of a fraternity in Bethlehem itself: one more 'tabernacle' with a tiny chapel which had been furnished, appropriately, with contributions from all the other fraternities. On board a boat from Alexandria during her journey in the Orient she wrote to Father Voillaume of how she felt the time had come for a more familiar mode of address than 'vous' to be used in the Fraternity. The 'tu' form was more generally used by the workers with whom the Little Sisters associated. At very least the Little Sisters working in the factories should adopt it. As an experiment, she informed him, Little Sister Yva, regional responsible for the Orient, Little Sister Jeanne and she were going to try it. The experiment would eventually become general practice in the congregation.

The end of January saw Little Sister Magdeleine once more in Rome. It was she who wrote yet another supplication to Pope Pius XII on behalf of her ninety-five Little Sisters now living in twenty fraternities. She was still appealing for permission to start the worker fraternity in Rome, but she also asked the Pope for the Fraternity to become a congregation of pontifical right. To date in the case of each new fraternity she had had to apply for authority to the bishop of the particular diocese in which it was to be founded, but with fraternities on the horizon as widely dispersed as Japan and the Soviet Union, committed now not only to the Islamic people but in Jerusalem to the Jews and elsewhere to other orientations, she was foreseeing the time when there would be too many dioceses involved and too great a diversity for the Fraternity to remain one of diocesan right. As always, prior to her audience with the Pope, Little Sister Magdeleine committed her arguments to paper:

> We come under the Roman jurisdiction and under the Greek Catholic jurisdiction, are devoted to the workers, to the Muslims, and shall be soon to the Jews, to the gypsies in France and the bedouins in the desert. How, in the light of all this burst of expansion, can we present ourselves as a diocesan congregation belonging to a French diocese at a time when the charge of nationalism is compromising the most magnificent missions?

Hand in hand Little Sister Magdeleine and Little Sister Jeanne went from their audience with the Pope to an audience with Mgr Montini who had remained supportive of the cause of a worker fraternity in a poor quarter of Rome itself. There followed a few days during which the two women were separated before meeting again in Morocco with a view to going on together to Beni Abbes, where a group of Little Sisters were due to assemble from the four corners of the world. It was while they were in Casa, Morocco, that Little Sister Magdeleine received a telegram with the news that her mother had died on 10 February 1950.

At the end of the war, having shared all the dangers endured by the Little Sisters at the fraternity in Lyon, Madame Hutin had returned to Le Tubet. She had become the first of a succession of parents who would spend their last days there, for Little Sister Magdeleine, in calling upon her Little Sisters to be prepared to give up everything, nevertheless did not require them to abandon their duty to and their concern for parents who had no other source of care in their old age. Madame Hutin had loved young people. She had once instructed her daughter, 'Whatever you do don't put me in with a lot of old ladies.' She had known the early Little Sisters as postulants, novices and professed. She had seen their faults, their difficulties and their growth. She had teased them, consoled them and remained a mother to them all throughout. Her daily saying of the rosary, her devotion to Our Lady of Lourdes whose statue was never far from her side, and her unshakeable faith had been seen by them as a form of silent participation in the growth of the congregation. Nor had the sacrifice she had made of her daughter's time and presence to the Fraternity been unappreciated, but it had undoubtedly been hard for her. The swift arrivals and departures of her 'shooting star' had been so unpredictable that the Little Sisters had frequently been careful to avoid Madame Hutin's disappointment by not telling her of her daughter's advent until she had actually set foot in the building.

For a long time Madame Hutin had suffered without complaint from a weak heart. In July 1947 while Little Sister Magdeleine was at Ste Baume, she had come so close to death that she was given the last rites. Her daughter then had rushed to her bedside, blaming herself, at least in part, for her mother's condition. Since Madame Hutin was by then permanently resident at Le Tubet Little Sister Magdeleine had felt it appropriate to sell the family home in Metz but she attributed her mother's heart attack to the pain of this last act of severance from her past life. 'No, you will not die,' she had protested vehemently aloud before her mother's inert body. The Little Sisters nursing her mother had stared at her in stupefaction but the sound of her daughter's raised voice had had a beneficial effect on Madame Hutin. The old woman had recovered to live a little longer. On that occasion, for all her distress, Little Sister Magdeleine had written to Father Voillaume to insist that her mother's illness must not interfere with the retreat planned for the Little Sisters at Sainte Baume. Their foundress's personal pain must not be allowed to be the cause of the sisters' slightest spiritual loss. When, nearly three years later, she was faced with the choice of whether or not to return to France to say her final farewells to a mother who had throughout her life 'surrounded her with strength and tenderness', once again her thoughts were not only for herself but for her Little Sisters. If her mother had still been alive it would have been different. As it was, she declined to travel back from Africa for the funeral out of consideration for all the other Little Sisters who would find themselves far from their families at moments such as this. Madame Hutin was buried on 12 February in the tiny cemetery above the pine-grove at Le Tubet. Little Sister Magdeleine was now the sole survivor of her sizeable family. 'She can only hide her suffering in silence,' wrote Little Sister Jeanne as she relayed the news to the Fraternity.

The gathering at Beni Abbes of fourteen of the first Little Sisters took place as planned. The foundations for a new fraternity of prayer and adoration were to be laid close to the hermitage of Charles de

Foucauld. A decision to turn El Abiodh not only into the location for the Little Sisters' annual sessions but into a permanent fraternity, and the first noviciate away from Le Tubet, also emerged out of the encounter. Its primary aim, however, was to commit to Charles de Foucauld a new stage in the Fraternity's development. Places spoke powerfully to Little Sister Magdeleine. On 18 February Father Voillaume arrived with a group of Little Brothers from El Abiodh having walked across the desert with their tent and eight camels 'like real nomads'. 'This meeting is so moving in such a place,' she wrote in her diary. 'Twenty-two Little Brothers and fourteen Little Sisters . . . sons and daughters of Brother Charles of Jesus coming to gather up their sacred heritage, and it is not only his hermitage and his garden, it is his thought and his message. . . . And it is vast, this message of universal love.'

A fortnight later, in the desert near El Abiodh, with the help of the Little Brothers, the first tent fraternity was finally initiated. The fraternity's first mass was celebrated in a corner of the tent set aside to be the Little Sisters' chapel. 'It is so moving to think that the Lord came down to our small tent, there, in the open desert,' Little Sister Magdeleine's diary recorded. It also recorded how everything perishable had to be hung up out of the reach of the multitude of what she referred to as 'guests'. These uninvited visitors took the form of rats, mice, jerboas, scorpions, lizards, scarab beetles and snakes. There was much to be learned. The proposed flock of twenty-five sheep, two rams and two goats had yet to be purchased. Little Sister Magdeleine, having tried the tent, pronounced it too large to be easily moved about. The nomad Little Sisters must have a smaller one but the large one would be retained as a place in which to receive instruction about the nomad life, a function which would justify its size. 'I am living again in the tent. . . . Today the women of the camp came to see me. I would like to stay here for ever and die here,' she wrote to Father Voillaume.

In a sense a nomadic life in a tent encapsulated all Little Sister Magdeleine's intuitions and dreams. It was a life of extreme simplicity lived amongst some of the most forsaken people, in a relationship of reciprocity, in which if anything the Little Sisters were to find themselves even more vulnerable than the most marginalised who came and went between the tents with their news, their problems, and all the warmth of spontaneous relationships. It was a life devoid of barriers with only the thin, woven strips of camel and goat hair to separate the fraternity and the sacramental body of Jesus from their Muslim 'friends' and from the great contemplative silence of desert and sky. It was a life of total dependence on and surrender to the will of God amongst people for whom the expression *inch'allah*, 'God willing', was not only a leitmotiv of conversation but also the guiding principle of their lives.

Little Sister Magdeleine did not articulate such thoughts but each time she had the opportunity to pause for a while in a nomad tent and drink the sweet green tea and eat the dates that were the hospitality of the desert people, it was with an ineffable joy. She had hinted at the depth of her feeling to Father Voillaume when first she heard she had authority to create the tent fraternity. 'If only you knew what this tent, I have been yearning for, for more than forty years, can represent for me.' Once she asserted that God spoke to her in two ways: the first was to make her see immediately and without any shadow of doubt what he required of her. In the second method it was she who initiated a project and then waited for an indication of confirmation. Characteristically, she likened herself to a weather-vane on a roof, wanting to be as responsive as possible to the least wind that came from God. The dynamic operating through Little Sister Magdeleine was something which she could not always and possibly did not even endeavour to explain. It found its most effective expression in practice, in something actually lived.

The same principle applied to the message of universal love which Little Sister Magdeleine discerned in the lived example of Charles de Foucauld. This message, the message of the gospel, of the Sermon on the Mount, was to be crystallised in the actual life of the Fraternity. It was Little Sister Magdeleine's conviction that the fraternities in each country should be 'lived' by Little Sisters of that country according to the culture of that country. Travel in war-torn places such as Beirut had made her acutely conscious of the dangers of nationalism. She did not want the Fraternity to be constantly identified as French or open to allegations of paternalism. The gospel message would best be understood by the people of a particular country if it was being assumed and lived by their own. At the same time the most powerful witness to universal love, to unity, to the truth that because of Jesus who became man there were no barriers or frontiers between people, would be provided by Little Sisters of different continents and convictions, Arabs and Jews, Germans and French, living in fraternity with one another. In order to achieve this end, a tangible witness to the love that could exist between all people, however, fraternities must first be established all over the world.

From El Abiodh Little Sisters Magdeleine and Jeanne made a brief visit to Algiers, Oran and then on to Morocco, followed by a tour of the fraternities in France and Belgium. In Little Sister Magdeleine's mind this latter journey was to pay her personal farewells not only to the fraternities there but also to the friends who had supported her since the earliest days. The plan was for Little Sister Jeanne increasingly to undertake visits to existing fraternities independently in order to leave Little Sister Magdeleine free to devote herself to countries that were further afield and, as she hoped, one day to Russia and the other Communist countries. In July Little Sister Magdeleine left her General Responsible in France and set off by boat for the Lebanon, Syria, Jordan and Israel. On board ship the Little Sisters endeared themselves to the crew by helping to peel the vegetables but were obliged to do it secretively for fear of causing offence to other religious among their fellow travellers. 'What can we do?' asked Little Sister Magdeleine in a letter to Mgr de Provenchères. 'We belong to a different world, we are so different from the others. We would like so much to draw near to them but it is too soon for us to understand each other.'

Travelling time was still an opportunity to write of a multitude of things, not least of the Constitutions. A 'skeleton' of rules was now being required to be included in them. She wrote too of how she had a growing consciousness of being nothing in the work of foundation. She was 'finished' but she also wrote of her conviction that when she reached Jerusalem, where she would need to support the Little Sisters and found the fraternity, she would have a strength that was not human, the energy of a twenty-year-old to do all that was necessary. Sure enough, when she reached Jerusalem not just one but two fraternities were established. The first was in the Church of Saint Veronica with a number of rooms requiring refurbishment attached to it. The property which belonged to Greek Catholics was actually at the VI Station on the Via Dolorosa, in the Arab quarter of the ancient city of Jerusalem. The other, made available only a matter of days later by the Sisters of St Vincent de Paul, was in the Jewish sector. Only the day before this building, which had been recently bombed, was offered to the Little Sisters, a member of another religious congregation in Jerusalem had told Little Sister Magdeleine somewhat sceptically that he would be more inclined to believe in her mission if she had found a house by the next day. To little Sister Magdeleine the establishment of the two fraternities was the perfect symbol of unity and a response to the suffering caused by the lack of such unity which could only have come from God:

> He alone could have created this windfall of love, to have us plant simultaneously, in each sector of Jerusalem, an Arab fraternity and a Jewish fraternity so close to one another but right where the barrier of hatred is, in order to place Little Sisters there whose mission, whose sole mission will be not to convert but only to try, by loving both sides with the same love, to work for greater unity, greater friendship, more fraternal love around them between the children of the same Father.

From Jerusalem she also wrote to her sisters of the desirability of local vocations which would avoid some of the negative associations of nationalism. A few months later, with the blessing of Maximos IV, she herself applied for Syrian nationality but, much to her disappointment, her request was never granted.

September 1950 saw Little Sister Magdeleine in Rome with Little Sister Jeanne and five more Little Sisters preparing to make their final vows. Nineteen fifty had finally brought consent from the Cardinal-Vicar of Rome for a small fraternity to share the life of the city's poor by living in a barrack hut, from which one Little Sister would go out to work. Humble but persistent, once more she asked Pope Pius XII for authority to have the general house in Rome and for the Fraternity to be erected as a congregation of pontifical right, telling him how it could not confine itself to any single race but was expanding to encompass the entire world. In November a group of Little Sisters and Brothers gathered at El Abiodh for the first stage in what was to become a concerted effort to seek out the most forsaken people and establish tiny fraternities round the world, which would share the life of the local people, be a reflection of the love of God amongst them and, it was hoped, be increasingly made up of Little Sisters from that country. One Little Sister who had joined the fraternity had felt a particular calling to the people of central Africa. It seemed appropriate to begin an expansion into central and southern Africa and so a party made up of eight Little Sisters, two Little Brothers, Father Voillaume and five of his friends, set off across the desert in a lorry. The vehicle bore the motto of Charles de Foucauld's family 'Never retreat' which, Little Sister Magdeleine was quick to point out, 'implied' the idea which she would have preferred: 'Ever further' or 'Even further'.

The ultimate destination of the group was the Cameroons. First, however, its members were to undertake what was really a pilgrimage to the places where Charles de Foucauld had lived: to Beni Abbes, El Golea, In Salah, Tamanrasset and Assekrem. In union of spirit with Brother Charles of Jesus, of which her physical proximity to the key places of his life was a profound expression, at El Golea Little Sister Magdeleine wrote down the pillars of her grand plan for the Fraternity. There were, she maintained, three general but essential ideas:

(i) The Fraternity was a poor, worker congregation. It was therefore to earn its living through manual labour in the humble social conditions of manual workers. In certain places where health conditions were poor and medical treatment was hard to come by, it had seemed appropriate for some of the Little Sisters to serve as nurses, doctors and midwives. In certain countries also it would prove to be the only basis on which the Little Sisters would be given visas, but although this was a role traditionally associated with women's religious congregations, it carried with it a certain status which Little Sister Magdeleine saw as likely to change the physiognomy of the Fraternity. The number of nurses was not, therefore, to exceed a tenth of the total number of Little Sisters.

(ii) The Fraternity was made for the most forgotten. Such people were to be found all over the world and not necessarily in distant lands.

(iii) The Fraternity was contemplative not only in inclination and spirit, but also in a concrete way by virtue of the existence of fraternities especially devoted to the adoration of the exposed Sacrament.

It was in the light of these three principles that the future fraternities were to be built. With unrelenting energy she went on to specify that as far as she was concerned no region was complete unless it had four kinds of fraternities: a regional fraternity, a fraternity of adoration, a worker fraternity, a fraternity for mutual aid and in certain regions a fraternity of formation and one which provided hospitality. Little Sister Magdeleine's resignation as General Responsible had in no way diminished the thrust towards new foundations or the degree of commitment she afforded every detail of the Fraternity's life. Nor had her determination waned to defy her physical weakness and her personal inclinations in the interests of obedience and the resulting reassurance that what she was undertaking was God's work.

In the south of Algeria Tamanrasset awaited her. There stood the long narrow building, nicknamed the 'frigate', where once Charles de Foucauld had lived and prayed. There too was the *bordj* or fortress where he had met his death. Then some eighty kilometres of difficult track away from what had developed by then into a sizeable village, lay Assekrem, the 'hermitage' where he had kept a meteorological station, perched some 2,800 metres up on a mountain peak and accessible only by a steep, narrow path which zigzagged its way through the loose stones of the mountain face. Little Sister Magdeleine was warned against accompanying the group on this phase of the pilgrimage which was to be made on foot with camels to carry the baggage. The air was thin and the nights were bitterly cold. Little Sister Magdeleine acknowledged her fear of the prospect, but was she to abandon the idea of making the ascent to Assekrem out of fear of fatigue and suffering? The question gave rise to a troubled debate in her. Her whole life to date had been a succession of acts of irrational faith to which God had always responded. She had followed blindly the way she felt he was calling her to go in the conviction that 'the faith that could move mountains' would always be rewarded. Had she been directed by Father Voillaume not to go to Assekrem it would have been different, but it was not out of obedience that she hesitated, it was because of her own fears. Was she to start now to govern her life by what was humanly speaking reasonable?

At some very profound level Little Sister Magdeleine needed to make the tortuous ascent to Assekrem in order to confirm that God was still sustaining her. Only with this reassurance, she confided to Father Voillaume, would she be able to go, as planned, to the far reaches of the earth. Reminding herself of Charles de Foucauld's assertion that fear was the sign of duty, she trembled nonetheless before all the suffering she knew must lie ahead of her. 'I still have terribly difficult things to do,' she predicted. 'If I flinch today for fear of the cold, of the walking, the altitude, to me it would be like the beginning of giving up on the whole thing.'

She made the punishing journey from Tamanrasset to Assekrem on foot. She could not keep pace with the camels but she and Little Sister Jeanne and a Little Brother who had recently suffered an attack of malaria followed behind at a slower pace on a track marked out for them by the others with arrows and small piles of rough pebbles.

Every step was difficult across the mountainous plateaux of the Ahaggar covered with their dark stones, through basalt pinnacles weathered by the wind and finally up the face of one of the highest peaks in a lunar landscape of needles and rocky protusions. Little Sister Magdeleine could not, however, have lived with her failure to make such an act of faith and when at last she spent the night in the rough stone hermitage once occupied by Charles de Foucauld and attended mass celebrated by Father Voillaume in what had once been his place of prayer, the journey was more than justified. The party of pilgrims made their way back down the rough paths to Tamanrasset trying to hold on to the fruits of the spectacular sunset and dawn, the fierce clarity of the mountain air and its transforming peace:

> trying to keep in our hearts all the light and strength that we had received up there to follow the route which the Lord has laid out for us and which is sometimes as rough and painful in a different way as the most rocky and precipitous slopes of Assekrem.

Christmas that year was spent at Tamanrasset. A crib was set up in what had once been the bread oven for the *bordj* and mass was celebrated in the chapel where Charles de Foucauld had spent long hours in prayer. By 26 December, however, the lorry with its extraordinary load was back on its route, first across Niger and Northern Nigeria, and then on to the Cameroons. In the mountains of Northern Cameroon it was the small tribe of the Oueldémés which particularly attracted Little Sister Magdeleine. The local bishop would have preferred the Little Sisters to start their fraternity among a larger, more significant tribe, but the Fraternity's vocation was to the most forgotten, to the 'least'. Thus it was amongst this small group of tribal people to whom hitherto no one had really extended the hand of friendship that it was decided to leave a handful of Little Sisters and Brothers. The site of the fraternity was finally determined by the availability of water. The Little Sisters and the Little Brothers would build mud huts after the fashion of the Oueldémés tribe, to accommodate themselves and a chapel, beside a stream of clear water which they found unexpectedly at the foot of a mountain occupied by the tribe.

In Southern Cameroon the intention was to start a fraternity devoted to lepers. A group of Little Sisters would begin a trial period at a leper hospital among people who, with maimed hands and feet, knew what it was to be rejected out of fear and ignorance. Whilst in Southern Cameroon, however, the plight of the local pygmies was brought to Little Sister Magdeleine's notice. Living in dense areas of forest in small encampments of huts made out of branches, they were despised and ridiculed by the people of the villages. Determined to visit them, Little Sister Magdeleine made her way into the bush in a party made up of local religious and their African pupils, led by a priest in a plumed felt hat and bearing a gun. So dense was the undergrowth that the group was obliged to struggle in single file behind its priest/guide who hacked a laborious way through the humid vegetation. Little Sister Magdeleine's sandals kept coming off. Eventually she gave up and walked barefoot which was, as she would record with humorous understatement in her diary, no comfortable state of affairs in the jungle. She stepped on ant hills: 'Those ant-bites are terrible,' she reported, 'especially ones from soldier ants that cling to your flesh and have to be torn off with real force. When they enter a house, all you can do is get out of it while they pass through. They devour everything: flies, spiders, even hens and cats.' She yelped with the pain of the ant stings but she persevered. When, finally, they found the first cluster of huts in the forest, even the African girls accompanying her would not go in. The pygmies, Little Sister Magdeleine pronounced, were amongst the world's most despised peoples. They looked so nervous and shy. They would number amongst her dearest brothers and sisters. She ate with them in the depths of the forest, seated on a banana leaf, then went on in search of a second encampment. Plans for a fraternity amongst the pygmies began to take shape. At least six Little Sisters would be required, two of whom would remain in a fraternity in the nearest village where they would have a small plantation. The others would have a hut in one of the more permanent pygmy encampments and would accompany them when they went out to hunt, with the women and the children.

For Little Sister Magdeleine the journeying continued. After the Cameroons it was back to Morocco and the Sahara for the fifth annual session at El Abiodh. There followed a brief interval in Europe. Then it was on to Beirut and the Lebanon, Syria, Jordan, Israel, Egypt, Belgium, Tunisia and, at the end of the year 1951, back to Algeria. By then the foundations had been firmly established for a group of fraternities forming the 'Sahara Region' centred around the fraternity of adoration at Beni Abbes. On 8 December she returned at last to the sand-dunes of Sidi Boujnan for the reopening of the fraternity which, with so much personal sadness, she had been obliged to close in 1946. It was, by her own account, one of the most beautiful days of her life. She would have liked to cry her joy aloud but she felt that, apart from the Little Sisters and friends who were close to her, no one would understand, for no one could know what Sidi Boujnan really meant to her. It was the birthplace, the cradle of the Fraternity, the place where she had encountered the nomads for the first time, a building each white-washed wall of which reminded her of the effort that had gone into its construction. For five years she and the nomads and the other Little Sisters who had come and gone had worked on the building together. For five years the nomads had shown her a friendship of extraordinary warmth and depth and never once let her down. Once, in a moment of solitude and self-doubt she had asked Athman whether there would ever be enough Little Sisters to justify the extensive construction work she had undertaken as one of innumerable acts of blind faith. The Muslim mason had reflected for a moment and then drawn from the depths of his own faith the reassurance that she needed: Yes, they would come.

The thirty-four fraternities which had been founded during the interim five years of absence could not make Little Sister Magdeleine forget such fidelity. Sidi Boujnan was still surrounded by tents and *zribas*. As word spread that 'Oukhti Majdalia' had returned, Little Sister Magdeleine was surrounded, dragged from tent to tent, escorted by young men whom she had known as the little boys who had made camels out of palm fibre. She had loved them too much for them to forget her. They still held the pink cards confirming that they had the right to remain in the area, for which she had fought on their behalf. Then it was the turn of those who settled as permanent residents, of Athman, Tahar his brother, and of Abdou, a young African labourer whose father had died of thirst in the desert in 1942. Little Sister Magdeleine had been indignant when his donkey had returned without its rider and the local administration had done nothing. She had set off herself into the desert to find him but it had been too late. Abdou's father was dead but the boy had not forgotten the way in which she had shared his sorrow. He was there together with a multitude of others to express his gratitude and affection. When Little Sister Magdeleine parted from them this time, she left behind her three Little Sisters, happy in the knowledge that they would be watched over by friends.

The process of consolidating existing fraternities and founding new ones would take her during 1952 not only further south in Africa but also on a first tour of Europe, to London where the neat rows of houses made her wonder how the Little Sisters would ever be accepted. As it transpired, although a fraternity would be initiated in London in the course of the following year, her approach got off to a bad start. No bishop would receive her without a letter of introduction from Mgr de Provenchères and by the time the required introduction arrived the English bishops had left for a Eucharistic Congress in Barcelona. Undaunted, Little Sister Magdeleine made for Barcelona where the Congress would provide her with an opportunity to meet bishops from other countries also. En route she paused in Belgium and Holland to found fraternities there, and afterwards came her first journey to South America.

The plan for expansion was not entirely a question of improvisation. Every project was submitted to the bishop of the location concerned. Little Sister Magdeleine would arrive and introduce herself at once to the local Church authority but always her first question related to the poor and the most forgotten. In Conceição de Araguaia she was instantly drawn to the Caiapos, a tribe of Indians renowned for their hostility. During the previous year the Caiapos had slaughtered fourteen Christians. Their reputation alone was enough to instil fear into other Indian tribes and the local white people also. The more people made ready to defend themselves with arrows and guns, the more people maligned them, the more she held them dear. 'You must soften them through prayer,' she committed them to the Little Sisters in a very particular way since for the time being they were otherwise inaccessible. An actual fraternity was begun instead amongst the Tapirape tribe, a group of just fifty people who were the only survivors of an encampment of eight hundred Indians attacked by the Caiapos four years previously. Among the Little Sisters left there was one with farming skills. They would have a plantation such as the Tapirapes had and grow sweet potatoes, rice, maize and other crops. They were, their foundress instructed them, to become Tapirapes and, having done so, to reach out from that vantage point to the other Indians. The idea was not simply to be a bridge or point of union between hostile peoples but to remain Tapirapes and as Tapirapes to love the Caiapos, the enemy who had murdered the remainder of their tribe.

In Chile she left behind her two fully professed Little Sisters who would become Chilean amongst the people of Chile. As a step towards the overall plan for the regions to be made up increasingly of people

134

from the country concerned, they would take and form postulants from Chile in their own country, rather than bringing them back to France. Then it was on to North America, to the United States and Canada. In Alaska it went without saying that it was to the poorest Eskimos of the most remote islands that Little Sister Magdeleine felt called. Despite the ravages of the climate, which she herself experienced, she could already see her Little Sisters fishing with the other Eskimo women. Alaska was very close to Siberia. It had once been part of the Soviet Union which lay just across the Bering Sea. The not so distant shores of the Soviet Union were like a beacon to Little Sister Magdeleine.

Russia was, she confided to Father Voillaume, ever before her. It was partly at least with Russia in mind that during a second tour of Europe in September and October of 1952 she determined to establish a fraternity in Fátima, the Marian shrine in Portugal. Not only was Our Lady of Fátima dear to the heart of the Pope, it was also to her that prayers for Russia were particularly addressed. A request to start a fraternity at Fátima had already been made in June to the archbishop of the diocese of Leiria. He had expressed reservations because of the number of Portuguese, Italian and American congregations already in the throes of constructing large buildings at the shrine. By September Little Sister Magdeleine was resolved to persuade him further. On 11 September, however, on the road outside Lourdes the vehicle in which she was travelling, driven by a Little Brother and accompanied by two Little Sisters, was involved in a serious accident. The car's tyres were badly worn, the road was slippery, the vehicle turned over in a ditch. One of the Little Sisters was badly bruised. Little Sister Magdeleine herself suffered a severe blow to the back and afterwards remembered feeling as if her thorax had been smashed in. She was taken to hospital in Lourdes where initially her condition was so serious that she could not be X-rayed. When eventually she was it was found that she had three ribs broken at the back and two more at the front plus complications with her lungs. A month's bed-rest was ordered but Little Sister Magdeleine had already prayed either to die or to leave the hospital within a week. She explained her intentions of going on to start fraternities in Madrid, Lisbon and Fátima and on 20 September she telephoned Mgr de Provenchères to ask his permission to continue her journey. He gave it, saying that the Lord who had always guided her would give her the strength she needed. Despite her condition, swathed in heavy bandages, she set off again with Little Sister Jeanne on a pilgrims' train to Bordeaux and then on to Madrid by plane. The foundation in a desperately poor slum area of Spain went ahead as planned. It was the first time Little Sister Magdeleine had even tried to walk since her accident but her pitiful struggle to the Little Sisters' house in the slum revealed to her the open hearts of its poverty-stricken residents. They brought her out a chair, gave her a glass of water. Everyone wanted to assist her in some way. The appropriateness of entering their neighbourhood in a state of poverty and suffering impressed itself upon her.

Furthermore, when, three days later, she and Little Sister Jeanne arrived at the residence of the Archbishop of Leiria after a seventeen-hour train journey, the Archbishop was more touched by her physical state than he would have been by any explanations. Little Sister Magdeleine had spent the night propped up on pillows, vainly attempting to cushion herself against the jolts of the carriage. When, in response to his question as to why she had not stayed in hospital, she informed him that it was because she had wanted to obtain from the Blessed Virgin a foundation at Fátima, the Archbishop's defences were bridged. He agreed to all her requests: a foundation; a noviciate; and the right, in the absence of an available priest, to expose the Blessed Sacrament by a process known as 'automatic tabernacle' which would open the tabernacle without the Little Sisters actually touching it. His consent was given in an attempt to make her remain and receive the medical care she needed. Instead, she went on to Fátima where she commended all the brothers and sisters to the Virgin and asked for the strength to continue her journey to its end.

In the words of Mgr de Provenchères she continued to 'travel the world, devoid of strength, suffering as she went, in order to sow the seeds of the fraternities'. She travelled on the backs of lorries, third class on ships, in native boats. On a boat to Naples she prepared the green beans for the other passengers, thinking of those who had to spend their lives preparing delicacies that they would never eat. There were times when she was very close to danger. During one of her South American flights the window of the aircraft shattered. Vain attempts to block the hole were made but the air blasted its way through the plane. She arrived at her destination nonetheless safe and sound. Her humour did not abandon her even when she was obliged to camp out between a pool frequented by crocodiles and a river that was home to piranha fish. Next morning tracks showed that four crocodiles had passed close to where she slept. She wrote with a certain amused satisfaction of how they had declined to bother with the sleeping group of brothers and sisters concealed beneath their blankets and sleeping bags, preferring the fish and tortoises in the water. She reported too that she had made the acquaintance of Brazilian ants which bit her 'just as cruelly as their sisters in the Cameroons.'

By the time, in October 1952, she went once more to see Pope Pius XII to report on the development of the Fraternity and to ask permission for a future 'general fraternity' to be located in Rome, there were sixty fraternities, 220 Little Sisters and twelve noviciate houses where Congolese Little Sisters or Little Sisters from the Orient, from the Cameroons, from Spain, Belgium or Canada could prepare for the religious life in their own countries. Together Little Sister Jeanne and Little Sister Magdeleine were about to leave on yet another long journey which would begin with Egypt, India and Vietnam and end with Japan, Korea, Papua New Guinea and Australia. Anywhere where the 'little' people were being crushed or despised by the 'great', the foundress felt impelled to go. The infant Jesus who had taken her by the hand at the very beginning of the Fraternity would, she was convinced, be her strength provided she followed blindly where he was leading. And frequently in unaccountable ways her faith appeared to be vindicated.

India had been calling to her since the death, as a result of a bicycle accident, of a Little Sister who had consecrated her life to that country. In particular the 'eternal city' of Varanasi, or Benares, with its 2,000 Hindu temples lining the west bank of the sacred River Ganges seemed to her the ideal place in which to have a fraternity of adoration. Long afterwards Father Voillaume would recall arriving in Benares with Little Sisters Magdeleine and Jeanne. It was a time when vestiges of British colonialism were still strong. Benares consisted of two separate areas, the ancient Hindu city and, alongside it, what was known as the 'cantonment', each with its separate railway station. It was in the cantonment that the Apostolic Prefect lived and here that Little Sister Magdeleine first resorted to inform him that she wanted to open a fraternity on the very banks of the Ganges. The Apostolic Prefect told her first that it would be impossible even to have a place of Christian prayer in the Hindu city and certainly not on the banks of the Ganges where the ancient temples were interspersed only with lodgings that were bought for extravagant sums of money by Hindus wishing to end their days there and so be freed from the cycle of

137

reincarnation. In response to Little Sister Magdeleine's insistence, he gave the inevitable answer that he would think about it, whereupon his visitor informed him that she would have to leave Benares next day so the foundation must be made immediately. Would it not be possible for a priest to show her round the Hindu city? Clutching his camera, Father Voillaume followed Little Sister Magdeleine and the guide that was accordingly found for her, to the *ghats*, the flights of steps leading down to the water's edge. Suddenly she stopped dead in her tracks. What she herself referred to as 'an irresistible attraction' caused her to inquire at a collection of old buildings set among the temples whether the Little Sisters could rent accommodation there. The house, which was so close to the Ganges that the water washed into it when the sacred river was in flood, did indeed have accommodation to let. The fraternity founded there remains to this day,

There were to be many other examples of such 'irresistible attraction' on the strength of which Little Sister Magdeleine defied all reasonable or practical considerations. The four steep flights of stairs that had to be climbed on foot to the sacristan's flat attached to the Church of Saint-Sulpice which formed a temporary location for a fraternity in Paris did not prevent her from immediately arranging the Little Sisters' furniture in her mind's eye. Nor did the narrow-gauge train through the Himalayas to the Tibetan border and Mount Kinchinsunga, the world's second-highest mountain, deter her from envisaging a fraternity amongst the mule-drivers who travelled between India and Tibet with their trading caravans. The fact that the mule-drivers were tall and strong and somewhat formidable in appearance simply made her decide to choose Little Sisters who were 'not too likely to be afraid' to come and live amongst them.

The war raging in Vietnam at the time did not alter Little Sister Magdeleine's plans to go there. In fact, three foundations were begun there, one of them in a leper village in Saigon itself. The consequences of the French involvement in the Vietnam war, however, were a source of deep personal distress to her. Because of her French nationality certain areas and towns had been closed to her. For her there were few experiences worse than such exclusion. She would have liked, she admitted, to divest herself of everything that identified her with her country of origin in order that her heart might be exposed to the world with its universal love for every human being.

It was in Vietnam that she put the finishing touches to what was perhaps the most ambitious plan of all: a journey right round the world to establish foundations on all five continents so that the Fraternity would become fully international and a concrete realisation of its goal of unity in love between people of all races, classes and backgrounds. Between 1 August 1953 and 28 August 1954, together with Little Sister Jeanne and, for the most part, Father Voillaume, she journeyed across Africa, America, Asia, Oceania and the Orient (see Appendix A, pp. 264–5), driven on by the love of God which Little Sister Magdeleine professed to experience as a 'fire', a 'brazier' that burned inside her. 'More and more, He shows me everything,' she wrote in January 1953 to Mgr de Provenchères, referring to the way in which God was guiding her, but the fact that the direction of her life was divinely inspired and her obedience to it complete did not make the journey any less one of suffering. Quite apart from the physical consequences of travelling over every conceivable form of terrain from mountains and rivers, through tropical jungle, over ice floes, in whatever means of transport presented itself, with an itinerary which would have eroded a far more robust constitution than hers, the struggle continued on other fronts also.

By the end of 1952 thirty-five diocesan bishops had approved the Fraternity's Constitutions and its desire to depend financially upon its own labour as a worker congregation. They had not yet, however, had the final approval of Rome. Nor were the Fraternity's activities as welcome in some Church quarters as they were amongst the forsaken people whose lives they sought to share. In Ireland, from where some of Little Sister Magdeleine's ancestors had come and where for this reason she had set her heart on founding a region before she died, the offer of Little Sisters was received with caution. Although later, in 1972, a fraternity would be established in Dublin amongst the 'travellers' there, when first approached, the archbishop declined to give his permission to have a fraternity in his diocese. The episcopal council could not accept the idea of religious working in factories or mixing with the masses. The 'little' people, the Indians, Eskimos, the bush people, the mushrooming population of Chile or the occupants of the Brazilian *favellas* adopted the sisters with great warmth but those whom Little Sister Magdeleine referred to as 'the great' sometimes condemned or failed to comprehend them. The Governor of Niamey in Niger professed to understand the Little Sisters' vocation, but then could not accept the idea of them making straw matting because that was slaves' work. It was, he was ill advised enough to add, 'a question of prestige'. The comment met with the kind of explosion of 'righteous

anger' to which Little Sister Magdeleine was quite capable of suc-
cumbing, though not without feeling upset with herself for doing so.

In the United States, the Archbishop of New York expressed the
view that the Fraternity was too new for his diocese, ordaining that
the sisters could not work in factories. In reality there was reason to
believe that the presence of the Little Sisters would be perceived as
a reproach to the Catholic Church there. North America in general
saw them as a congregation for the poor which did not really have a
role in a relatively rich country. A visit to Universal Studios in Hollywood reinforced Little Sister Magdeleine's view to the contrary.
Immediately she wanted to consecrate a fraternity to the very 'special
Hollywood milieu where as yet the Church was not present'. She felt
a fondness for the North American people in whom she identified
'youthful souls devoid of complications' but North America would
prove more inaccessible than many other parts of the world because,
as she put it, it represented 'riches, progress, the quest for efficiency.'
Yet she persisted. Her dream of a fraternity in Hollywood was never
actually fulfilled but elsewhere her dogged determination paid off.
The Archbishop of Washington, never quite ever able to say 'no', but
only 'we'll see', eventually succumbed to the annual approach made
to him by a somewhat nervous Little Sister at the foundress's behest.

The very speed with which she was spreading her Little Sisters
around the world rather than taking longer to form them and consoli-
date existing fraternities was not always understood, even by those as
close to her as Father Voillaume. In June 1951, still in the process of
working out an appropriate relationship between herself and the General Responsible, and recognising that, despite her resignation, it was
she who was taking the initiative for the foundation of so many
fraternities, Little Sister Magdeleine had written to her spiritual director to tell him that she was worried that this was not in keeping with
the spirit with which she had resigned. Father Voillaume had
responded with words of reassurance: 'I can assure you in the name
of the Lord that you cannot and should not for the moment abandon
your role as foundress, whatever may be the ensuing difficulties and
suffering.' He was not always, however, as swift in his endorsement
of all that she was doing. Looking back over their relationship, after
Little Sister Magdeleine's death, Father Voillaume wrote of how, even
though she saw him as her spiritual director, he had been unable
really to 'direct' her. He had been able to give her the reassurance
she had sought concerning the authenticity of the graces that guided

her, and he had answered to her continuing thirst for obedience, but as her confidence grew that the impulse to create fraternities throughout the world came from the God who held her hand at all times, it was she who, he acknowledged, in some ways directed him, encouraged him, illuminated his way. There was between them frequently an extraordinary synchronicity of thought but there were also times when they caused each other pain, or rather, as Father Voillaume was later to insist, he had caused her pain. By virtue of the fact that Little Sister Magdeleine was following her star so fervently, he could not formulate projects of his own. Because of the strength and simplicity of her faith, for Little Sister Magdeleine everything was relatively straightforward and clear. Things were not quite so self-evident for her 'director', particularly since Mgr de Provenchères had delegated to him the powers he had as bishop supervising the foundation of a new congregation. Father Voillaume did find himself borne along by the same impulse that was driving Little Sister Magdeleine but his role was not to be as unquestioning as hers, and the restraining voice of his reason which sometimes she knew how to value was nonetheless at others a source of frustration and sadness. To Mgr de Provenchères she wrote on one occasion of how the way in which God was causing her to travel ever further afield and at such speed 'disconcerted' Father Voillaume. 'So we argue because I am certain that I must follow God's plan and I would like Father to see that. And I suffer at being obliged to argue. You know my desire to be all smallness and obedience in relation to him.'

It was a comment which substantially summarised their relationship as they travelled together. Nor were they exempt from the usual irritations arising from two very different personalities thrust together in a common cause. The fire that burned in Little Sister Magdeleine could not resist expression in the casual encounters of airport lounges or station cafés. She could not help talking to people and telling them all about her plans for the Fraternity. For Father Voillaume, who chose his moments for serious discussion more carefully, her spontaneity was sometimes an embarrassment, and her attempts to enlist his opinions about such significant issues as the Constitutions or points of spirituality while he was driving a car or waiting for a train were not always welcome. Yet they journeyed together from South Africa, with its apartheid system which struck so deeply at the ideal of unity Little Sister Magdeleine carried in her heart, but where she had to agree to keep silent in order to avoid being expelled from the country, to the bushpeople of the Kalahari, onwards and ever onwards for nine months until finally, in Vietnam, commitments elsewhere obliged Father Voillaume to part from the Little Sisters. Little Sister Magdeleine went on to Australia and the Aborigines, amongst whom she founded a fraternity in a camper van.

On the roadside, in the passenger seat of vehicles, in snatched moments during the day and late into the night, while those around her were sleeping, she worked on the rules and spiritual principles of the Fraternity which required constant modification in response to its rapid developments. From Ceylon she wrote to Father Voillaume in June 1954: 'I am working relentlessly on the Constitutions. They have become the means of transmitting all the work of my heart and soul. They have taken up an enormous place in my life.' She maintained her journal, she kept in touch with friends throughout the world and she wrote regularly to her Little Sisters. She relayed to them the spiritual messages that came to her out of the circumstances in which she found herself. She knew that the life on which they were embarking was hard. She had made a point of experiencing its rigours for herself, but she called them to the same blind obedience which lay at the heart of her own life. She urged them to charity, simplicity and openness and to what she referred as a state of spiritual childhood.

At a gathering of sisters and brothers at Beni Abbes she spoke to them of how this spirit was made up of trust and total self-surrender in the hands of God. She resorted then as she would on many occasions thereafter to the image of a small child whose father pretends to toss him over a cliff. The child laughs at the precipice beneath him because he is in his father's arms and he knows that his father could never let him fall. The state of spiritual childhood was one of simplicity and joy which was yet compatible with the greatest knowledge and the finest intelligence. God had led by a star, not only the shepherds but also the wise men, into the presence of a little baby without grandeur or majesty. Little Sister Magdeleine was quick to dispel any confusion with some childish caricature suggesting her sisters should become like little girls. The law of contrasts had a role to play. One had to be fully adult in order to become totally childlike, in the same way that one had to be strong in order to be infinitely gentle, and wise in order to allow oneself to be foolish. Two years later, in April 1952, she wrote a 'message' which was to form the concluding part of her 'will and testament' as she had written it in the 'green booklet'. Added to her previous writing under a section entitled 'Childlike in heart you will receive the little infant Jesus of the manger from the Virgin Mary, his mother', it saw the receipt of the infant Jesus as the crowning point of the Little Sisters' religious life. It emphasised the importance of the state of spiritual childhood which was a condition of entry into heaven. It also appealed to the reader to be 'always a small child with your heavenly Mother'. It was to her, the 'Mediatrix of all graces', that Little Sister Magdeleine entrusted the Fraternity.

The Virgin Mary was assuming a growing prominence in Little Sister Magdeleine's life and hence in that of the Fraternity. 'I do not know quite how it happened,' she maintained, 'but very gently and progressively, the baby Jesus has led me to his Mother.' From Ceylon she wrote to Father Voillaume on 11 June 1954 of how she had entered a period of peace in which the Blessed Virgin was entering more and more into her life and enabling her to off-load what was most painful, what was too sensitive and too extreme in her. Had it not been for the Virgin, she protested, she would have given in to despair. This dependence found concrete expression in the resolution to found the fraternities of adoration whenever possible close to Marian shrines. All the fraternities would have an image of 'Our Lady of the Whole World'. 'I think the Holy Spirit is in the process of blowing a storm,' she wrote in that same month, 'because many things are becoming clearer about the organisation of the Fraternity.'

By then there were 105 fraternities and 100 novices. Still protesting in the privacy of the chapel that she could take no more, she nevertheless watched the growth of the Fraternity and the transformation of her Little Sisters with a certain satisfaction. It was still largely Little Sister Magdeleine who set the guidelines which shaped that transformation. It was she who directed what was to become an ongoing search for an appropriate form of poverty and standard of living for the Little Sisters, now living amongst people whose poverty took such manifold forms. She set down the instructions for Little Sisters going out to give talks about the work, defining their vocation, for example, in relation to the 'missionary role' which at first had not seemed applicable to their lives. Whilst she had made it clear from the beginning that the aim of the congregation was not a missionary one in relation to the people of Islam, contact with the Oueldémés tribespeople or the pygmies of the Cameroons had revealed that there were people who actually looked to the Little Sisters to hear the gospel message. 'We do not have the right', she modified any absolute assertion that they were not missionaries, 'to refuse bread and water to people dying of hunger and thirst.' Nor did they have the right to hide the light which had been given to them under the pretext of having a vocation to the 'hidden life'. The Little Sisters were increasingly obliged to turn down the role of catechists in the interests of remaining faithful to their vocation to the hidden life of Nazareth. However, the manifest needs of some of the people they encountered gave rise in 1954 to an announcement which Little Sister Magdeleine afterwards described as like 'dropping a bomb', namely the creation of a new group called the Little Sisters of Christ who would assume a more specific role of religious instruction. The news was welcomed by some but was a cause of anxiety to others and in fact in 1963 the Little Sisters of Christ would become the Little Sisters of the Gospel, a separate and autonomous congregation.

Little Sister Magdeleine was by no means afraid of dropping such 'bombs'. She was capable of admonishing her sisters in the strongest terms when they fell short of her ideal of obedience or charity. From the hill of Bethany, surrounded by the conflict between Arabs and Jews, she reproached them for the fact that when she arrived in fraternities wanting to take refuge from all the violence and disdain that existed between people, she did not always find the haven of peace she had hoped for. Sometimes the words that passed between Little Sisters were less than gentle. Sometimes forgiveness was not always as forthcoming as it should be. Little Sister Magdeleine was swift and uncompromising in her determination to point out such shortcomings and the pain they occasioned in her. At other times she would tell her Little Sisters to keep their defects to the end of their days in order that they might be merciful with others. For her pride was the ultimate sin and one which she would not tolerate under any circumstances. 'Disdainful, proud eyes are painful to me,' she once acknowledged, and in her determination to stamp out pride when she came across it in her sisters, she knew she could be excessively severe. 'Some Little Sisters are still hard to shift,' she would state baldly after her attempts to stress the importance of being 'light' and ready to go at the slightest notice wherever the Lord intended had fallen on a certain number of deaf ears. 'It makes the journey so wearing.'

In general it was still she who took responsibility for the spiritual welfare of the congregation. She was also concerned with more practical considerations such as the habit which she saw as a visible sign of the presence of the Church amongst the poor and the presence of

144

Madeleine Hutin with her parents, maternal grandmother, brother André and sister Marie in Paris, 1907.

The first five General Responsibles of the Little Sisters of Jesus. *Front from left to right*: Little Sisters Jeanne, Magdeleine, Iris-Mary. *Rear left*: Little Sister Annie and *right*: Little Sister Carla.

With Father Voillaume at the foundation of the first worker fraternity.

The gypsy fraternity in France in 1950.

Working on the building site at Tre Fontane, Rome in March 1964.

The tent fraternity at El Abiodh Sidi Cheikh, Algeria.

Little Sister Magdeleine and Little Sister Jeanne with friends in Sidi Boujnan, Touggourt in 1967, twenty-five years after the fraternity's foundation.

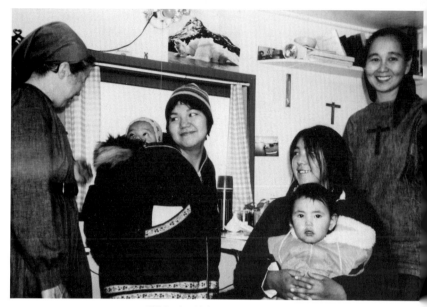

With the Eskimos in Alaska.

Restoring a derelict building to house a fraternity in Ikuta, Japan.

The first visit by Little Sister Magdeleine and Little Sister Jeanne to Moscow.

With Brother Roger of Taizé during his visit to Tre Fontane in 1980.

With members of the Salvation Army at Tre Fontane, Rome in 1978.

With Pope Paul VI and Father Voillaume at Tre Fontane in 1973.

Little Sister Magdeleine in her tiny office with Pope John Paul II during his visit to
the general fraternity in 1985.

The two foundresses, Little Sister Magdeleine and Mother Teresa, together at Tre Fontane in 1975.

ittle Sister Magdeleine and Little Sister Jeanne with the 'Shooting Star' on arrival in Moscow.

ne of the many attempts to reproduce Our Lady the Whole World, with the double gesture of ary offering her child and the infant Jesus reaching out to give himself to the world.

Little Sister Magdeleine at Tre Fontane in 1976, in front of a picture of Charles de Foucauld donated by Pope Paul VI.

Little Sister Magdeleine at work in Tre Fontane in 1972.

The plaster model of the infant Jesus preserved as Little Sister Magdeleine left it in her rooms at Sidi Boujnan.

the poor to the Church. She applied herself in detail to the question of to what extent the Little Sisters' dress should be adapted to reflect the dress of those whose lives they shared, concluding that whilst it was appropriate for the Little Sisters to modify their habit to conform with the style of certain peoples amongst whom they lived, the Eskimos for example, or the Indians or the nomads, it was also right to retain the essential characteristics of the habit of the Fraternity: the poor and ordinary material, the blue colour and an adequate length. In order to preserve a family spirit between the growing number of fraternities and to enable her to know how they were developing, she required each one to keep a diary, and she had very definite views on how the diaries should be kept. To ensure that they became a real element of unity and a means of self-improvement, the Little Sisters writing them were to apply themselves to the task wholeheartedly and intelligently. They were to avoid writing about banal things, not to fall into the trap of journalistic sensationalism and, above all, to avoid giving offence to any of the Fraternity's friends by, for example, making fun of drunks or mentally disturbed people. Little Sister Magdeleine also issued her Little Sisters with very specific practical directives relating to the details of their daily life, to the amount of sleep they should have, the time they should spend on meals, how they should cook and clean. They were never to hitch-hike alone and not after nightfall (eight o'clock in summer). Their baggage was not to exceed twelve–sixteen kilogrammes. Although she herself did not like the arrangement, her concept of the religious life was still sufficiently traditional for her initially to order the Little Sisters' day around the ringing of bells.

The need to shape the Fraternity both in spirit and practice was all the more pressing for the fact that Little Sister Magdeleine could see the time for her departure behind the Iron Curtain drawing closer. Privately she harboured an aspiration to go into the Soviet Union, remain there and possibly even find her way into a concentration camp. Already in 1953 she had set her departure date for 1955. By August 1954 she was praying for the courage to go through with a project which she had already presented to the Pope for his blessing. She had completed her tour right round the world but when she looked at her map of the world there still remained a large dark shadow, an area to which she had not as yet gained access. Her final goal was to penetrate behind the Iron Curtain, to die there in order 'that the infant Jesus and the Blessed Virgin might reign there'. By then, she maintained, only one mission which was very close to her heart remained outstanding this side of the East/West divide: that of endeavouring to make Charles de Foucauld known to the world as 'Little Brother Charles of Jesus'. In April 1953 at Assekrem she had undertaken to spend the rest of her life working to that end. The name 'de Foucauld' carried with it associations of class, power and French nationalism and colonialism which she believed belied the message of universality for which he had stood. It was for such reasons that in December 1952 she had decided to drop the 'of Father de Foucauld' from the name of the Fraternity. It was for the same reasons that by the time, in 1953, evidence was being gathered for consideration of his beatification she was convinced that he should be beatified under the name of 'Little Brother Charles of Jesus'. It was a name that could be translated into any language and was comprehensible and acceptable to the poor.

Otherwise she was satisfied that most of her undertakings were nearing fulfilment. By then even a long-nurtured dream of a circus fraternity was on the horizon. As a child she had loved circuses. In July 1953 she had visited one in Brussels and, touched by the hidden suffering of those who risked their lives day after day in order to entertain others, of the clowns who were obliged to smile when they would perhaps rather weep, she had felt called to send some Little Sisters to them. The atmosphere between performances, she recognised, had little of the glamour suggested by the ring. Her Little Sisters, she had felt for some time, could be a presence of the Church amongst them but even she had not dared at first to suggest such a venture whilst the Fraternity was still being subjected to so much criticism on other counts. By 1954, however, two Little Sisters had provisionally joined the Pilatus Circus in Switzerland. The apparently impossible was appearing increasingly possible.

In less than ten years, the Fraternity had indeed spread to encompass the world. Quite apart from the European Little Sisters – among them French, English, Belgian, Italian, Swiss – there were Americans, Brazilians, Canadians, Chileans, Congolese, Egyptians, Indians, Japanese, Lebanese and Mexicans. Between 9 and 18 September the Fraternity was able to hold its first General Chapter at Le Tubet. The occasion, which proved to be 'a magnificent witness to unity', brought together 180 Little Sisters and fifty others who were considering a vocation to the Fraternity. Little Sister Jeanne was unanimously elected by the twenty-five capitulars to continue as General Responsible and nine General Councillors were appointed each with responsibility for a group of regions. The Chapter explored many issues: poverty, the different forms of the fraternities, the annual sessions at El Abiodh, the training of novices. It approved, with the support of Father Voillaume, the rapid spread of the foundations founded with just one professed sister and a postulant. Most important of all, however, was the submission for approval of the Constitutions. The Constitutions upon which Little Sister Magdeleine had worked under the most extraordinary circumstances were the fruit of constant discussion not only with Father Voillaume but also with her Little Sisters. The search for the right spirit and the appropriate expression was not one which Little Sister Magdeleine conducted without calling upon the input of those who must live it. Nevertheless she had felt that certain concepts such as 'the offering of one's life in immolation', the 'search for the last place', the 'desire for abjection', the 'desire for martyrdom' might appear too unreasonable. The overwhelming vote to retain them in the revised Constitutions was for her one of the greatest joys of her life. It was an eloquent demonstration that the spirit of the Fraternity was as she had felt from the beginning it should be.

In October 1954 Little Sister Magdeleine took the revised Constitutions to Rome to lay them before the Sacred Congregation for the Oriental Churches to which the Fraternity had been answerable since 1949. In the crypt of St Peter's Basilica five more Little Sisters were to make their final professions. It was also an opportunity for Little Sister Magdeleine, who was only on this occasion to see Pope Pius XII as part of a general audience at Castel Gandolfo, to write to him of the progress of the Fraternity. At Little Sister Magdeleine's request, the Fraternity was to be considered for erection to a congregation of pontifical right. Now she asked that even if it were to be granted such a privilege, it remain under the jurisdiction of the Congregation for the Oriental Churches. The Fraternity as a whole was still committed to the people of Islam through prayer and self-immolation. The Congregation for the Oriental Churches was, she felt, best equipped to guide them in this direction. In the Orient the Little Sisters had by this time become very much part of the Melkite, Coptic and Armenian communions and were due shortly also to become part of the churches of the Chaldean, Syrian, Maronite and Syro-Malankaran Rite. Little Sister Magdeleine asked also once more for the right to have the General Fraternity in Rome.

With these requests made, it seemed at the time that it remained only for her to make ready to leave for the Iron Curtain countries. Her anticipated departure was to be delayed, however. The only condition the Church authorities had set upon her leaving the Fraternity was that the congregation be adequately established before she went and that the new Superior General together with her council be ready to govern it. Yet obstacle after obstacle seemed to conspire to delay her. Little Sister Magdeleine's habitual response to obstacles was sheer perseverance. She had an undauntable capacity to see her ventures through to the very end, but she also identified a sign that it was perhaps right to wait a little longer. There were still ends to be tied up: the struggle for the right to have Little Sisters actually locked up in prison as voluntary prisoners was still, for example, going on. There were final journeys to be made. The ensuing months were devoted to, among other journeys, a return to Algeria to Sidi Boujnan and Father Voillaume's session at El Abiodh. She made a last tour of Africa, one of those journeys which she loved in which nothing could be predicted: no plane service, buses or even lorries, just thousands of miles of hitch-hiking with ten Little Sisters across the desert. Once more she made the arduous climb to Assekrem. The tensions leading up to the Algerian war of independence were mounting, however. By September 1955 it was becoming apparent that it would be ill advised to hold the annual session at El Abiodh. Instead, it was held in a large summer house of a seminary belonging to the Congregation of Propaganda Fide next to the Pope's gardens at Castel Gandolfo.

The beginning of 1956 Little Sister Magdeleine spent at Le Tubet working with Little Sister Jeanne on the creation of a General Secretariat. The energy she poured into this caused a bout of illness. Yet she went on working day and night. Her diaries and her correspondence must be brought up to date. She slaved on the Constitutions in order to leave her Little Sisters with a work in which 'everything had been considered, weighed, prayed about and corrected'. Endlessly she weighed every word for fear of inviting the least false interpretation of the ideal she sought to convey. Little Sister Jeanne's father fell gravely ill and died soon afterwards. It became difficult to anticipate a swift departure. Nor did the process of founding new fraternities decelerate. In England foundations had been started in London, which was to be a regional fraternity and also an artisanal fraternity, and in Leeds which was a worker fraternity. After a comprehensive tour of all the Marian shrines of England and Wales, Little Sister Magdeleine had settled on Walsingham as the location for a fraternity of adoration for which the Little Sisters had to wait a number of years. Now she wanted to set up a study fraternity in Oxford where the Little Sisters could study theology and learn English.

In Marseille a fraternity was begun, right in the heart of the prostitutes' quarter where the Little Sisters would try to bring a little humanity into the lives of the women who solicited on the streets of the port. Living amongst them, befriending them, listening to their problems, providing them with a haven without judging them, the Little Sisters afforded them a respect which they found nowhere else. From poor and broken homes, sometimes alcoholics, sometimes mentally ill and illiterate, surrounded by all the associated social and moral vices of criminality and sexual deviation, the Fraternity's prostitute 'friends' were very close to Little Sister Magdeleine's heart.

In August 1956 she ventured for the first time behind the Iron Curtain on a journey made in secret to Yugoslavia, Hungary and Czechoslovakia. On her return she and Little Sister Jeanne spent a night in Bellechasse prison. The experience was to prove the prelude to a request from the governor of a prison in Hagenau for a Little Sister for each section of his institution: 'Send me five,' he wrote to their foundress, 'and the atmosphere in the prison will be transformed.' At one time, Little Sister Magdeleine acknowledged, she would have liked to give her life for prisoners. 'As in the case of the lepers, the nomads, Africa, the Lord has given me all these vocations so that the Little Sisters can fulfil them. But in what calling shall I end my days?' A few days spent behind the closed frontiers of the Communist world had heightened the desire to return, but as her final departure drew imminent fear of what lay ahead became more pressing: 'I have Russia ahead of me and I am afraid of leaving,' she admitted. She made a last pilgrimage to Fátima and she called for an 'onslaught of prayer' for those who were suffering in the Eastern bloc but also for those who were causing the suffering. 'We must pray with love,' she directed her sisters. 'Reprobation, hatred must be kept for evil and error but never for any man, however perverse he might appear.' It was love that would save the world, the love of the Virgin Mary giving her tiny child to people throughout the world with a gesture which no one would be able to resist. Little Sister Magdeleine was still trying to find an artist who could adequately convey the mysterious image she carried so constantly with her and which she yearned to transmit to others in the form of 'Our Lady of the Whole

World'. The Little Sisters venturing even into those places which others considered inaccessible, into Afghanistan, Iran, Syria and elsewhere, were essentially the bearers of the Christmas message, the message of God made man in all his vulnerability, but Little Sister Magdeleine was still finding new ways of giving practical expression to that message. By July 1957 she had discovered yet another final mission to accomplish before setting off as a bearer of a message of love behind the Iron Curtain.

A number of Little Sisters from countries as wide-ranging as Italy, Switzerland, France and Vietnam felt called to use their particular instrumental and vocal gifts to spread the message of the manger, not only at Christmas but throughout the year. The idea had been conceived of a group of Little Sisters who, after the fashion of the medieval troubadours, would travel about, spreading the message and the spirit of Christmas through music and song. She submitted this idea for approval by various Church authorities and received it. She also endeavoured to build into the organisation of the Fraternity a means of safeguarding the interests of and preparing Little Sisters for certain groups which she considered particularly important to it because they were the realisation of ideas upon which Charles de Foucauld had placed great emphasis. Charles de Foucauld had said, 'Go to the most suffering members of the body of Christ.' Little Sister Magdeleine found in his directive the inspiration for a 'section' devoted to the care of the sick. There would be fraternities specially devoted not only to lepers but also to those suffering from tuberculosis and the mentally and physically handicapped, but there would also be within fraternities with a different orientation individuals who were particularly devoted to work amongst the sick. All those consecrated to the sick would belong to one section which would share their problems and represent their interests, independently of the requirements of their particular fraternity or region.

Similarly there would be a section for the 'nomads' to include not only those in the tent fraternities but also those who travelled with the circus, the gypsies and the travelling folk. A third section would be for 'prisons, prostitution and drug addiction'. She also wanted a section for the 'diffusion' of the message of the Fraternity not only through the activities of those who gave talks or performed as troubadours but also through the skills of those who created crosses, cribs, renderings of the baby Jesus and other images central to its spirituality. For Little Sister Magdeleine such images were a means of conveying a spiritual message 'via the eyes'. The fifth and final section, for which Little Sister Magdeleine would retain personal overall responsibility, was for Communist countries. In June 1957 she went to say her farewells to Pope Pius XII. Together she and Little Sister Jeanne had a meeting with him in a room adjoining his office. There she entreated the Pope, 'in the name of the infant Jesus, the real founder of the Fraternity, in the name of Our Lady of Fátima, Our Lady of Russia and Our Lady of the Whole World', to allow her and those who would accompany her to leave before the end of July. The vast red area on the map of the world awaited her: 'I no longer have any desire', she told him, 'but to give my life for Russia, in Russia.'

It was in September that Little Sister Magdeleine finally parted from the last group of Little Sisters who had accompanied her as far as Vienna, believing that she would never see them again. On the morning of 7 September, in the company of a Little Brother who was to be her driver, she turned her back on the small fraternity in Austria's capital and began a journey that was to take her first to Czechoslovakia, then to Poland and finally to Russia. Once more she was following blindly, regardless of the human and emotional cost. Some time later, looking back on the pain of separation from those to whom she had been closest, she wrote in characteristic language of how 6 and 7 September were the most difficult in all her life as foundress of the Fraternity: 'That crossing of the frontiers into the Eastern bloc countries seemed to place a barrier between the Little Sisters and me for ever.'

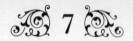

The Church's Approval

As it transpired, Little Sister Magdeleine's separation from her sisters was not to prove as permanent as she had anticipated. The journey through Prague and then on to Czestochowa in Poland, where she joined the pilgrims wending their way to the Marian shrine, went as planned. From there she continued to Cracow and Warsaw and began the necessary procedures for obtaining visas for other Eastern European countries on her agenda: Albania, Bulgaria, Romania, Czechoslovakia and Russia. On Monday 4 November 1957, however, she received an unexpected telegram from the two Little Sisters who were by then living under cover in Prague: 'Expecting you before Thursday.' For reasons of secrecy they could say no more and Little Sister Magdeleine was unable to contact them. She had left them, secure in the knowledge that they had visas to remain in the Czechoslovakian capital for one year, but she could only imagine now that some serious problem had arisen. Under normal circumstances it would have been quite impossible to obtain a visa for Czechoslovakia within twenty-four hours, but she put her faith as always in the 'Master of the impossible' reassuring herself that if the visa was not forthcoming it would be for a reason. By the evening of the following day she had been granted a visa, and on the morning after that, at the very last minute, she managed to get herself a seat on a plane.

In Prague it emerged that the Little Sisters' visas had been withdrawn in reprisal for the French government's refusal to allow a prominent Czech figure to enter France. The Little Sisters had wanted to consult their foundress as to whether they should take steps to try and return. Little Sister Magdeleine's own visa for Prague was only for forty-eight hours. She had no visa permitting her to return to Poland. Not knowing quite which way to turn, she headed for Zürich where the only available plane seat was destined for Rome.

Taking it for a sign, she duly despatched a telegram to Little Sister Jeanne, announcing her return.

After several years of respectful but unrelenting persistence she had eventually obtained authority to have a noviciate in Rome. When authorisation was first received in the summer of 1956, she had not as yet found a location for it. Something had told her that it should perhaps be over some catacombs. More and more, she had heard talk of a piece of land situated near a place of pilgrimage where the Virgin was said to have appeared, opposite a Trappist monastery at Tre Fontane. Charles de Foucauld had begun his monastic life as a Trappist. Little Sister Magdeleine interpreted an accumulation of such factors as an indication that it was to Tre Fontane that she was being called to take the noviciate. The prize land on the outskirts of the 'eternal city' in the vicinity of the Trappist monastery had, however, long since been bought up. By November Little Sister Magdeleine had been offered the use of some wooden barrack huts which were duly dismantled, transported from Milan and stored courtesy of the Trappists at Tre Fontane. On 5 December 1956 Little Sister Magdeleine had gone to the abbot of the monastery and told him of her distress at being unable to find a site for her Little Sisters. Ten days later she received word that he and his Council had agreed that she should set up her international noviciate on their land. The very next day the Little Sisters found themselves in a small wood of eucalyptus trees, opposite the grotto which, although as yet not officially recognised by the Church, had in practice become a place of Marian pilgrimage.

A young monk appointed to show Little Sister Magdeleine the site and act as her interpreter was struck by the way in which, for her, God was a loving person who was part of her whole life and responsible for everything that happened. Afterwards he noted how she had, quite naturally, remarked at several junctures upon how 'God protects us, God is good, the Good Lord helped us', without any affectation or ostentation. It was, he wrote, as if she lived quite naturally in a spiritual atmosphere. He had been struck, too, by the fact that she looked as if she had suffered. Her face was thin, her look was penetrating and her features drawn. Her attitude was rather serious and reserved like that of 'a soul sharing in the Passion and death of Christ on the cross to give life to others and give birth to an institute'. Her clothes were poor and simple. In the middle of winter her feet were bare beneath her sandals. Over her shoulders she wore a hooded cloak and on her head the simple 'veil' of a twentieth-century woman worker. In her the young monk recognized the poverty of the Gospels, a poverty that was not just external but internal also, a poverty that was total, which translated itself into her whole bearing, an attitude of inner prostration before God in faith and adoration. He found in her no affectation of humility. Quite simply and in the unspectacular way of true humility, she *was* humble. To him she talked very simply of 'our Constitutions', 'our foundations', 'our apostolate'. In her own written account of the event she commented on 'How the Blessed Virgin has spoilt us.' 'For years I had been seeing the Little Sisters installed in Rome in a eucalyptus wood but on the other side of the road, never imagining that the Trappist Fathers would one day give us one of the most beautiful corners of their land.'

By 1957 the Little Sisters had themselves cleared an area among the eucalyptus trees at Tre Fontane and reassembled the wooden barrack huts in which the international noviciate was to be housed. Little Sister Magdeleine, on her unexpected return to Rome, had intended only to meet with Little Sister Jeanne to establish with her how best she could return to the Communist countries on which she had set her sights. As it transpired, however, Mgr de Provenchères was at Tre Fontane for a session of the General Council, and he asked that she return to the Fraternity. Accordingly Little Sister Jeanne took her back to Tre Fontane, there to be engulfed by an enthusiastic crowd of Little Sisters, overjoyed to see her again after the sorrowful farewells of the previous September. The aborted plan to leave for ever was taken as a manifestation of the will of God, on the strength of which Mgr de Provenchères decided that from then onwards Little Sister Magdeleine should divide each year into two: six months were to be spent travelling behind the Iron Curtain and six months were to be spent with her Little Sisters.

Her 'definitive' departure had in any case not been understood by some outside the congregation. For reasons of necessary secrecy even members of the Fraternity had not been party to the details of Little Sister Magdeleine's intentions behind the Iron Curtain. Ostensibly, as far as the world at large was concerned, she had abandoned the congregation she had founded to set off as a tourist, in a van specially converted by the Little Sisters for the purpose and nicknamed, as she herself had been 'l'étoile filante', 'Shooting Star', in the company of a Little Brother, in pursuit of an objective that was scarcely defined. At the very least, to some her actions appeared eccentric. She still suffered from the fact that there were those who thought she was by nature someone who could not bear to stay in one place for very long, whereas in fact she craved stability. Not for the first time, she announced that the initial years of explosive extension were to give way to a period of more gradual and progressive development, a period during which the Fraternity would establish its roots more soundly.

Some criticisms Little Sister Magdeleine could dismiss as the product of human caution of the kind that must be subordinated to obedience to the will of God. Undemonstrative though she generally was in her affections, she loved her Little Sisters with a maternal tenderness which would come to light on occasions such as her 'final' departure from them. From her 'Shooting Star' then she had written to them with manifest sorrow and deep tenderness. Yet, much as she loved them, she would not spare them the dangers which she regarded as part of their vocation. The first Little Sisters to join her had even been required to sign a paper stating that they were ready if necessary to die of starvation. When Brother Charles of Jesus had conceived of his 'Little Brothers of the Sacred Heart of Jesus' in Morocco, he had stated that for all his longing for companions, he would prefer to remain alone rather than be joined by those who were not really called by Jesus or disciples of his heart. In January 1903 he had written in this context:

> I ask three things of those who want to come: firstly that they be ready to give their life's blood without offering resistance, secondly that they be ready to die of hunger, thirdly that they obey me despite my unworthiness until such time as, some of them having been tested by a short period of community life, it will be possible to elect a superior who I hope will not be me.

It was enough to warrant Little Sister Magdeleine's seeing such absolute commitment, which was in any case very much part of her own temperament, as an integral and necessary part of the Little Sisters' vocation. Such extremism, her readiness to send young girls into places of danger, was not understood by everyone. When in July 1951 a young postulant died of a tropical disease contracted in the Cameroons, she had felt 'all the pain of a mother's heart' but it did not persuade her to change her attitude, that to protect them would be to strike at the roots of their vocation to be poor amongst the poor to the point of suffering and even death. 'I love my Little Sisters as

155

a mother loves her children,' she wrote to the administrator of Maroua in response to attempts by the French authorities there to have her raise the standard of her sisters' accommodation and living, 'but I shall never hesitate to send them into places of danger. It was above all for that that I founded the congregation.' To her Little Sisters she wrote that they should respond to criticisms on such grounds that even in the very best-equipped congregations working in mission countries there were still people who fell victim to the climate. They were also to point out that no one was as concerned about the poor people who died of deprivation and poverty, and that there were far less beautiful causes for which people were willing to risk their lives without engendering criticism and reproaches. This was not to suggest that Little Sister Magdeleine did not sometimes think that the world might be right in fearing for the lives of her Little Sisters. Confronted with the horrors of the fighting in Vietnam, she did experience a fleeting moment of doubt, but then she saw again the manger with the infant Jesus lying on a bed of straw, the shepherds, the apostles and all those who in their weakness had mysteriously brought about the most extraordinary conquests, and she told herself that the Lord wanted this poverty and vulnerability in order that they might be only the instruments of a work that was exclusively his.

As in the case of many of Little Sister Magdeleine's expressed opinions, her views on the appropriate living and working conditions for the Little Sisters were by no means devoid of apparent inconsistencies. Responding always to the need of the instant, she was quite capable of stating adamantly at one moment that she felt that people were far too concerned with the Little Sisters' health and not enough with the dreadfully hard life of the poor, and at the next, urging Father Voillaume to take into consideration that the Little Sisters were not to be treated like men. Hand in hand with a vision that was frequently absolute went a certain realism. Little Sister Magdeleine might well expect her sisters to contend with snakes and rats and hostile insect life, but she knew that they were not for the most part born nomads, Eskimos or gypsies. They did not therefore have the natural resistance of those whose lives they sought to share. The Little Sisters would not survive unscathed the cold of winter in a holey tent or a draughty caravan. It was for this reason that she ensured that they had more permanent accommodation to which they could repair at intervals. Similarly she did not send Little Sisters to share the real conditions of Eskimo lives without giving them first a period of adjustment in a poor house in a small nearby town.

As far as the level of poverty which the Little Sisters were required to assume was concerned, Little Sister Magdeleine was the first to be troubled by the least intimation of feeling rich amongst the poor. It was a dreadful experience for her to feel well dressed and well fed amongst the unclothed and the hungry. Even whilst urging her Little Sisters to think of the suffering of the rich with their intolerable burden of class prejudice and all the material encumbrances that prevented them from 'flying freely' towards God, she did not want them to appear rich in any way. When in 1948 the possibility had arisen of the Little Sisters wearing stockings, she vehemently opposed the idea on the grounds that both in Europe and in Arab countries stockings were considered a mark of wealth. Arriving in New Bell in the Cameroons in August 1953, she was devastated to find that the wooden cabin she had originally helped to erect, which had been accidentally destroyed by fire spreading from the sanctuary lamp, had been replaced by something grander. It was much taller than the neighbouring huts. It had large windows, timber pillars, a roof which was quite different from the others and which therefore made them seem all the more poor and dark. 'We are no longer one with them,' pronounced Little Sister Magdeleine. In her mind's eye she could see all the tiny fraternities she had chosen with so much love being transformed for all kinds of good reasons into comfortable houses. Little Sister Magdeleine wept at the prospect of this betrayal of the Fraternity's vocation. People had always predicted that they would be unable to maintain their poverty. They would not be required to abandon it as yet, however. The bishop who had installed the Little Sisters in the new cabin took it back, and the Little Sisters began work on a hut like all the other African huts, which the local Europeans considered unfit for habitation. Two years later, she visited the fraternity that was in the process of construction next to Charles de Foucauld's hermitage at Beni Abbes. Dismayed by the magnitude of the imposing pillars which were clearly destined to support a sizeable building in the shape of a cross, she took up a pickaxe and set about demolishing them.

Little Sister Magdeleine had an eye for beauty which manifested itself in many ways. Her appreciation of the wonders of nature, of art and craftwork, even the satisfaction she manifestly derived from seeing her Little Sisters properly and uniformly arrayed in their habits, bespoke a developed aesthetic sense. To her such beauty was a revelation of God, but more beautiful than the natural grandeur of Assekrem or the brilliance of the desert stars was, she maintained, the smallest act of love. She was realistic enough to know that poverty could be sordid and that such poverty was not desirable for her Little Sisters. The fraternities, be they in a tent, a gypsy caravan or a highrise apartment, must be clean and tidy. They must not be too beautiful. At the same time she understood that simply by virtue of the fact that the Little Sisters' homes were kept clean and tidy and were not constantly overrun by children, they might well appear more attractive than their neighbours', but then even in the poorest families, she pointed out, where there was a woman of taste things could appear well ordered.

She had herself a gift for making a very unpretentious room attractive. The buildings she helped to construct with her own hands at Sidi Boujnan, with their wooden chests and the niches built into the walls to avoid the need for shelves, were beautiful in their simplicity. She adorned them with the gifts she had received from her Arab friends: 'sand roses', the 'flowers' formed by the action of the wind and the elements on the desert sand, or with the local craftwork which she always tried to encourage; and a very basic room was thus transformed. 'This problem of our poverty is such a source of suffering to me,' she acknowledged. 'As soon as you use a little taste to arrange a fraternity, it loses its look of poverty.' For all the simplicity of the materials used, the buildings erected at Sidi Boujnan and El Abiodh also reflected the size and spaciousness of the French colonial era. But then the numerous courtyards each had a specific purpose which was not inconsistent with the Fraternity's vocation. Elsewhere, accommodation was infinitely more modest: huts, slum houses, council flats were more the locations to which she gravitated, depending upon the usual accommodation of the indigenous poor. In any case, were the Little Sisters to live all in one room simply because their neighbours sometimes had to live ten to a single room? Little Sister Magdeleine knew that in order to retain the inner resources necessary to reflect the love of God to those around them, her sisters needed a minimum of space. However simple the structure, ideally they should have a dormitory, a living area in which to receive guests, an area set aside as a chapel, and wherever possible a separate room for the 'responsible'.

In a sense it would never be possible for the Fraternity to achieve the real poverty of the poor, for simply by virtue of belonging to a congregation the Little Sisters benefited from a security to which the really poor could never lay claim. Little Sister Magdeleine felt that the Fraternity's calling was not so much to the poverty of the destitute beggar dressed in rags as to the poverty of Jesus of Nazareth and the poor working classes. Furthermore, each Little Sister could live out the vocation to poverty in a different way: some, by their work in factories, on farms or as artisans, were most readily identifiable with the Jesus of Nazareth; others were poor by virtue of the fact that they were totally dependent on the labours of others for their livelihood, perhaps because they were themselves sick or because they were specially oriented towards a particular work of love among the suffering. 'Jesus – caritas – Jesus – love': Little Sister Magdeleine invariably gave precedence to love. Which was given greater significance in the Gospels: poverty or love? It was love that was to be the Little Sisters' priority. Asked to define the Fraternity in a single word, its foundress chose not poverty but unity.

The fact remained, however, that the Little Sisters were being required to live in extraordinarily difficult circumstances for which, because of the rapid expansion of the Fraternity, they were not always as well equipped as they might have been. When in 1953 a nomad fraternity was begun in the region of the Ahaggar, the Little Sisters' diary recorded, not without a certain humour, how because the thirty goatskins, which they had purchased one by one, had yet to be sown together, they had eventually set off from Tamanrasset with the chapel tent and another small tent belonging to the local doctor. The nomad fraternity was actually to consist of two professed sisters from the fraternity at Tamanrasset, two Little Brothers and an Arab friend. They also had with them a flock of goats, and two donkeys belonging to a European woman who had lived for many years in Tamanrasset, a colourful character of strong will but good heart, known affectionately as Tante Miche. After a terrible sandstorm they spent their first night in the shelter of a rock, some twelve kilometres from Tamanrasset. Next morning they took their livestock six kilometres to the nearest water. That evening they managed to lose the goats which had been grazing peacefully in the vicinity of the tents. Next they lost the two donkeys. A torrential rainstorm blew up marooning the Little Sisters with the Little Brothers in the chapel tent. At the end of the fortnight, they had lost all their animals. And so the chapter of incidents went on.

Other disasters, such as the death of the Little Sister in the

159

Cameroons, were manifestly more serious. Some might be considered avoidable; others were simply the hazards that formed an inevitable part of life in close proximity to war, prostitution or prison occupants. What did concern Little Sister Magdeleine was that her sisters should be spiritually equipped to deal with such situations. Their general formation, the establishing of the appropriate balance between their life of prayer and adoration and their active work, were a continuing source of concern. It was rumoured at times that Little Sister Magdeleine preferred to keep her Little Sisters in a state of intellectual poverty in order to preserve their simplicity. In fact she had continued to give considerable priority to the Little Sisters' studies. They were required by the Constitutions to undertake certain obligatory years of study and to continue this intellectual formation throughout their lives. In theory at least, the rhythm of the fraternities was specifically structured to enable them to study theology and thereby render themselves 'open to the knowledge of God'. In general she kept close control of the first generation of young sisters, knowing that through them she was laying the foundations for the future. 'The first will be the sacrificial ones,' she had predicted as early as 1943, 'those who will be sent out as the advance guard and on whom we shall have to be able to depend.' Nevertheless she did recognise, for example, that founding a fraternity with just one professed sister and one postulant was far from ideal, that sometimes they were moved about with a rapidity that was not in the best interests of the stability of the fraternities, and that at times her Little Sisters, and more specifically their young superiors, lacked knowledge, maturity and experience. 'You have superiors who are not up to their role. I know that even better than you,' she told them in no uncertain terms. 'But didn't I tell each one of you again and again when you first came, that you could not have at one and the same time both the advantages of a brand new congregation and those of a well-matured and established congregation in which all the superiors have passed through a long and serious formation?' People with the kind of temperament that needed the security of 'human prudence' were not made for what Little Sister Magdeleine herself saw as a small family still full of imperfections and deficiencies.

She was tough with them, telling them not to join if their ideal, though possibly much more beautiful, did not coincide with that of the Fraternity. Those who did join were to go off to far distant lands without so much as glancing behind them, and they were not to be afraid either of suffering or of solitude. One Little Sister would recall many years later how, when first she had been considering entering the congregation, the one question Little Sister Magdeleine had asked her was whether she was prepared for loneliness. Young as she was at the time, something in the way the older woman posed the question had made her realise that it was born of personal experience and engraved it for ever on her memory. If Little Sister Magdeleine was demanding, she was also unpredictable and sometimes difficult to relate to, not only because the supernatural lights that guided her could make her appear quite irrational, but also because her natural personality was both fiery and not devoid of quirks. For all the breadth and distance of her metaphysical vision, her eye for detail was such that she simply could not tolerate things that were not quite as they should be. Because, also, love could be poured into the smallest detail and transform it, everything, even the most everyday considerations, assumed importance. She liked drawers, compartments and charts, and ordering information and details into coloured sections. At international gatherings she liked her Little Sisters to sit together according to the continents from which they came, and when the numbers became too large for such clear order to be maintained she did not hesitate to articulate her disappointment.

She did not approve of Little Sisters singing religious music in parts. Nor did she like solo singing. Primarily she was concerned that during worship people should not be over-preoccupied with elaborate music. She was also anxious that the display of individual talents on the part of some sisters might occasion a sense of inadequacy in others. Yet this apparently did not enter into her thinking when it came to the Little Sisters' handicraft where individuals were happily allowed to shine. Dancing, on the other hand, was an area in which sensitivity once more prevailed. For Little Sister Magdeleine dancing was inextricably linked with the idea of courtship between men and women and thus not something she considered suitable for her Little Sisters. Little Sisters who shone at African dancing or other forms of ethnic dance with no such associations had difficulty in dissuading her from her blanket condemnation, and when they did so it was to discover that in her eyes that was not dancing, it was either 'rhythmic movement' or 'farandole'; and it was only 'dancing' that she did not like.

A picture that was not straight would scream at her. Doors to fraternities must not be too large. When she arrived in a fraternity,

Little Sisters expecting an affectionate greeting after a period of separation could well find themselves reproachfully informed instead that the colour of their habit was not the correct blue. Fraternity cows should be black and white. Little Sister Magdeleine was very fond of certain shades of red. Red was the colour of blood. It was the colour of love, of the Sacred Heart and of martyrdom. For this reason she wanted to 'rehabilitate' red at a time when for some it was a colour associated largely with Communism. Certain shades of yellow, on the other hand, she could not abide. She did not want anything in the fraternities to be yellow. Nor did she consider floral patterns appropriate, and her dissatisfaction and disappointment when she found that her predilections had been disregarded were made clearly apparent.

Yet the Little Sisters followed her. They signed the piece of paper that they were prepared if necessary to die of hunger, perhaps because they were young and did not really know then what such a death entailed, but also because they sensed in the Fraternity, in the spirit of Charles de Foucauld, in the writings of Father Voillaume and in her, something new and vital. When those who had been among the first to join looked back on the sessions at El Abiodh, they remembered their fear of scorpions when they slept in the disused hospital buildings, the overcrowding as the numbers swelled to over a hundred, the tent that had to be erected to shelter them from the relentless heat of the Algerian sun during Father Voillaume's talks. They remembered on one occasion the Little Sisters falling sick one after another with stomach upsets, and they remembered Little Sister Magdeleine's distinctive ways. To ensure a free exit for anyone overcome by heat or illness she wanted a way left clear down the middle of the assembled sisters. The memory of her arriving to inspect the rows of Little Sisters sitting on the ground, and inquiring in characteristic fashion, 'But where is my little passageway?' was a vivid one; but it did nothing to deter their enthusiasm. They rode on the backs of lorries, albeit hoping that they would be able to sit on sacks of dates to cushion the discomfort of the dirt tracks. When she took up a pickaxe to destroy something she considered too comfortable for them, they followed suit. And when they heard the news of the death of their sister in the Cameroons they volunteered to replace her because they sensed the mysterious presence of what they would variously call a breath of inspiration, the wind of the desert, the action of the Holy Spirit.

There were, however, some who left the congregation. With the rapid growth of the Fraternity there had been little time really to test the validity of some vocations. It was part of Little Sister Magdeleine's vision of the Fraternity as a reflection of unity in which there were to be no barriers between people, that it should be open to all. Because of her own experience of ineligibility for established religious orders because of ill health, Little Sister Magdeleine had been determined from the very beginning that illness should not be an obstacle to becoming a Little Sister. Little Sister Magdeleine's initial journeys to the Cameroons and her concern for lepers had brought her into contact with a young African woman who felt she had a religious vocation but who, because she was suffering from leprosy, had little hope of ever fulfilling her calling. Little Sister Helena, who, for her part, was overwhelmed by the arrival of an extraordinary European woman who had travelled in a lorry across the Sahara, and by the respect and affection Little Sister Magdeleine showed to her as a black person and someone with leprosy, became the first African Little Sister to join the Fraternity. Young women suffering from tuberculosis and other illnesses were also able to join. Provision was made within the Fraternity for those requiring treatment or convalescence and who were not able to be as physically active as some others but who were no less capable of contributing to the spiritual and contemplative life of the congregation. Those who had known what it was to be invalided or rejected for their physical weakness would be better able to understand those outside the Fraternity undergoing similar experiences.

For similar reasons the Little Sisters of Jesus would not decline people sometimes considered by other religious congregations of the day as ineligible because of family background or previous moral behaviour. Provided they had a vocation, Little Sister Magdeleine saw it as part of the Fraternity's calling to embrace people who had been in prison, who were former prostitutes or who had otherwise experienced for themselves the weaknesses to which some of the friends of the Fraternity were prone. She did her utmost to combat the possibility of such considerations becoming a source of disharmony within the Fraternity by forbidding her sisters to talk about their backgrounds. In France a name alone could reveal much about the social status of its bearer. The Little Sisters were required not to make reference to or even hint at their family names.

There were times, however, when the Fraternity's openness to all did pose problems for its community life. Some who joined were afterwards found to be obviously unsuitable and had to be asked to leave. Others left voluntarily because they did not find what they were seeking in the Fraternity. Little Sister Magdeleine was on occasions taken by surprise and upset by such departures but she encouraged her sisters to be open about and accepting of those who had felt it right to go. In March 1956, at a time when she had felt blocked at Le Tubet but still anticipated her final departure for Communist countries, Little Sister Magdeleine had written a letter expressing her confidence in each of her Little Sisters and referring to 'several painful departures':

> You must keep in your prayers those who do not renew their vows because they are not made for the Fraternity. I would so much like it also to be part of our spirit, to be able to speak openly and without mystery of these departures. It is quite simply a matter of having tried a form of religious life and recognised that one has made a mistake.

Some of those who had left, however, had done so feeling aggrieved and critical, and word of their complaints filtered back to Rome. It was at a time when the Fraternity's application to become a congregation of pontifical right was being considered. On 14 December 1959 Mgr de Provenchères arrived in Tre Fontane to look, together with Little Sister Jeanne and her council, at the state of the Fraternity. There was nothing unusual about such a review. It was a task that he undertook annually. On 16 December, however, with obvious emotion, he announced quite unexpectedly that the Little Sisters were to receive an Apostolic Visitor. Faithful daughter of the Church that she was, for Little Sister Magdeleine a visit by an envoy from the Pope could only be a cause of joy but it was clear to her from Mgr de Provenchères's attitude that this was to be something painful. It was not without an air of ominous expectation that he told them: 'Remember that your Christmas grace is to be a child in the arms of the Church.'

On 8 September 1939, the day on which the Fraternity had been founded, the woman through whose hands it was initiated had asked God that, as a sign that the foundation was in accordance with his will, for twenty years there be no serious difficulties with those who represented the Church in relation to it. She had added that if during those first twenty years there were any such difficulty, she would take it as a sign that the Fraternity was not in accordance with the will of

God, and would 'disappear'. For twenty years there had been no serious problem except perhaps the refusal of the Congregation for Propaganda Fide to assume responsibility for the worker fraternities. Even that, however, in the vision of Little Sister Magdeleine, had proved to be wonderfully providential because it had brought the Fraternity the remarkably fruitful relationship it had with the Congregation for the Oriental Churches. Cardinal Tisserant, head of that Congregation, had always been so encouraging. His secretary, Cardinal Coussa, a man of Syrian origins with an exceptional knowledge of Canon Law, had enjoyed finding ways of making new developments possible within the framework of that Law. He had brought to Propaganda Fide's view of the Fraternity and its Constitutions what one Little Sister described as 'a certain oriental freedom'. As for Pope Pius XII, he had kept a close and paternal eye on the Fraternity. When in June 1957 Little Sister Magdeleine had gone to see him for the last time before leaving for Russia, she had started to tell him about the Fraternity. The old man had interrupted her with a smile. 'Oh, I know everything that concerns you and the work that you are doing.'

The Pope who had made himself so accessible to the Fraternity, however, had died in 1959. By the time the Apostolic Visit was announced in 1959, Angelo Roncalli had become Pope John XXIII, with whom Little Sister Magdeleine had had no direct contact. The twenty-year period of freedom from difficulties with the Church had elapsed three months previously. She did not know exactly what the visit would entail or what it was precisely that the Visitor was being required to examine or sanction. It was not without a certain undefined apprehension that Little Sister Magdeleine greeted the arrival of the Apostolic Visitor, an Oblate priest of Mary Immaculate, on the afternoon of 16 December. Officially, the Apostolic Visit was due to commence on 22nd. Some two hundred Little Sisters had converged upon Tre Fontane to see their foundress that Christmas. On 21st she gathered them all together to ask them to prepare for the festival of Christmas with love. She also spoke to them about the Apostolic Visit and asked them to welcome the visitor from the bottom of their hearts because he came from the Holy Father. In that way they would demonstrate their attachment to the Church even if it was to cause them suffering. Mgr de Provenchères parted from them on the morning of 22nd, having tried to reassure them that despite all the criticisms he had heard about the way in which their habits were not always as neat as they might be and their veils were sometimes adrift and even, more seriously, about the frequency with which they changed fraternities or the limitations of their formation, he had never heard any bishop complain about them in connection with the vital issues of poverty, prayer, obedience, humility or charity. He also made a point of stressing to them the unity of thought and spirit which existed between Little Sister Magdeleine and Little Sister Jeanne.

Later that day the Visitor introduced himself to the Little Sisters with an address which could only further unnerve them. It underlined the importance of such a visit and the authority and powers of the Visitor. An Apostolic Visit was, he pointed out, more significant than a Canonical Visit. It was in fact 'a visit by the Holy Father through the intermediary of his representative', who consequently assumed all associated powers. The representative had overall jurisdiction over the Fraternity. He had unlimited rights to see all documents and letters. In practice the Fraternity's Superiors would maintain their role but their authority was subject to that of the Pope and hence now to his representative. The reason given for the Visit was that before pronouncing its approval by making the congregation one of pontifical right, the Church required information. For twenty years, he acknowledged, everything had been undertaken 'hand in hand' with the Church of Rome. There had been no shortage of criticisms, the Little Sisters were informed, but the Church had blessed the 'apostolic daring' of Little Sister Magdeleine who had always wanted to reach out to the hundredth sheep amongst the mass of humanity that lived far removed from the Church. Having heard differing assessments of the Fraternity from diverse sources, the Holy Father did not want to be influenced by others but rather to study the question for himself. That was why, the Visitor explained, he had sent his envoy to take a look at what they were and what they wanted.

There were perhaps other unmentioned factors at play. The possibility has been mooted that the support of Cardinal Tisserant which Little Sister Magdeleine had so valued over the years now conspired against her. Cardinal Tisserant was a Frenchman. Like Little Sister Magdeleine, he came from Lorraine and was as direct in manner as she was. He did not fit the Italian diplomatic mould and towards the end of his life was also the subject of sharp criticism. The Apostolic Visit coincided with the resignation of this influential but not always popular churchman who had shown the Little Sisters so much solidarity. The combined reasons for the Visit were doubtless manifold and complex. With hindsight it was apparent to many that there was some justification for it and that good eventually came out of it. On one point, however, those involved were unambiguously clear, namely that they could not fully understand or condone the inquisitorial methods employed by the Pope's envoy.

'I shall question each Little Sister individually,' he announced. 'They are to tell me anything that is wrong with the Fraternity and if they tell me that everything is fine with their Superiors, I shall not believe them.' Despite the Visitor's attempt to balance the assertion of his authority by emphasising that the Visit was to take place in an atmosphere of prayer and fraternal love, the announcement immediately upset the Little Sisters. They were even more distressed to learn that the Visitor required Little Sister Magdeleine to leave Tre Fontane and the Little Sisters who had gathered there to see her, in order that he might more freely assess Little Sister Jeanne's government of the Fraternity. He had first assembled the councillors to inform them of his intentions. The councillors representing different continents had made a point of stressing their unity but it was apparently precisely this unity which was a source of concern. In the view of the Visitor if there was no opposition, there was no democracy, no freedom of thought or action. When he told them of his decision to separate Little Sister Magdeleine and Little Sister Jeanne for a while, one of the councillors ventured to protest that the two were really one person. 'Precisely,' was the response. 'They are supposed to be two.' Inevitably the Visitor's line of approach begged the question as to whether one of the purposes of the Visit was not in fact to establish whether Little Sister Jeanne was in proper control of the Fraternity.

The clarification of the respective roles of the General Responsible and the foundress had been a delicate task, as those directly concerned had known full well it would be. As early as February 1950 Mgr de Provenchères had expressed his satisfaction that Little Sisters Jeanne and Magdeleine understood their respective positions. He had pointed out to Little Sister Magdeleine that from the point of view of Canon Law, Little Sister Jeanne was everything and she was nothing, a position which he knew the foundress would wholeheartedly endorse. At the same time obedience and charity required Little Sister Magdeleine to be at Little Sister Jeanne's disposal in so far as it was in the interests of the congregation. Little Sister Jeanne's mission, the Archbishop had maintained, did not require her to govern the Fraternity without the help of the woman who had founded it. Their respective positions, he had predicted, would require of the new Prioress much strength and prudence and of the woman she succeeded ever more humility and charity. Little Sister Magdeleine was to be of as much service as possible whilst being as self-effacing as possible. He had suggested that she draw her inspiration from the words of John the Baptist: 'He must increase, but I must decrease' (John 3:30).

If there was a difficulty at all between the new General Responsible and the foundress it derived from the fact that neither wanted to take precedence over the other. It was for this reason that on Christmas day 1950 at Tamanrasset together they offered to the infant Jesus the 'first place' which neither of them wanted to occupy. Little Sister Magdeleine knew well that she could not have done what she had done without Little Sister Jeanne. Night and day Little Sister Jeanne had been there for her with her youth, her abilities, her loyalty and her quiet discretion. By nature Little Sister Jeanne needed more sleep than Little Sister Magdeleine, but from the point of view of her health and in every other respect Little Sister Magdeleine needed her and she was always there when required. Together they lived side by side in shared devotion to the infant Jesus and in rarely articulated devotion to each other. The letter Little Sister Magdeleine wrote to the woman to whom she had entrusted the government of the Fraternity from Cracow in September 1957, believing that she had parted from her for ever, was unusual in its expression of affection and revealing in respect of their relationship:

> If only you knew what suffering separation from the Little Sisters and from you is capable of causing me. Every day I feel it more.
>
> You are very close to me. You have been so good, my Little Sister Jeanne. . . . I shall never be able to repay the devotion you have given me day and night, for ten years or more. . . . No one has ever suspected the depth of my tenderness because I am not demonstrative. . . .
>
> I have made you suffer. . . . I was worn out with tiredness, so I did not weigh my words. . . . And you, you never showed that I was hurting you. I ask your pardon, my Little Sister Jeanne, who have been the treasure the Lord has given me.

Father Le Sourd, a priest and friend of the Fraternity for many years, remembered being struck, not long after Little Sister Magdeleine's resignation as Prioress, by how 'very beautiful' it was to see 'the ease and spontaneity of Little Sister Magdeleine with her capacity to react swiftly to the most unexpected situations and the discreet but effective presence of Little Sister Jeanne'. Little Sister Jeanne was by no means weak. She was a strong character in her own right. In the words of Father Voillaume she 'was the General Responsible and she knew how to take responsibility'. She and Little Sister Magdeleine had different ways of approaching people, different modes of expression. Together the two women had nonetheless achieved an extraordinary unity. Mgr de Provenchères saw the fact that if Little Sister Jeanne said something, Little Sister Magdeleine would say the same as a very beautiful characteristic of the Fraternity. He claimed never to have seen such unity of vision in two so very different temperaments.

If for Little Sister Jeanne it remained difficult temperamentally to take precedence over the foundress, it was a difficulty that was openly acknowledged, and even made a source of humour between them. When on 27 September 1952 Little Sister Magdeleine had arrived with Little Sister Jeanne in Fátima, only a few days after doctors had told her that she should have a month's bed-rest following her car crash, they had found a room in a small local hotel. Early next morning mass was celebrated in the sanctuaries but since the Little Sisters would have to catch a bus to get there and Little Sister Magdeleine was in a dreadful physical condition, Little Sister Jeanne had told her not to go. The owner of the hotel, however, not fully appreciating the situation, began to reproach Little Sister Magdeleine for her failure to attend mass. He had seen people who were in a far worse state than she was at mass in the sanctuaries. In no uncertain terms, he told her that the congregation she had founded was doomed to failure with a General Superior with such a lamentable lack of faith. It was one of the rare occasions on which Little Sister Jeanne lost her temper, informing the local hotel owner sharply that it was she who was the General Superior and she who had ordered Little Sister Magdeleine not to go. The man's words had undoubtedly touched a nerve but Little Sister Magdeleine would afterwards tease her General Responsible about the assertiveness of which she had suddenly shown herself capable.

For all her capability, Little Sister Jeanne had continued to think it inappropriate for her to assume the role of explaining the spirit of the Fraternity to visiting bishops and others, while the foundress, whom God had afforded special graces, was still close at hand. To the more hierarchically minded, however, this policy reflected badly upon Little Sister Magdeleine who was suspected of not allowing the General Responsible her rightful role. It was, in part at least, allegations along these lines, which appeared even to embrace the possibility that, powerful and charismatic personality that she was, what Little Sister Magdeleine had founded was something in the nature of a cult, which the Visitor appeared to wish to investigate.

From the very first conversations between Little Sister Magdeleine and the Visitor it became apparent that he had difficulty in understanding not only the unity which existed between the foundress and the General Responsible and between them and the councillors, but also the Fraternity's devotion to the infant Jesus, the absence of what the Church more usually recognised as religious ministry or 'works', its poverty based on the lack of dowries or income from capital and their contemplative life in the midst of the world. The Church authorities were inclined to draw a clear distinction between contemplative orders and apostolic orders. They were also inclined to assess congregations for the purposes of such classification in a very concrete way. The Church could not judge them according to the inner workings of the soul; it defined them therefore according to the outer structure of their life. The contemplative life thus meant a rule which expressed a separation from the world, silence, recollection, offices day and night. Apostolic orders, by contrast, were those consecrated to the active ministry of evangelisation, who did not therefore live in cloisters or keep Grand Silence. The Little Brothers had begun their life as a congregation which could quite clearly be defined as contemplative and then moved, with the evolution of the worker fraternities, towards closer contact with the world. Little Sister Magdeleine herself had begun in Boghari with a more active apostolate which had led to an ever more pressing recognition that she was being called to a life which in its close contact with people was nonetheless centred on prayer and adoration. The establishment of an appropriate balance between the structured programme of prayer and the long working hours required of factory workers in those days was not an easy one. Nor did the precedence afforded to charity make it easy always to find the silence and spiritual space that was nonetheless essential to the spiritual health of a fraternity. The maintenance of monastic silence in the fraternities made little sense when the sound of neighbours' squabbles or the arrival of 'friends' at any time of the night or day called to different priorities. In practice, for the Little Sisters a flexible daily rhythm of prayer was constructed where possible around a morning office, mass, one hour of adoration of the Blessed Sacrament, recitation of the rosary, reading and meditation on the Gospel, half-hour community meetings and an evening office. Ideally half a day was devoted to silence each week. Where possible also, once a month a whole weekend would be devoted to prayer, and every year contained a period of retreat.

As early as 1947 when a number of Little Sisters made their vows and received their habits at Le Tubet in a ceremony attended by a crowd of guests, Father Voillaume had ventured to say to Little Sister Magdeleine that since the sisters' ideal was contemplative, the occasion should perhaps have been a more contemplative one. With the reasoning of a churchman of the day he had added that a life of contact with people should not really be called contemplative and that she should not juggle with words. 'Words which are the expression of an idea do not always have the same nuance of meaning,' she had responded to him, adding, 'no human language being rich enough to convey that idea, but they are enormously important . . . to change the word is to betray the idea.' She had urged him then to stand firmly by what she knew was a new form of religious life: 'The contemplative life, you yourself have said it, is a life of friendship with the Person of Jesus, it is a much deeper inner life, in contact with God. Why should this friendship, this contact, not be able to co-exist with a call to souls, even a call to crowds?' What in fact both Father Voillaume and Little Sister Magdeleine had moved towards was a new understanding of the contemplative life, at the roots of which lay Little Sister Magdeleine's assertion that prayer was a way of life and that contemplation was a state of intimacy between God and the soul by no means confined to structured worship or dependent on rigid adherence to the external trappings of the religious life. This was not to dismiss the importance of such structures but it was to recognise that a contemplative vocation was as dependent on the free action of the Holy Spirit and the openness of a childlike heart turned constantly towards God, be it in the midst of the desert or on a factory production line. 'Don't define, live,' Father Voillaume instructed his Little Brothers in a letter he wrote from Beni Abbes in February 1950. 'You will know more easily what to live by looking at Jesus.' Later in the same letter he told them:

> Jesus wants you to be the light of the world, the salt of the
> earth, the leaven in the dough. And understand this well: He

wants you as light, salt, leaven and that is 'to be' those things. It is not a question of doing. All your desire, all your work is to be so united with Jesus that you become light, salt, leaven with Him. The rest is not up to you. Jesus also wants you to be present in the midst of humankind. You must therefore allow yourself to be consumed by those who are hungry and thirsty for the justice of God.

Similarly Little Sister Magdeleine, in a section of her 'green booklet' entitled 'You must bring your contemplative vocation into the midst of the everyday life of mankind', reassured her sisters that the contemplative vocation was not to be feared as something so lofty that it was inaccessible to most. Rather it was 'a completely simple, trusting and loving attitude of someone talking intimately with Jesus'. It was 'the affection of a little child for his father, the confident sharing of a friend with a friend'. Charles de Foucauld in his 'spiritual writings' had written: 'When we love someone, we want to speak to him endlessly. Prayer is nothing else: a familiar conversation with our Beloved. We gaze at him, we tell him we love him, we rejoice to be at his feet.' 'As you work, as you come and go, as you pass among the crowds,' added Little Sister Magdeleine, 'to be a contemplative will mean simply that you try to turn to Jesus within you and enter into conversation with him, as with the one you love most in the world.' There would still be those, however, who would maintain that it was quite simply not possible to be a contemplative and to work in a factory.

Before Little Sister Magdeleine left Tre Fontane the Visitor informed her that she must rewrite the Constitutions taking into account his remarks. To do so would be, in her view, to strike at the very spirit of the Fraternity. The Visitor so manifestly did not understand the childlike spirit which was at the basis of the congregation, calling upon its members now not to be 'little' but 'grown-up'. Yet she accepted when the Visitor, ill equipped as he seemed to teach the ideal of the Fraternity, offered to stand in for Father Voillaume, who for reasons of ill health was unable to give the talks at the forthcoming session. Only good could come from an envoy of the Church, even if appearances seemed to suggest otherwise. With the same faith she undertook to write what would be the eleventh edition of the Constitutions, trusting in the 'Master of the impossible' to safeguard what she remained convinced was his handiwork. On the evening of 15 January she left Rome, as directed, for the fraternity at Montée d'Avignon, in Aix-en-Provence, leaving Little Sister Jeanne in Rome to have her leadership of the congregation assessed.

For Little Sister Magdeleine it was a desperately difficult departure. She suffered because of the separation involved but she was even more distressed at the thought of the simplicity of her Little Sisters being shaken by the reservations and criticisms of a representative of the Church. She was afraid that doubt would be introduced into the Fraternity which had been so exclusively constructed on faith and trust and on her own 'blind' following of the will of God. The unity in love which existed between her and Little Sister Jeanne was the very principle at the heart of the Fraternity. She was fearful that because of her something essential might be changed. From between the carefully controlled lines, with which she explained the events of the Apostolic Visit in her collection of letters, resounded a note of desperation. 'I understand better now,' she wrote, 'how sometimes one can find oneself confronted by trials which no one can rationalise and for which there is no consolation.' The Visit was for her the supreme test precisely because obedience to the Church she loved was so fundamental to the spirit of the Fraternity. 'Against an adversary of the Church we would struggle vigorously to defend our vocation to littleness, to seeking the last place, to the contemplative life, to the submissiveness of a small child,' wrote Little Sister Magdeleine. 'But how can we defend ourselves against an envoy of the Church?'

It was to prove a period during which almost everything for which the Fraternity stood was called to question. The General Responsible found herself increasingly at a loss as to how to direct the Little Sisters to respond to this representative of the Church who was yet so uncomprehending of the Fraternity's ideal. At the beginning of March 1960 Little Sister Jeanne came to Le Tubet to await the arrival of the Visitor on the 8th. On the 18th, the Visitor's day of rest, she and Little Sister Magdeleine spent the day together, examining their consciences as to what their attitude should be.

The Visitor was apparently troubled by the lack of clearly defined continuity in Little Sister Magdeleine's thought and vocabulary. Little Sister Magdeleine explained the successive changes in her thought and in the Constitutions in terms of her response to the indications of Divine Providence that she had always believed she was following. She explained it also in terms of the changing requirements of the Fraternity's expansion, without her personal volition, from its initial exclusive consecration to the people of Islam to its extension throughout the world. She explained the creation of the different forms of fraternity in response to the numerous vocations which had presented themselves but she wrote too of how in the creation of each one she had sought to reconcile the intense desire to remain in the presence of the Blessed Sacrament and the yearning to be so 'inserted' in the midst of humanity that they would be the 'leaven in the dough'. She explained the Fraternity's attachment to the Congregation for the Oriental Churches. She explained the importance given to Islamic countries.

There were points on which she was prepared to acknowledge personal error. In obedience she accepted the closure of certain fraternities and noviciates, but as she worked again on the Constitutions it was with deep sadness that she realised that there were some issues which she would never be able to concede: total poverty, smallness, the state of spiritual childhood, the contemplative life. It was too expedient a line of reassurance to suggest to her that the Visitor was neither the Church nor the Pope, but only an emissary, and that he was capable of error. Her inability to be like a child in relation to him was a source of extraordinary sadness and regret, but already the seeds of division were being sown amongst the Little Sisters who were being questioned about their superiors' least shortcomings and denied even the right to silence. Some of them were already saying that they would leave the Fraternity if its spirit was to change. There came a point where in the interests of this spirit and of the 'treasure of unity' which she believed God had entrusted to her, Little Sister Magdeleine felt it her clear duty to defend the Fraternity's ideal. Even with Father Voillaume, she told herself, she had argued when he had given advice to the Little Sisters which she had felt was better suited to the Little Brothers. She could see the Fraternity being turned into a well-organised congregation but devoid of the sense of freedom and suppleness that had hitherto characterised it.

The knowledge that the ideal was in danger of compromise cast a shadow over everything. On Easter Saturday 1960 when the Little Sisters at Montée d'Avignon, sang 'Christ is Risen' under her window, she found herself unable to respond to their calls. They must not see the sadness she felt was written on her face during this season of joyful resurrection. Next day when the sisters from Le Tubet arrived in their turn to sing what was known as the 'Song of the Foundations', and applauded to bring her to the window, she could hear only the applause which the Priest Visitor had condemned as evidence of

174

infatuation with her personality. Despair set in. Her birthday was usually a day of celebration in the Fraternity but on 26 April that year she spent the day in Marseille to avoid a recurrence of what had happened at Easter. She was sure that she had done nothing to focus the affections of her sisters on her personality. If anything she felt that quite the reverse was true. She had such a fear of anything which might screen them from the love of God. For the duration of the Apostolic Visit she wanted to remain in silence and in solitude. She could not bring herself to celebrate or be joyful among her sisters until she could herself see the light again.

She saw very few of her Little Sisters during that period but many of them wrote to her expressing their sympathy and support. She had the understanding too of Mgr Mercier and many other bishops but they could not be seen to oppose the Apostolic Visitor. Mgr de Provenchères could preach only patience and hope. With his advice and guidance, however, Little Sister Magdeleine continued her work on the Constitutions and wrote letter after letter defending the Fraternity and its spirit against the various allegations raised by the Visitor. By May she had received what must have been one of the most painful blows. It became apparent to her that letters which she had written and extracts from talks given to the Little Sisters were in part responsible for the Apostolic Visit and that some of her Little Sisters had actually contributed to its severity. A minority of Little Sisters had, it seemed, complained about the absolute way in which devotion to the infant Jesus was presented to them. Little Sister Magdeleine found herself having to protest that her emphasis on the spirituality of the manger was not to suggest that the infant Jesus was to be the sole focus of their devotion. She had in fact always struggled to ensure that the Little Sisters did not talk about the infant Jesus when they were referring to the Eucharist. If some had misinterpreted her thinking it was either because she had expressed it badly or because they had misunderstood or because young responsibles had been unable to explain it to them properly. In this, as in so many other things, it was impossible to avoid all distortion and deformation. She could only make an effort to strive for greater precision.

Little Sister Magdeleine was very accepting of differences of individual calling, often seeing in them signs from God as to the overall direction the Fraternity should take. When one Little Sister asked to devote her life to being part of the Fraternity but as a hermit, the foundress respected her need for greater solitude and silence and

175

agreed, emphasising only that her case was exceptional. The free action of the Holy Spirit and the richness and diversity of the life of Jesus might well, she felt, find more complete expression in forms which varied and complemented each other according to differences of milieux and the nuances of individual callings. The Constitutions reflected this respect for what she had referred to as 'individual vocations'.

The Visitor, however, objected to what he understood by the expression. At his intimation she duly changed 'individual vocation' to 'individual orientation' but she had to make the point that to dispense with the idea itself would be a serious loss to their calling. 'Individual vocation' to her did not mean in any way a lack of openness to the will of God. The Little Sisters were required to accept being sent anywhere in the world, if necessary in contravention of their personal wishes. The vocation of the Fraternity as a whole, however, presupposed a gift of friendship to a particular people or a milieu, a personal gift which implied a choice and attraction which was spiritual in nature, but which must always be subject to obedience and often sacrificed to a greater good. She cited the example of two Little Sisters who were totally dedicated to the people of Japan and Alaska. If they were asked to go to the opposite corners of the world, she was sure that in obedience they would do so joyfully, but in their heart of hearts they would maintain their love for the people of their first choosing and for whom they had offered themselves when they made their final profession. Beyond Little Sister Magdeleine's careful attempts at explanation all the frustration at the inadequacy of words was yet discernible. If, in obedience, everything which touched on this 'personal calling' must be suppressed, she would obey but she did not want to do so with the thought that she had not been understood because she had been unable to explain it properly.

The process of enquiry continued with Little Sister Magdeleine remaining quiet but for the letters of explanation she wrote to the Apostolic Visitor. She stopped sending directives to the Little Sisters even though she had previously done so with Little Sister Jeanne's blessing. She carefully appended green labels to those letters which she did write with Little Sister Jeanne's authority, stating clearly that they were written on behalf of the General Responsible. She professed to have many faults, to have made many mistakes and written some silly things in her life as a foundress. Her relations with the Visitor were full of assurances that she would submit herself totally to the will of the Holy See no matter what sacrifice was required, but when, on 13 June, she received a parcel with part of her revised Constitutions returned covered with corrections and annotations made by him, she resolved that it would be better to remain a diocesan congregation than to change the ideal of the Fraternity so completely. Fortunately the Apostolic Visitor had concluded his alterations with the statement that this was not part of his official mission and that she was not therefore obliged to take his corrections into account. With all the disappointment of one who six years previously had gone so full of hope to ask Pius XII and Mgr Montini for their help in making the Fraternity a pontifical congregation, she shut the sheets of paper away in a drawer to await the end of the Visit.

One month later a chapter still outstanding, relating to the Little Sisters' work, was returned, it too completely amended. Little Sister Magdeleine claimed to console herself with the idea that the more obviously unacceptable corrections there were, the better chance the Fraternity had as far as the Church was concerned, because the Church would not wish to see the ideal of Little Brother Charles of Jesus so disfigured. In truth, however, she was almost beyond such consolation. She made brief journeys to Italy and Austria. She spoke still of her yearning to go to Russia. She could still derive joy from the gift of two turtle doves that flitted about her office and perched at intervals on her shoulder. There were too the sympathy and solidarity of friends and bishops such as Mgr Mercier who wrote to her of his visits to the tent fraternity in Algeria; and there was a visit to Le Tubet by Cardinal Tisserant, the circumstances of whose resignation from the Congregation for the Oriental Churches had occasioned in him very similar feelings to her own. Still there remained with her the thought that if she were to die, a substantial part of the Fraternity's problems would be solved.

When in October 1960 she received an unexpected letter from the Apostolic Visitor in Rome suggesting that she come to Tre Fontane to attend a session being held for those about to take their final vows, it was only with mixed feelings that she went. The Little Sisters themselves had written to the Apostolic Visitor asking him to allow Little Sister Magdeleine to come. For their sakes she did so but it was with a heavy heart and in the conviction that she would be walking something of a tightrope. 'If I don't speak, people will think I am sulking. If I speak they will think I am taking your place,' she wrote to Little Sister Jeanne. On 13 October she arrived in Rome to find

177

herself surrounded by Little Sisters, eager to welcome her. She would have liked, she later wrote, to have gone straight away to weep discreetly in the presence of the Lord. Instead she was carried along by her well-intentioned sisters to the community room, where she could no longer hold back the tears. She cried openly, regretting her lack of control even as she did so, because they could not fully understand the reason for her distress. To date she and Little Sister Jeanne had done everything they could to protect them from the anguish their superiors were undergoing.

Little Sister Magdeleine did not attend the vow ceremony held on 30 October 1960 in the crypt of St Peter's Basilica. It was a reflection of her desire for self-effacement and also part of her way of making her 'definitive' departure for the Iron Curtain countries in 1957 that thereafter she did not attend any of the Fraternity's official ceremonies. Nevertheless fifty-four Little Sisters made their final vows into the hands of Little Sister Jeanne, in eleven different languages: German, English, Arabic, Spanish, French, Greek, Italian, Persian, Portuguese, Somali and Tamacheq. Next day Little Sister Magdeleine had a meeting with the Visitor. She had prayed for inspiration and after ten months of restraint, finally considered it her duty to pour out all that she felt in defence of what God had entrusted to her to transmit to a new religious family. The Apostolic Visitor, by her own account, was stupefied to find himself in the presence of a completely different person, and she was even more so to hear him say: 'But why didn't you speak to me like this in the first place?'

Yet on her return to Aix-en-Provence the correspondence she received throughout December offered little cause for hope. The Apostolic Visitor found the text she had written for him on the subject of the state of spiritual childhood edifying. He was grateful for Mgr de Provenchères' assurances that since their last meeting the Archbishop had made a special point of confirming that the General Responsible and her council were in appropriate control of the Fraternity and for his directions to the Little Sisters that they must for their part be clear in distinguishing the roles of and their own attitudes towards the foundress and the General Responsible. He received letters from the Little Sisters respectfully indicating that their loyalty and affection for Little Sister Magdeleine was based not on human attachment but on the fact that she was so clearly and simply a pointer towards God, and affirming their belief in the spirit of the Fraternity. By the third week in December, however, Little Sister Magdeleine was convinced that in human terms there was nothing more she could do. An essential part of their vocation, particularly their contemplative vocation, was seriously in danger of compromise. The Little Sisters decided to make a novena to the infant Jesus 'with a faith that would move mountains and fill valleys to overflowing'. On 17 December they started to pray – 'Jesus save us lest we perish'. Afterwards Little Sister Magdeleine referred to how privately she had added an expression of her desire that the Visitor should be as glad of this deliverance as the Little Sisters themselves.

The novena finished on Christmas morning. On 31 December Mgr de Provenchères telephoned the Little Sisters to wish them a happy new year, adding that he had a small present to give them but that he could not disclose it yet. On 6 January they received another letter from the Visitor which was no less disconcerting than his previous ones. On 18 January, however, to the Little Sisters' utter amazement, a telegram arrived from Mgr de Provenchères who was in Rome at the time, bearing the totally unexpected words: 'Visit over'. The sisters could not believe their eyes. The Visitor had informed them that they would remain under his control for several years. For Little Sister Magdeleine it was no coincidence that the news arrived at the beginning of a Week for Unity. The unity which she considered the Fraternity's supreme gift had been so severely threatened. She saw in this astonishing deliverance also the intervention of the many friends throughout the world who had been touched by the Fraternity's suffering, and the handiwork of the Christmas Christ-child. A letter from Mgr de Provenchères following hard upon the telegram revealed that officially the Visit had concluded on 23 December. The Prior General could now resume the government of the Fraternity within the framework of the Constitutions. In practice the Little Sisters could now proceed as they thought best, except with regard to those points on which the Priest Visitor had written an actual precept. It would be wise, the letter pointed out, to take into account his advice but it remained advice. 'Accept this news peacefully and with joy,' counselled the Archbishop, 'without going back over what has been painful during the last months.' The Fraternity, Little Sister Magdeleine recognised, must forget about its bruises and get back on its feet but she did not think it would happen overnight.

Unofficially it was suspected by some that there had come a moment when Cardinal Tisserant and Mgr de Provenchères had pointed out that the intervention of the Apostolic Visitor was in danger of stifling something precious. The end of the Visit was mysteriously abrupt. Its outcome was that the Holy See was satisfied after detailed enquiry that there were no fundamental grounds for complaint. The indult allowing fraternities to be opened with only one professed sister was not to be renewed and the number of noviciates was to be reduced, but Little Sister Magdeleine's teaching on the significance of the infant Jesus and the message of the manger was found to be sound. Sanction for the Fraternity's life as workers amongst the poor would only be confirmed with official approval of the Constitutions but Mgr de Provenchères was hopeful in the light of the encouragement forthcoming from many sources that it should not present undue difficulty. In a sense, however, the liberty of the Fraternity was restored without any real conclusion, and for a while, at least, even the extent of that liberty appeared to be in doubt.

A further piece of heart-rending news awaited the Fraternity. As a final consequence of the Apostolic Visit the Little Sisters of Jesus were no longer to be answerable to the Congregation for the Oriental Churches which had supported them so faithfully over the years and to which they were so deeply attached. Instead they were to come under the jurisdiction of the Sacred Congregation for Religious. Little Sister Magdeleine's request to Pope Pius XII in 1954 to remain under the jurisdiction of the Congregation for the Oriental Churches, even in the event of the Fraternity becoming a congregation of pontifical right, had been granted. A letter from the Secretariat of State dated 23 April 1955 had confirmed that Pope Pius XII accorded them this right. In vain, however, Little Sister Magdeleine wrote an appeal to Pope John XXIII pointing out the special relationship deriving from the fact that all the Little Sisters offered their lives for the redemption of their Muslim brothers, that the Fraternity had foundations belonging to all the oriental Churches and that it was part of its vocation to be a fraternal presence amongst the separated Eastern Churches. Little Sister Jeanne took the supplication to Rome in person, but the decree had already been signed. Little Sister Magdeleine remained convinced that if she had been afforded direct contact with the Pope during the Apostolic Visit and the opportunity to explain to him in person the importance of the Fraternity's attachment to the Congregation for the Oriental Churches, he would never have authorised the change. As it was, the Little Sisters were confronted with a fait accompli. On 14 March 1961 they received official notification of their transfer to the Congregation for Religious. It was not, Little

Sister Magdeleine was at pains to point out, that the Fraternity had anything against their new Congregation but removing it from the Congregation for the Oriental Churches was like 'wresting a child from its mother'. Privately she feared that the Congregation for Religious would not allow the Fraternity the same freedom to develop afforded to it by its predecessor.

On 13 May 1961 Little Sister Magdeleine wrote the final full stop on her new version of the Constitutions. A few days later Mgr de Provenchères presented them in Rome. Other revisions were required thereafter. The period that followed was one of an attempt to bring greater order into the structure of the Fraternity. Authority was reorganised into three tiers with local, regional and general responsibles; instead of four councillors there were to be eight. In general considerable energy was directed into giving it a more solid framework. These and other changes had to be accommodated in the Constitutions with the guidance of Mgr Paul Philippe of the Congregation for Religious. It was a period of construction also in an even more concrete sense. Each year it had been Little Sister Magdeleine's practice to give special attention to a particular new foundation. In 1961 it was the construction of a home for parents at Le Tubet. During a stay in Jerusalem in June 1958 the need to build such a home for those parents who had no alternative support in their old age had 'imposed itself' on her mind. She had decided then and there that the first one was to be in Aix: the house must be big enough, with a garden; each 'parent' should have two small rooms, one in which to sleep, one in which to receive guests and eat in case of need; there should also be a living room with small tables at which people could eat in groups. By 1961 the time had come to render concrete what she considered to be one of the fundamental characteristics of the Little Sisters' vocation: 'the love for our parents which our religious life, far from diminishing, should cause to increase in the love of our beloved Brother and Lord Jesus'.

In Rome too building work was to begin. Little Sister Magdeleine would later record 1962 as having been a year marked by the construction of barrack huts at Tre Fontane. First, however, part of the forest of eucalyptus trees with their twenty-metre-high trunks must be cleared. With the help of students from the Germanicum, the German-speaking seminary in Rome, the Little Sisters then set about stacking and sawing up the felled trunks. Little Sister Magdeleine had for some time been envisaging the General Fraternity in Rome but she had set her sights at first on the Pretestato catacombs as a suitable location. For the time being the intention was for the huts at Tre Fontane to accommodate only the General Novitiate but the work involved in the clearing and levelling of foundations for that alone was demanding. Little Sister Magdeleine worked alongside her sisters with vigour and her customary practical capabilities, shovelling the earth and assembling the component pieces of the huts, but for a while it was apparent to some that something indefinable had gone out of her. The treatment she had received at the hands of a representative of the Church she loved had undoubtedly touched her to the quick.

For all her suffering and the openness with which she spoke of certain aspects of it, she was not, however, one to be depressed. On the contrary, she was someone in whom her sisters identified an underlying peace. Her resilience had taken her round the world whilst still suffering from the aftermath of a road accident. Having sat up half the night working, she would still be bright and intelligent next morning. At Christmas 1961 she had announced to her sisters that, looking round at them, she had decided they had become a little too serious. 'As we get older, we must not lose our joy,' she told them. She wanted them to be a smile in an unhappy world. Amongst all the pain in the world there were still magnificent things to be found. On Christmas night they should ask for joy.

A growing relationship of trust with the Congregation for Religious restored some of her own courage. With hindsight she would write of how in March 1962, 'After the difficult times of 1960 and to some extent of 1961, we began to spread our wings again and to look afresh at the map of the world.' She began to travel once more, although for the most part within Europe: to attend the blessing of the foundation stone for the new house in Aubonne which the troubadours were to occupy; to Berlin; to several Iron Curtain countries.

On 11 October 1962, Pope John XXIII opened the Second Vatican Council, an event which was to bring a succession of bishops to Rome and to Tre Fontane. For Little Sister Magdeleine the Council was a 'Council of Unity'. She relished the sight of bishops from all over the world fraternising together. Watching them emerging from St Peter's, all races mingling together and the 'observers' mixed with the bishops, was for her an unforgettable experience. When the Pope who had instigated the occasion for this gathering and assigned it the task of renewing the religious life of the Church, died in June 1963, Little

Sister Magdeleine received the news with profound sadness. She had not had the personal contact with him that she had enjoyed with Pope Pius XII but that did not affect her devotion to him. As Little Sister Jeanne wrote to the Fraternity, the Little Sisters had found in him the living realisation of what was the very basis of the Fraternity's ideal: 'unity, universal love, a preferential love for the poor'. Little Sister Magdeleine was in Yugoslavia when, on 21 June, she learned of the election of Cardinal Montini as his successor on the radio news. The discovery finally brought release from a persistent anxiety:

> In a second, this news banished the nightmare in which I had been living during and even after the Visit. It did not matter how much everyone reassured me, I was still in a state of anguish about the future. Why should what had happened once, not happen again?

In Cardinal Montini she found again Pius XII and all fears for the future were at last dispelled. Cardinal Montini had given her encouragement from the very earliest days when first the Little Sisters had been criticised for travelling about with rucksacks on their backs. He had followed the evolution of the Fraternity closely and been involved with her annual meetings with Pope Pius XII. She immediately resolved to return to Rome for the enthronement of the new Pope Paul VI. A gesture of particular affection for the Little Sisters at a general audience they attended and a letter expressing Paul VI's apostolic blessing upon them was enough to confirm her renewed confidence. She wrote to her Little Sisters,

> And now we must go forward with renewed courage but also with greater lucidity than before. . . .
> We shall always provoke misunderstandings and anxieties along our way. Don't let us be surprised by them. They will arise firstly from our shortcomings and deficiencies. . . . They will also arise from the fact that the Little Sisters do not always know how to explain our ideal very well and use unfortunate words to defend it which inevitably give rise to controversies. . . .
> But the failure to understand will also derive from the fact that the world looks for efficiency more than for the unobtrusiveness of the hidden life and that Bethlehem and Nazareth will always remain a mystery to it.

On 21 April 1964, while Little Sister Magdeleine was at Montée d'Avignon in Aix, she received a telephone call from the Little Sisters in Rome to say that the Congregation for Religious, having approved the Constitutions for seven years, had, on 25 March, signed the 'Decree of Praise' for the Fraternity. The Fraternity of the Little Sisters of Jesus had thus finally been made a congregation of pontifical right. The Decree of Praise recommended it highly. It also recognised the Little Sister's vocation to a contemplative life centred on the Eucharist and lived at the heart of the world, the world of the poor in particular. For its foundress there was a trace of sadness attached to what was essentially a confirmation of the Fraternity's ideal and hence a source of overwhelming joy. It meant that the General Fraternity would no longer be answerable to Mgr de Provenchères. He would remain nonetheless, she insisted, an adviser and father to the Fraternity.

Little Sister Magdeleine had been unable to obtain the site at the Pretestato catacombs on which she had originally hoped to locate the General Fraternity, but the building work which sometimes went on into the night at Tre Fontane was bearing fruit. On 24 March the Little Sisters had even installed central heating in the existing accommodation. Little Sister Magdeleine had not been alone in feeling grave qualms about such a step but it had had to be acknowledged that the Little Sisters coming from far warmer climes for the international noviciate would otherwise find the Roman winter intolerable. It was yet another case of charity ultimately taking precedence over the witness to poverty which was yet so precious to them. The new General Fraternity would be housed in the steadily growing number of wooden barrack huts amongst the eucalyptus trees. On 31 May, on what Little Sister Magdeleine emphasised was the feast of Mary, Queen of all the world, it was at last officially transferred to Rome.

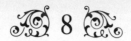

8

One with Them

'I<small>N</small> 1957,' L<small>ITTLE</small> S<small>ISTER</small> Magdeleine was to tell her Little Sisters more than thirty years later, on the occasion of the fiftieth anniversary of the Fraternity, 'I could no longer bear the idea of any iron curtain being able to shut off one single country from the message of Brother Charles.' In the same way that she had known in the case of other countries that she must seek out the lost sheep in places of physical and spiritual neglect, she had simply *known* that she must go next to the countries with Marxist regimes. Accordingly, she had resolved that little by little the iron curtains she found so intolerable would open, or at least half open, to her Little Sisters. Even in 1989 she could not disclose the whole story but the extension of the Fraternity to the countries of the Eastern bloc, inspired as it was by an intuition and kept a closely guarded secret from all not directly concerned, was nonetheless the product of a concerted and far from unsystematic effort.

The first journey undertaken by Little Sister Magdeleine together with seven sisters and a brother in September 1956 to Yugoslavia, Hungary and Czechoslovakia had been used as an opportunity to establish contacts with the churches there. Their strangely adapted van, adorned with an image of the Virgin Mary and the infant Jesus against the background of a red star, had drawn curious stares from all they passed, but they had managed to initiate friendships. They had been taken round churches by local people. They had attended mass wherever they could and they had sown the seeds of what would become lasting relationships with church leaders. The ultimate aspiration was first to send Little Sisters from the West into the Eastern bloc countries, if necessary clandestinely but always without jeopardising the safety of the people concerned, and eventually to have, as elsewhere in the world, Little Sisters who were actually from those countries. In Yugoslavia it was possible, even on the occasion

185

of that first visit, to leave behind two Little Sisters and a postulant to live for a while with a community on the outskirts of Belgrade.

Little Sister Magdeleine's second journey behind the Iron Curtain, which ended so unexpectedly in Rome in 1957, was undertaken in a second 'Shooting Star', the original one having been given to a nomad fraternity. The second model was fitted out, to Little Sister Magdeleine's evident satisfaction, with even more attention to detail, with a wardrobe, wall cupboards, drawers, a cooker, a sink with running water and a collapsible altar and a concealed tabernacle. She took pleasure in describing to those who had not seen it the way in which the vehicle had a partitioning wall which meant that the front area could be used, according to the time of day, as the chapel, refectory, kitchen or 'cell' for the driver; while the rear served as her own office and 'cell'. Arriving in Prague in this vehicle in September 1957, she met up with the first two Little Sisters destined for Czechoslovakia. For a while they were received into a Christian family in Prague. In the mornings they did housework. In the afternoons they learned Czech, but it was they who experienced the visa difficulties which eventually occasioned Little Sister Magdeleine's untimely return to Rome. She did so, after a three-week stay in Poland, bearing with her the impression of a Christian faith still very much alive in difficult conditions. With a blanket over her head and shoulders after the fashion of the Polish women on pilgrimage, she attended mass in the basilica at Jasna Gora. By then one Little Sister was already living in Cracow with the family of a Polish professor, and Little Sister Magdeleine soon found herself disclosing to their circle of intimate friends future plans for a fraternity close to the Marian shrine at Czestochowa. Among that circle of friends was a priest known then simply as 'Father Charles'. Karol Wojtyla, the future Pope John Paul II, became and would remain a friend of Little Sister Marie-Germaine and of the Fraternity.

Mgr de Provenchères's decision to take Little Sister Magdeleine's unexpected return to Rome as a sign, and his stipulation that from then onwards she was to divide her time between the Fraternity and her activities behind the Iron Curtain, did nothing to dampen her determination to do the work to which she felt she was being called. One way or another she was going to 'the other side', she had informed her sisters in 1957. Either it would be to paradise or beyond the Iron Curtain. Frightened, and sometimes shedding tears in her mobile 'cell', she had, however, had time to reflect during the journey she made alone with the Little Brother who served as her chauffeur. She had recognised the importance of putting her Little Sisters' interests first, something which she felt she had not always done, allowing herself instead to be 'eaten up' by other people wanting her attention. She had also wondered about the wisdom of making her journeys without any of her Little Sisters for companionship and support.

In January 1958 a solution seemed to present itself in the form of a suggestion by Mgr de Provenchères that two Little Sisters should pass their driving tests and study mechanical engineering at a garage, so that Little Sister Magdeleine could cross to 'the other side' with two of her sisters as drivers. Later that same year Mgr de Provenchères wrote a confidential letter to Cardinal König, Archbishop of Vienna, who was to authorise the foundation of a new fraternity in Regelsbrunn, Austria, on the banks of the River Danube. Ostensibly this was the fraternity of adoration for the Austrian region, a rural fraternity supporting itself with its own orchard and farmland. In fact this fraternity was to have a special orientation about which the Archbishop was asked to remain silent. It was to be the place to which those Little Sisters with a special orientation to Marxist countries would come to prepare themselves to go, as circumstances permitted, behind the Iron Curtain.

There were, among those joining the Fraternity, a number of Little Sisters who felt a special calling to the people of Communist countries. They were encouraged in their vocation to the point of being required to learn the language of the country to which they might one day be called upon to go. One of them would study Russian for ten years before she was actually able to enter the Soviet Union. Throughout the years of the cold war she worked at the language with difficulty and without any real prospect of ever being able to use it in the way that she hoped. Finally, when the opportunity did arise, Little Sister Magdeleine told her that she had known all along that one day she would go. She had never said so, however, during those testing years of perseverance. 'Little Sister Magdeleine had these intuitions which she couldn't present to us in rational terms,' the sister concerned would recognise with hindsight, 'and if you did not have the same faith it could be very difficult to live with.' Yet considerable care was put into turning the intuitions into practical reality.

At Regelsbrunn, the Little Sisters prayed especially for Communist countries. There they had the opportunity to study the language of the countries which lay beyond the Austrian border, and it was from there that they left to stay in those countries, if and when they were granted visas. In 1958 whilst applying for visas for her own forth-coming journey to Czechoslovakia, Yugoslavia and a first visit to Bulgaria, Little Sister Magdeleine also found a small house in Austria, in Mariazell, another place of Marian pilgrimage, to serve as a pro-visional noviciate. By August 1958 she could write to Cardinal Tisser-ant from Mariazell that there were now forty Little Sisters who had volunteered for Eastern bloc countries.

On 17 August she herself set off again with two sisters as drivers in the 'Shooting Star'. She was less distressed, knowing that the intention was to return to the Fraternity after a two-month journey, and for her there was always comfort to be derived from the knowledge that inside the van, concealed in a tabernacle behind an icon of the Virgin Mary, was the Reserved Sacrament. Before it burned a lamp which had been given to her in Jerusalem. She also had with her in the van the infant Jesus in a cradle made in Kenya by a Kikuyu woman, together with a 'bambi', a small monkey and other reminders of the fraternities scattered throughout the world. The 'Shooting Star' and its inmates were now a 'proper fraternity' with a daily rhythm of communal prayer characterised largely by its simplicity and including some brief personal intentions. This fraternity would travel the roads of the Iron Curtain countries as a tabernacle, a presence of prayer and of Jesus, bearing with it 'a little of the Lord's love'. At the Czech frontier on that occasion the border guards were fascinated by the interior arrangement of the camper and by the small mementoes which Little Sister Magdeleine felt 'softened the hearts' of those who visited her mobile fraternity. The guards pronounced the 'Shooting Star' 'prima', but added that it was small for three of them to live in.

Once across the frontier, the idea came to her that the journey through Czechoslovakia should be a Marian pilgrimage. She therefore decided that they would allow the Lord to determine their route, adding that she realised that it was difficult for the drivers who wanted to know their destination in advance. Driving Little Sister Magdeleine was in any case a challenging experience. She was as demanding of her Little Sisters' driving skills as she was of their undertakings in any other field. They must not drive too fast. She was nervous of speed even when there were very long distances to be covered. Above all, however, she would not tolerate an aggressive or irritated response even to the worst offences committed by other drivers. Verbal prot-estations if another car cut in front of the 'Shooting Star' would elicit from Little Sister Magdeleine a firm and reproachful: 'Sister . . . , what did you say?' Taxing though it undoubtedly was, her approach to other drivers was entirely consistent with her approach to the rest of humanity. It gave precedence to charity and elicited from her sisters the 'littleness' she sought at all times. 'That was how we were to be before God and humankind and that was how I was to be as a driver even if another person had not treated me with much kindness or consideration,' one Little Sister who spent some considerable time driving the foundress would afterwards reflect.

With God as their guide and the drivers endeavouring to rise to Little Sister Magdeleine's exigencies that third journey behind the Iron Curtain took the 'Shooting Star' on eight pilgrimages in Moravia, Bohemia and Slovakia. It gladdened the foundress's heart that through the presence of three Little Sisters, it was possible to express the Fraternity's ideal of unity. Little Sister Magdeleine had always wanted to take the gospel message of love to those whom others would not reach. The fact that behind the Iron Curtain the Church was being persecuted had undoubtedly served to strengthen her resolve but she was also aware that within the Church there was a strong anti-Communist dynamic and that too was unacceptable to her. She wanted to make contact with other Christians, but she wanted also to reach out to the Communists she encountered, to talk to them, show them that they were loved, that she was one with them. For both these purposes it was important that the members of the fraternity in the 'Shooting Star' should be clearly recognisable as religious who had come to the people of the Eastern bloc from the 'free world'. Little Sister Magdeleine's attachment to the habit even whilst travelling in places where it might attract unwanted attention was to be understood in this context. 'For everyone, we are Little Sisters,' she wrote. 'Above all I am holding on to the habit. We have only shortened our skirts a little. When we go out we hide our crosses with a dark red neck scarf.' With characteristic sensitivity to detail and attributing to others her own strong views about colour, she added that the red scarf could not always be worn in case it saddened priests and religious of the country who did not like red very much.

As religious, they were warmly received by many in Czechoslovakia. There were, however, some tense moments when the need for concealment was brought sharply home to her. As the 'Shooting Star' crossed the frontier back into Austria, the Czech border guards searched the camper. Spotting the icon on the door to the concealed tabernacle, one of them asked what was behind it. Filled with apprehension that he might discover the Reserved Sacrament, Little Sister Magdeleine opened up the two small doors to reveal another icon. 'An icon of the Virgin,' she told the guard who called his comrade to join him in the search, but after what seemed to her like centuries of waiting, he allowed her to close the doors without probing behind the second icon. An hour later she was still trembling, but all that the border guards had really found suspicious was the papers and notebooks she carried with her at all times so that she could continue her work on the Constitutions. They had wanted to know what she wrote on them but satisfied with the answer, 'Our history,' they finally waved the Little Sisters through.

Despite her nervousness above all else that the Reserved Sacrament might be discovered, the journeys continued. In September 1958 on the road to Zagreb she saw women with scarves on their heads working as labourers on building sites or on the construction of roads and immediately in her mind's eye she could see Little Sisters labouring in a similar fashion. Next year she left two more Little Sisters in Yugoslavia, one of whom would subsequently change her name and apply for Yugoslavian citizenship. The journeys to Czechoslovakia, Yugoslavia and Poland in particular became regular events, although not always quite for the full six months of the year she had originally intended, because of the requirements of the Fraternity elsewhere. Other than in Yugoslavia it was not possible for the Little Sisters' presence to be overt. It was not a case of establishing open and permanent fraternities, but the sisters came and went behind the Iron Curtain as the authorities permitted. Compromises had to be made on the lifestyle and the form of work undertaken. They went not illegally, but clandestinely, as students, as cleaners and au pairs and earned their living by other similar means. Contrary to the Fraternity's policy elsewhere it was sometimes necessary for them to live with members of the French community rather than with people of the actual country. At a second General Chapter held from December 1963 to January 1964 the question was raised of abandoning the habit to which Little Sister Magdeleine was so firmly attached in favour of 'civilian' clothes. The answers to a questionnaire on the subject pointed to overriding support for its retention other than in exceptional circumstances. The Little Sisters who went behind the Iron Curtain were considered to be in such circumstances. Little Sister Magdeleine attributed considerable importance to the sisters' overt wearing of the cross, which she saw as a symbol of and a way of witnessing to their love for God and of God's love for humankind. In Damascus she had stated without any room for compromise that the Little Sisters would agree to any condition necessary for a 'deeper insertion' amongst the people there, except the suppression of the wearing of the cross. Behind the Iron Curtain, however, she accepted, apparently without undue difficulty, the need to conceal it. There the Little Sisters frequently wore ordinary clothes and they lived sometimes with middle-class, professional families.

Little Sister Magdeleine's journeys in a succession of 'Shooting Stars' led to the gradual, quiet extension of the Fraternity to successive Communist countries. The creation in 1959 of a section devoted to them was something by which she set great store and to which she would later attribute much of the fruitfulness of the work undertaken behind those 'half-open curtains'. It was because responsibility for the Fraternity in the Eastern bloc countries was the only one which she did not relinquish on her resignation as General Responsible that in 1960, the one year in which because of the Apostolic Visit she was unable to undertake her annual journey, she repaired not to Le Tubet but to Montée d'Avignon in Aix-en-Provence. Montée d'Avignon was the 'headquarters' in France for the Eastern bloc section, or 'sector' as it was then known. At that point there were four Little Sisters in Poland, one of whom was herself Polish. Two years later when Little Sister Magdeleine returned briefly to Poland for the second consecutive year, there was only one Little Sister left there. Important relationships were being cemented nonetheless. When, at the time of the Second Vatican Council and the resultant convergence upon Rome of Church leaders from all over the world, a succession of bishops came to Tre Fontane, Cardinal Wyszynski, Primate of Poland, numbered amongst them. On 21 October 1962 he addressed a gathering of Little Sisters, blessed them and visited what was gradually evolving into a 'village' of wooden buildings. On 8 December, the first session of the ecumenical council came to an end. The Little Sisters gathered in St Peter's Square to witness its conclusion and next day Mgr Karol Wojtyla, by then Archbishop of Cracow, celebrated mass at a fraternity in a very poor quarter of Rome.

Still Russia, in all its inaccessibility, called to Little Sister Magdeleine. Since 1946 she had been talking of having Little Sisters who were not just in Russia but who were actually Russian, but for a long time even the initial step of gaining access herself eluded her. In 1959 she had written directly to Mr Khrushchev as the only person she felt able to grant her request, explaining that as a member of the Fraternities of Charles de Foucauld she was interested in the problem of leprosy throughout the world. She had, she told him, visited leper hospitals and asylums in France, Italy, Morocco, the Cameroons, Iran and Korea. Now she wanted to visit leper hospitals in the Soviet Union. She presented herself as a compulsive tourist who had already covered thousands of kilometres in her camper van and with regard to whom the Soviet government need have no fear of subversive propaganda:

> I can give you my word that I have *never* – and I'm sixty-one years old and have travelled all over the world – perpetrated the least act of propaganda against any government because I love all countries and all people beyond all divisions of class, nationality or race. And it is in the name of this universal friendship that I ask you for the favour of a visa for Russia.

Despite such bold assurances, the favour was not forthcoming. Little Sister Magdeleine continued, however, to apply persistently for visas and finally, in 1964, at a time when the Soviet Union had scarcely opened its doors to visitors, her tenacity paid off. She and three other Little Sisters were granted tourist visas. Together with Little Sister Jeanne and two others, one of whom had been faithfully learning Russian in anticipation of this moment, she set off in the 'Shooting Star' through Yugoslavia, Hungary, Czechoslovakia and Poland to the Russian frontier. There the vehicle was searched in minute detail but the sisters, on this occasion dressed as Little Sisters but without their crosses, encountered no real difficulty. It was a source of satisfaction to their foundress that here, as elsewhere behind the Iron Curtain, without the cross the Little Sisters' habit could pass for ordinary dress.

In Russia they were supposed to adhere to a preordained route. The police stopped them several times on their way to Kiev for being out on the roads too late at night but, as Little Sister Magdeleine later reported, the Little Sisters' smiles disarmed them. They promptly took a resolution always to approach Russian officialdom with a smile. At the camping site where they spent the night the administrator engaged them in conversation:

'Everyone here says you are *monachki*' [nuns].

'It's a bit like that but not altogether. We are a new religious group known as a Fraternity. We live in small groups and work to earn our living.'
'Does each of you work for herself?'
'No, we share everything in common.'
'But that's Communism.'

The tourist visit continued via Moscow. Little Sister Magdeleine was not really interested in tourism. It pleased her to have her photograph taken in front of the many crosses that adorned the elaborate spires of Russia's ancient churches but that was because of all that those crosses represented for her. In the Tretiakov museum, it touched her to see rooms full of icons removed from the city's churches and monasteries. Her primary concern, however, was always to make contact with people. Wherever she could she joined in worship with the local Soviet people. 'In the Orthodox churches that are open', she wrote, 'we admire the fervour of the faith that animates the faithful who are living in such difficult times and who are mocked and condemned for their fidelity.' It was hard, however, to make personal contact even with members of the Orthodox congregations without compromising them. That first visit was undertaken therefore more with the simple idea of being a prayerful presence along the route. In Montée d'Avignon Little Sister Magdeleine reported to her sisters that she had not felt that her movements in Russia had been subject to constant surveillance. If they had been there would undoubtedly have been some comment on the breaches of the conditions of travel she had committed by leaving the tourist route at times and talking to people . . . 'Because what the government wants is that those they call "foreigners" – that word which should be banished from all vocabularies – should not see the poor areas or the villages that have not yet been modernised and above all that they do not tell people about the life in the West (especially about salaries).'

On 8 September 1964 the Fraternity, now made up of some 930 Little Sisters, celebrated its twenty-fifth anniversary and that of Little Sister Magdeleine's final profession. Numerous telegrams of congratulations arrived at Tre Fontane, among them one from Pope Paul VI himself. Another was from Mgr Karol Wojtyla who was once more in Rome for the third session of the Vatican Council and who joined Little Sister Magdeleine a few days later to have dinner with the Little Sisters of the Eastern bloc section.

Her initial visit to the Soviet Union proved to be the first of a total of eighteen. At the time it was difficult to explain the importance of such 'tourist trips'. The full extent of the Little Sisters' activities had to remain a secret and there were those within the Fraternity itself who found it hard to justify in their own minds the use of a camper to travel around for a purpose that was not obviously definable. To those living amongst the desperately poor of Latin America, for example, it seemed an unaccountable luxury. However, like the many years devoted to learning Russian for no obvious purpose which was suddenly shown to have been eminently wise when the Little Sisters took their first faltering steps into the Soviet Union, the use of the 'Shooting Star' was gradually to be vindicated. In countries where rooms were frequently bugged and Christians often lived in fear, it provided a meeting point, a place of hospitality, devoid of microphones. The autonomy it afforded gave the Little Sisters access to people in a much more discreet way than if they had been dependent on hotel rooms and taxis.

Almost every year until 1989 Little Sister Magdeleine would return to Russia, quietly building up friendships with members of the Orthodox Church, with Mgr Nikodim, Metropolitan of Leningrad and a man deeply interested in ecumenism, with the occupants of a monastery that was open to tourism, with those who met in secret to pray. She would speak to them of the Fraternity, and its ideal of universality came to them like a breath of fresh air precisely because they felt so cut off from the rest of the world. In their isolation and separation the idea of living in dialogue with others was particularly attractive. Difficult as it was to establish real contact with the Communists, Little Sister Magdeleine persisted quietly in her objective of befriending not only the persecuted Church but all those who had not yet seen the face of a Christ who loved them. For her it was never a question of being *for* some and *against* others, rather it was a case of being *for* some but still *open* to others. She did not call upon her Little Sisters to be silent in the face of racial or social injustice or oppression. Sometimes it was necessary in order to avoid eviction from a country. Sometimes it was right for them to be voiceless with the voiceless, but the Constitutions afforded them the right if necessary to compromise themselves both publicly and privately to proclaim the requirements of the gospel and defend the rights of the poor. In the factories it was left to their individual consciences as to whether or not they joined trade unions. Their foundress reminded them only that in considering whether to become shop stewards or accept other positions of leadership they should bear in mind the possible distance this might create between them and the least considered.

When it came to Communism, Little Sister Magdeleine remained resolutely open. Communism was not all bad, she reported to her Little Sisters. It had rehabilitated the working class. She made friends with the tourist guides who showed her round, with the police, and with the soldiers who stood guard outside houses occupied by people from the West to which no Russian was supposed to have access. She directed her Little Sisters that they must inform the guards with a smile when they were going out or coming back. They must thank them for looking after the 'Shooting Star' while it was parked outside, and even for 'keeping watch' over them. It was not the kind of treatment to which their custodians were accustomed. The curious selection of small gifts she carried with her in the 'Shooting Star', things which were rationally difficult to justify in the restricted space of the camper, often came into their own. When the occasion demanded and Little Sister Magdeleine found herself in possession of precisely the right token of friendship to offer, she would point out with a trace of triumph the way her apparent folly had been shown to be foresight.

In 1974 an initial three Little Sisters went to live clandestinely in Russia, each in a different place, for reasons of secrecy and security. Later one of them would recall how, living as she was with a French family, she had difficulty in making contact with the local people. Because of her laboriously acquired knowledge of Russian she was able to pass the time of day with people in the street. She took the family's children to the park and chatted with the grandmothers who looked after the children there, but beyond that she had been unable to make any real friendships. The day had come when she had resigned herself to being just a prayerful presence amongst the Soviet people. That in itself was something. At that precise juncture, however, her employers sent her to deliver a parcel to friends living in a small village some forty kilometres from Moscow. On the very same day a priest came to the house to bless it. To date the Little Sister had not disclosed her real identity to anyone apart from her employers, but Father Alexander Men immediately inspired her confidence. She spoke to him of the Fraternity and of her vocation. He had heard of Charles de Foucauld and read some of his writings, and he invited the Little Sister to join him that evening at an ecumenical meeting to be held at his house. It was the middle of the Russian winter, pitch-dark and bitterly cold. The village was at the very limits of the boundary beyond which the residents of Moscow could not go without permission. Her employers had had reservations about sending her there in the first place. Worried, she decided nonetheless to take advantage of what she knew must be a unique opportunity. In a small wooden house next to the church, a group of young people – Catholics and Orthodox and Protestants from the Baltic states – gathered in a room illuminated only by the light which burned in front of an icon. This group of young people would introduce her to others who met to pray together in secret and so, thanks to Father Alexander Men, the number of the Little Sisters' Russian friends mushroomed.

It mushroomed by a similar process in other Iron Curtain countries (see Appendix B, pp. 266–7). Little Sister Magdeleine visited every Eastern European country except Albania, and even in the case of Albania hope of sending her Little Sisters there one day was kept alive by the creation of a fraternity of the Eastern Rite in Eianina in Southern Italy, amongst people who had come from Albania some four centuries previously in the aftermath of the Turkish invasion. The fraternity there was to be devoted specifically to the creation of links with Albania and to the study of the Albanian language. Little Sisters actually from the various countries gradually entered the Fraternity: in Yugoslavia in 1961; in Poland in 1962; in Hungary in 1969; in Czechoslovakia in 1973; in the Soviet Union in 1979; in East Germany in 1981; in Romania in 1992. There were Little Sisters from the West in Bulgaria between 1967 and 1977 but thereafter their visas were not renewed.

Obstacles were sometimes forthcoming from unexpected quarters. In 1969 two German Little Sisters spent a period of time in an observation camp in East Germany to establish whether they could take up more permanent residence there. At the end of their stay permission was declined. A few years later it emerged that the police had made enquiries about them with the Cardinal of Berlin. The Little Sisters had assumed that the invitation they had received from a local bishop would be adequate but the police required the authorisation of the Cardinal and it was he who, not being fully aware of their situation, had declined to give it. Extraordinarily, however, Little Sister Magdeleine never experienced any real difficulties with the Communist authorities, even in the Soviet Union. She gave her name as Elisabeth Madeleine but it was inconceivable that the Soviet police did not know what she was. Every year she would encounter the same policemen at the frontier. Every year, they searched the 'Shooting Star' thoroughly, sometimes delaying its passengers for up to eight hours. On occasions they would seize books because they thought she was carrying too many, foraging through their pages to ensure that they did not contain undesirable messages or illegal currency. They once placed an embargo on a suitcase full of small statues of the infant Jesus. She dealt with them with her customary directness, stating simply that she and her sisters were 'women consecrated to peace', but she was never actually prevented from entering. Each year she was eagerly expected by the nuns in an Orthodox convent and by the people of a poor parish amongst numerous other friends, and each year she arrived to bring them a vision of a different world. *Perestroika* would eventually make it possible for the Little Sisters in Russia, Czechoslovakia and elsewhere to come out into the open and thus reveal the fruits of what Little Sister Magdeleine had initiated with her extraordinary journeying. At the age of ninety she would still be undertaking her trips behind the Iron Curtain.

In the years that followed the Apostolic Visit her travels were confined largely to Europe and the Eastern bloc. The Fraternity was still growing in terms of both the number of Little Sisters and the number of fraternities but at a far steadier rate than during the earlier period of explosive expansion. In March and April 1967, only three months after the fiftieth anniversary of the death of Charles de Foucauld had been marked at Tre Fontane by a mass celebrated by two bishops and twelve priests, she embarked on what her Little Sisters called her 'return' to the Sahara but what she referred to as her 'farewells'. Travelling in a van, she was too ill on that occasion to make the climb to Assekrem but she joined a gathering of sixty Little Sisters at El Abiodh who had come together for a 'year of renewal'. She also visited the fraternity at El Golea close to the tomb of Charles de Foucauld. Each day during her stay there she went to the tomb to pray that her Little Sisters might be even more generous, charitable and smiling than they already were, and to recite the prayer of Brother Charles of Jesus which she had made a prayer of the Fraternity:

Father,
I abandon myself into your hands:
do with me what you will.
Whatever you may do,

I thank you;
I am ready for all,
I accept all.
Let only your will be done in me,
and in all your creatures.
I wish no more than this, O Lord.

Into your hands I commend my soul;
I offer it to you
with all the love of my heart,
for I love you, Lord,
and so need to give myself,
to surrender myself into your hands, without reserve,
and with boundless confidence,
for you are my Father.

'Close to this tomb,' she wrote, 'in this desert setting, how can my heart not be filled with God, that is to say, filled with gentleness and love.'

While she was at El Abiodh she had received a letter from Athman, who had helped her in 1939 to build the first Algerian fraternity at Sidi Boujnan. He had not seen her since 1954 but he wrote to her of how she was sadly missed, asking her to come to Sidi Boujnan:

> We shall see you with our eyes and we shall speak to you with our mouths, we shall eat with you, we shall be reunited with you and it will be a happy and blessed day. And we shall talk about old times, asking God, *inch'Allah*, to give you health and strength.

Little Sister Magdeleine went to Sidi Boujnan. She saw again the walls she had helped to construct, devoid of cracks despite the gloomy prognostications of some who had watched them being built. A telegram expressing gratitude and good wishes for her return to the 'cradle' of the Fraternity arrived from Mgr Mercier, and for the four days of her stay her nomad friends and those who had settled in the vicinity flocked to see her: Athman, Tahar his younger brother who had years ago helped with the painting of the buildings, and countless others. She told them about the extension of the Fraternity and about its universality, and they listened with undiminished interest, remarking to the Little Sisters with obvious pride that they had known

'Oukhti Majdalia' before they had. 'You know,' Athman added, 'she was never cross and her face was never severe, and yet everyone wanted something from her.' 'At that I protested a bit,' Little Sister Magdeleine afterwards recorded, 'because I used to get angry too ... but love embellishes everything.' She talked with her Algerian friends of the Arabs she had met in the Orient, of Christians and Muslims, of the evolution of women and of Algerian independence. During the war the Fraternity had been obliged to withdraw from Algeria all the Little Sisters who did not have a specific vocation to live among Muslim people, or who could not stand the strain. There had been some concern that the move would be seen as an abandonment of its Muslim friends of so many years' standing, but the people of Sidi Boujnan had understood. Nor was any subject now too sensitive because they knew that she rejoiced with them for their freedom, that she understood them and loved them. As a last act of remembrance of her earliest years amongst them, she went round the tents once more as she had used to, with a donkey loaded with semolina, sugar, tea and sweets – a small gesture of gratitude for so much help and friendship received.

The relationship of love, respect and understanding which she had experienced in such a special way amongst the first friends at Touggourt was one which she wanted to see extended to all humanity. The yearning for it, for a unity which transcended all divisions, became a persistent driving principle. It was an ideal which had its biblical roots in the words of St John's Gospel: 'And the glory which thou gavest me I have given them; *that they may be one, even as we are one* (17:22). In Little Sister Magdeleine it found obvious expression in her reluctance to accept the concept of any iron curtain, or indeed of any insurmountable barrier between people. In July 1954 the yearning for unity had taken her and her Little Sisters across frontiers never previously opened to Christian religious, into Afghanistan. Contrary to all predictions Little Sister Magdeleine had been given a visa. She had travelled across Afghanistan, wearing her habit and her cross, and she had even been invited to send Little Sisters there to work as nurses in a hospital. Again, unity had taken her beyond the boundaries of Communist Europe. By September 1979 the desire for unity was expressing itself in the determination to breach the barriers that separated China from the remainder of humanity. Ever since the Fraternity's extension to the far corners of the world she had been considering the possibility of entering its most populous country, and in 1979 the fact that she was eighty-one years old and physically very frail was not to be allowed to deter her. She had no alternative but to take an organised tour of Peking, Nankin, Shanghai and other places of tourist interest, but in her eyes it was, as always, a pilgrimage which would almost certainly be the prelude to future foundations. In October 1979 she and Little Sister Jeanne and Little Sister Carla, who in 1981 would herself become General Responsible of the Fraternity, formed an anonymous part of a group of twenty taken to see the Great Wall of China, the mausoleum of Chairman Mao, the Forbidden City, the Peking Opera, the Ming tombs, a number of factories and various other attractions which the Chinese authorities considered appropriate viewing for visitors to their country.

Bearing her usual assortment of gifts – small models of the infant Jesus, pictures of the Pope, European newspapers – Little Sister Magdeleine managed to draw confidences and establish bonds of friendship. At secret gatherings, she explained the life and spirit of the Fraternity, showing pictures of the Little Sisters in tents, caravans and factories, of Little Sisters in Korea and Vietnam working in the rice fields. The idea seemed to correspond with the aspirations of young Chinese Christians who were part of a growing religious revival in China but who hitherto had known only a more traditional form of religious life: 'Religious living amongst our Chinese poor in the countryside, in the factories, what a joy . . . come quickly.' A local priest wrote to the Little Sisters afterwards, telling them that China in its poverty had need of them, thanking them for the spiritual sustenance they had brought with them, asking them for their discretion but urging them to come. 'How could I not see the hand of God in all these circumstances?' inquired Little Sister Magdeleine, marvelling at the way in which, after pleading fatigue, she had managed to separate herself from her tour and been brought safely to a series of fruitful encounters. On her return to Rome, where she was greeted with garlands of Chinese lanterns, she reported the events of her stay to her Little Sisters as always in simple language out of consideration for those for whom French was not their native tongue, with customary respect for those whom she had visited and with equally characteristic determination that there should be Little Sisters of Jesus in the People's Republic of China.

'Make your vocation to become one of them more and more real. Let it not be just words,' Little Sister Magdeleine directed her sisters. She wanted them to be 'small' and 'simple' like children because a child did not instil fear and so could tread where others could not. She wanted them to live as the nomads did amongst the nomads and work in the rice fields with the Vietnamese but that was not enough. If she wanted them actually to 'be' whatever the people to whom their lives were consecrated were, actually to 'become' Vietnamese, it was in order that they might assume the sorrows, pains, potential causes of conflict, the joys and the capacity for unity in love, of those whose lives they shared in the most profound way. It gladdened her heart that there came a point where the majority of Little Sisters in Asia were Asians from China, Korea and the Philippines, but she was also pleased to have Italian and French Little Sisters there to bear witness to the fact that it was possible to live happily together in such diversity. For similar reasons Little Sister Magdeleine wanted all the continents to be represented on the governing council of the Fraternity. She knew that an issue aired in the presence of an African, an American, an Arab and a Jew could not be discussed in the same way as if they were absent. The presence alone of someone directly involved in a debate called for the recognition that that person was also being inspired to something and worthy of respect. The universality of the Fraternity so close to Little Sister Magdeleine's heart was inextricably linked with her ideal of unity. That was why, when in November 1966 for the first time the Little Sisters making their profession at Tre Fontane came from all five continents, it was a source of particular joy to her. The Fraternity was becoming a living demonstration that fraternal love was possible between Little Sisters of so many different nationalities.

Unity, as Little Sister Magdeleine put it, 'haunted' her. It was no cursory remark that Patriarch Athenagoras of the Orthodox Church made to her when he received her in Turkey in July 1971. 'When I look at you,' he told her, 'I find in your face the reflection of my own. We have the same desire for unity.' Unity within the Roman Catholic Church, unity between the different Churches, remained close to her heart. The search for ways of establishing an ecumenical fraternity went on. Little Sister Magdeleine worked on the possibility of having Protestants participating as Little Sisters. The approach of the Roman Curia seemed to be to allow the experiment to happen and then see whether it was canonically possible and so she persevered in her belief that it was. Links with the Taizé Brothers were cemented to the extent that the possibility of having a fraternity at Taizé was considered. Friendships were also made with the Grandchamp Sisters belonging

201

to the Swiss Lutheran Church, with the secular institute of the 'Servants of Unity' linked to it, and with the Salvation Army. When in 1966 the Archbishop of Canterbury, Michael Ramsey, went to Rome for a meeting with Pope Paul VI, the Little Sisters at Tre Fontane recited an Anglican prayer for unity which was used for the first time that year in Catholic churches in England. Gladdened by what she saw as one more step on the path to unity Little Sister Magdeleine made a point of relaying to her sisters to what extent the Pope saw the visit as the reconstruction of 'the bridge which united the two Churches' which had collapsed centuries previously.

The same intense desire for unity lay behind her drive to bring together the various inheritors of the spirituality of Charles de Foucauld. She made every effort to tie the knots of friendship between the various congregations which had grown up over the years and was delighted when at intervals they came together to explore their respective vocations. In July 1966 something in the region of a hundred representatives of the 'family' of Charles de Foucauld met at Taizé to discuss: 'The contemplative vocation of all Christians and the manner of fulfilling it in the contemporary world.' Equally the ideal of unity lay behind her abhorrence of such words as 'foreigner', or 'blacks', of the manner in which 'black' was habitually imbued with negative associations, or even the pejorative tones that were sometimes applied to the word 'old'. When referring to the parents' home at Le Tubet she called on her sisters to try to refer to 'our elderly parents' or similar expressions and in a less derogatory manner. Like the gulf between the sexes, the generation gap was yet another to be spanned.

In China, on a people's commune to which she was taken, she asked the director whether the young people there wanted to stay in the country or go to the city. The director responded with conviction that they wished to remain in the country to be with their parents. She was highly impressed by the love and respect for parents which she saw as a Christian virtue and which she found everywhere apparent in China: at the cinema, in the streets and homes. It was, she pronounced, a virtue which her Little Sisters would do well to cultivate. In her own advancing years Little Sister Magdeleine retained a great love for young people and in particular, as she herself admitted, for boys and young men. She had grown up in the company of brothers and perhaps for that reason was at ease with young men, but she valued youthfulness in general, carrying with it, as it often quite spontaneously did, some of the qualities of the state of spiritual childhood. She encouraged the optimism of young people and their ventures as she did those of all the increasing number of people who came to Tre Fontane to seek her advice and help. In the 1970s Little Sister Magdeleine was particularly touched by the thousands of hippies who had taken to the road in defiance of a materialistic society. They were so frequently hounded by the police and met with unkindness and incomprehension yet some of them, she was quick to point out, had much goodness in them. Little Sisters went to sell their craftwork alongside the hippies at a market in Avignon. At Tre Fontane hippies were to be made welcome. A room and a place to wash was set aside for their use.

The President of Niger complete with his entourage of ministers, Patriarch Maximos V, Mgr Nikodim, cardinals and bishops from all over the world, Mother Teresa, friends from Algeria, old and young, people with dubious motives or suspected criminal status, the rich and the poor, the powerful and the weak – were all, Little Sister Magdeleine decreed, to be received with the same welcome. She herself treated cardinals and prostitutes alike for nothing appeared to shock her and all humanity, containing as it did the same spark of divine goodness, was worthy of the same respect and love. She was exactly the same with her friend Ciro, a boy who had been in prison several times, as she was with visiting prelates. Ciro adored 'Mamma Magdalena' who was his 'anchor'. They would talk for a long time together and Little Sister Magdeleine would listen to him attentively. Often she would give him what he asked for and then add with a smile which was simultaneously maternal and mischievous: 'If you could just tell fewer lies.' Little Sister Magdeleine could study the face of a dirty tramp and comment afterwards with approval that he had 'a proper Little Sister's smile', and she could respond to a bishop asking her for some thought to take away with him and manifestly expecting words of spiritual profundity, with the disconcerting question: 'Do you bishops always have to be so well dressed?' Similarly, she would write to her friends in Algeria in much the same vein as she wrote to the General Secretary of the Soviet Communist Party.

In July 1988 her seventeenth visit to the country she loved with unshakeable feeling was marred by a particularly lengthy and rigorous search of her 'Shooting Star'. In vain she told the border guards that Russians were not subjected to this sort of treatment when they came to France. It was, as she afterwards reported with an expression drawn from her youth with which her sisters were very familiar: 'like trying to play the flute with a cornet'. Their questions were very specific:

'Why do you travel like this at your age?'

As always she replied:

'Because I love Russia.'
'It must be tiring for you.'
'But what does it matter when you love?'

After a similar experience on her return journey, on 15 August 1988 she wrote to the General Secretary of the Soviet Communist Party, Mikhail Gorbachev, to suggest that there was room for improvement in the kind of welcome visitors to his country received. First she expressed her gratitude to him for the courage he had shown in acting on behalf of the Christians of his country against what had hitherto been Soviet government policy. She had, she assured him, herself witnessed the true 'liberation' that had resulted from it. She went on to comment on the treatment she and her fellow occupants of the camper had received from the frontier guards as they had entered and left the country:

> It is such a shame to be treated as an enemy when one comes as a friend. In France, Russians are most certainly not received like that.
>
> Could *perestroika* not change slightly the methods employed by customs officers which give the USSR such an unwelcoming face? I have only experienced them in Russia and Czechoslovakia of all the countries through which I have travelled so frequently.
>
> I have deliberately not supplied the names of the frontiers out of consideration for the customs officers.

The letter, which concluded with an expression of her wish that there might be ever more unity and love between the nations of the world, was signed 'Elisabeth Madeleine' of a Paris address. A response came back within the month from the deputy director of customs control in the Soviet Union expressing his regret to 'Honoured Madame Madeleine' that she had found the behaviour of customs officials offensive and assuring her that her next visit to the Soviet Union would not be tarnished by any such actions.

When Mikhail Gorbachev was criticised in the press Little Sister

Magdeleine rose swiftly to his support. She defended him in much the same forthright way as she had defended her friends in Algeria when they had needed food or the right to stay in the vicinity of Sidi Boujnan. In the same way that she would invariably spot the 'Christian virtues' in countries that were officially atheistic, the powerful and the rich incurred no more judgement on her part than did the poor to whom she was committed to giving a preferential love. It was not the role of a Little Sister to judge. For this reason their foundress had written into the life of the community the idea of 'not denouncing'. Because of the manner in which the Little Sisters shared the life of the poor they were often party to confidences. Living as they did in circus communities, amongst the prostitutes, gypsies and prisoners and others who were no strangers to vice or crime, sometimes these confidences were of potential interest to law enforcement agencies. It was important that the trust of people who frequently had no other source of comfort was not abused, that they should feel secure with those who were there amongst them to be their little sisters. Little Sister Magdeleine was one to respect the dictates of individual consciences but, except where life was at stake, she did not see it as consistent with their vocation to denounce even criminals. Their calling was to have compassion for them, to suffer with them, and to respect them precisely in their wretchedness, regarding them always as their own brothers or sisters.

At the roots of such compassion lay knowledge of their own fallibility:

> In each person there is a hidden, secret racism whose roots are deep in the human heart. We don't admit it, but we always look on our brother or sister with a superiority complex, and the proof of that is that we judge them.

Early in her life in the Fraternity a coloured South African Little Sister was disconcerted to be told by Little Sister Magdeleine that she must love white people too. She had thought that she had broken through that particular barrier many years previously but her foundress's words touched a chord of recognition all the same. A sister who was for some time responsible for welcoming people at Tre Fontane found herself on one occasion being reproached for not receiving everyone with equal warmth: 'She told me to examine my conscience and when I did I realised that there were two people whom I had difficulty welcoming. They were full of airs and graces, people who

205

were used to having doors opened wide to them. I acknowledged this to Little Sister Magdeleine. She understood my reaction but she said, "Of course we must welcome the poor but we must not forget that there are others with another form of poverty".'

No breach of this commitment escaped her notice. When she visited fraternities, the sisters would sometimes try to ensure that there were not too many interruptions. One fraternity was regularly visited by a number of tramp friends and the day of Little Sister Magdeleine's visit proved to be no exception. The Little Sisters' attempts subtly to curtail their visits, however, finally induced Little Sister Magdeleine to call them to her. 'I don't understand the language you're speaking,' she admonished them, 'but you are trying to send away everyone who comes here, and that I cannot tolerate.' 'Unity' of welcome meant that she was equally insistent on the absolute gratuitousness of any hospitality offered. The Little Sisters must refuse any form of remuneration, even the purchase of their craftwork, if such a purchase was made with the intention of compensating for the cost of a guest's stay. She was determined that those who did not have the means to pay for the hospitality they had received should not be made to feel the suffering and humiliation of their poverty. She was equally resolute that the Little Sisters should have the same relationships of gratuitous friendship with all whom they received. Sometimes in practice the Little Sisters' refusal to accept gifts could cause embarrassment to those who had the means to pay. Little Sister Magdeleine's decision that no money should change hands even between the Little Brothers and the Little Sisters in fraternities where the brothers came regularly to the sisters for meals, was sometimes a source of complication rather than simplification of relationships. More important than any such consideration, however, was the principle of family and fraternal relationships which saw in the guest a real brother or sister sent by God.

Confronted with anyone in distress, no matter who or what they might be, Little Sister Magdeleine was the first to want to understand or show them love. She could be very organised but when she was with a person needing her attention, time no longer mattered, and if she caught other Little Sisters looking at their watches in similar circumstances she would call upon them to be more sensitive. She herself was wholly present to individuals in a way which was quite extraordinary and which made no exceptions even when her time or her hospitality was actually being abused. Her non-judgemental love, focused on the divinity in each human being, resulted in great openness of mind and vision. Little Sister Magdeleine would remark upon how companionship, devotion between women, could be a very positive thing. When asked why some Little Sisters fell in love, she replied: 'The heart is made for love. They are made for love'.

God had so loved the world that he had sent his son to span the abyss that existed between him and his creation. Through the incarnation a unity had been established between God and each individual, between the divine and the human. Jesus in his humanity was the divine model. In the vision of Little Sister Magdeleine, who had set out to follow the example of that model, the barriers not only of nationality, race or class but also of inhospitality, discrepancies of age or financial means, moral judgement or differences of dogma were all as 'concrete' as the Iron Curtain. They were all obstacles to unity, a unity which was not just to be read on her face but of which her life was the very embodiment, for she herself was a woman for whom there were no frontiers in any sense of the word. There was in her no separation between what others might consider the important and the insignificant, between the transcendent and the empirical, between the spiritual and the temporal. Hence her assertion that prayer was 'a life', her insistence on the contemplative life at the very heart of humanity, and her rejection of the 'wall' that existed between the Church and a certain section of the world. The Church, she had been resolute from the first, must somehow emerge from behind it and rejoin the people where they were.

It was sensitivity to this fact that had taken the Fraternity into the factories, into the world of gypsies, prisoners, prostitutes and circus performers. In 1966 it took the Little Sisters into the Luna Park, an amusement park which had grown up in close proximity to the land owned by the Trappists at Tre Fontane. Little Sister Magdeleine's reaction to this as to the construction of a motorway near the fraternity at Le Tubet was that the Little Sisters should welcome the sound of the music that blared from the loudspeakers of the funfair rides and the noise of speeding traffic, as contact with the world. In February 1966 a group of Little Sisters set up their stand alongside the many other fairground attractions in the Luna Park. The stand was dedicated to spreading the message of the manger. It was called *Notte di Luce* (night of light). There children and young people could come to 'fish' for small wooden toys, carved and painted by the Little Sisters, and even if the 'fishing' was unproductive they rarely went away empty-handed. The Little Sisters were helped in the initial installation of their stand by a group of seminarians who, Little Sister Magdeleine pointed out, were happy to assist because they recognised that the presence of the Fraternity amongst all the other games and stands was an application of the Second Vatican Council's decree relating to the Church in the modern world.

Little Sister Magdeleine welcomed wholeheartedly the enormous impetus given by the Second Vatican Council to changes of attitude in the Roman Catholic Church towards other bodies, both Christian and non-Christian, and to a less authoritarian approach within its own life. Officially the Council ended in December 1965. The attempt to incorporate the spirit of renewal, of what the Council referred to as 'aggiornamento', into the actual life of the Church was to take much longer than the three years spanned by the Council itself, however. Little Sister Magdeleine herself believed that this would not be an instant but an ongoing process. She made a study of the Council's documents and set about endeavouring to pass on its spirit to the Fraternity at once. As one of her Little Sisters wrote in 1969 of Little Sister Magdeleine's response to its requirements: 'Through her, since the Council we have been in a continual state of "aggiornamento"'. The Council, however, required that all religious congregations call a special Chapter with a view to renewal in the sense of greater fidelity to the gospel and at the same time of total fidelity to the aims of their particular congregation.

Accordingly on 25 January Little Sister Jeanne, who had been re-elected General Responsible at the previous General Chapter held in 1964, wrote to the Little Sisters announcing a Special Chapter of Aggiornamento in the forthcoming December. Six years having elapsed since the previous General Chapter, it too was due. To spare the cost of travel expenses and the prospect of two prolonged absences on the part of those who would take part in the Chapters, the Congregation for Religious gave permission for the General Chapter to be held immediately after the Special Chapter. In November 1969 therefore representatives from the fraternities all over the world converged on Tre Fontane. They had been sent a questionnaire in advance. The first of its questions read, 'Are there certain texts from the Conciliar Decrees that you would like to see integrated into the Constitutions or the Appendix?' The second called upon the person completing it to indicate in what respects the Fraternity had not yet entered sufficiently into the spirit of the Council. The Special Chapter proceeded to examine the life of the Fraternity in relation to the Council's call:

(1) to have as the supreme rule of its religious life the following of Christ.
(2) to maintain faithfully the spirit of its founders.
(3) to be in communion with the life of the Church.
(4) to be in a position to bring more effective help to humanity.
(5) to give the prime role to spiritual renewal in the process of adapting to the requirements of our time.

The Fraternity's consideration of its life in respect of these points was by no means complacent. There was, it was fully recognised, room for growth and improvement in the actual expression of its spirit, particularly as the diversity of needs which it encountered as an increasingly international congregation made itself apparent. In Little Sister Magdeleine's view the endeavour to enter into the spirit of the Council and, more importantly, to retain it, was an enormous challenge. At the same time, however, what was very apparent when it came to considering whether texts from the Council should be included in the Constitutions was the similarity of the spirit expressed by both. 'I was struck', one Capitular summarised the views of many, 'by the extent to which the spirit of the Fraternity and the spirit of the Council were one and the same. But in order better to comply with it, we need to ask for the grace of simplicity, generosity and faith.' Adherence to the spirit of the Second Vatican Council was in many respects a matter of total fidelity to their vocation as Little Sisters. Little Sister Magdeleine's intuition of Little Sisters whose one model was Jesus and who were to bring their contemplative vocation into the midst of the everyday life of humanity had to a substantial degree pre-empted the Council.

On 22 November 1969, at an international gathering of Superior Generals, Pope Paul VI had provided certain guidelines for them to follow in their religious life:

> The religious life does not deprive you of real development as a human person. It does not make you strangers to the needs and aspirations of the earthly city. In order to be saved, your brothers and sisters in the world have, in fact, need of the example of created beings that are fully free, fully dedicated to the work of their salvation, fully bereft of all that oppresses

others with anxiety, fully joyous in their sacrifice, fully human because they are inserted in the One who is the principle and the measure of man, God the Father who saves us in Christ and who has marked us with the invisible but effective seal of his Spirit.

For Little Sister Magdeleine it was a confirmation of what she had written in her 'green booklet', using a different vocabulary but in the same spirit nearly twenty-five years previously:

Do not set up barriers between the world and yourself; do not think that as a religious you have a special dignity to safeguard. Penetrate deeply among people by sharing their life, by friendship and by love. Give yourself to them completely, like Jesus who came to serve and not to be served; you, too, become *one with them*. Then you will be like leaven which must lose itself in the dough to make it rise.

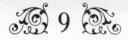

9

Only Donkeys . . .

IT WAS AN UPHILL CLIMB all the way. Sometimes Little Sister Magdeleine would say that she felt as if she was ten years ahead of her
time. Confident that truth and love would triumph in the end, she
had always been sure that what she had struggled for in relation to
the Church would come quite naturally with the passage of the years,
but she had been involved in breaking new ground and the going had
been hard. After the Apostolic Visit she did not write in quite the
same way as she had done previously, even to Father Voillaume, of
her spiritual anguish or inner suffering. It was as if, as the Fraternity
began gradually to find its shape, her suffering was experienced less
at the level of the spiritual and more as a result of the difficulties
encountered in particular countries or the degree to which the community did or did not correspond with her ideal. It was there nonetheless. Sometimes she acknowledged that she felt as if she were climbing
a steep mountain and that just when she appeared to be making some
headway she would be pulled downwards from behind. Often she
would sense the necessity for material changes to be made. She would
see the need to alter a fraternity, to acquire a car or take some other
step that might appear to be in contradiction to the Fraternity's life
to date and, as always, she would want to move swiftly. For all her
aspirations to 'littleness', she could be quite authoritarian in her
methods if she felt the end justified the means. Similarly, whilst she
wanted poverty for the Fraternity, she was quite capable of subordinat-
ing that commitment to the requirement to accomplish a particular
mission. In such circumstances it was sometimes her Little Sisters
who held her back.

Little Sister Magdeleine's yearning for paradise had not abated and
as her advancing years brought the prospect of wish fulfilment closer,
she was by no means blind to the importance of the Fraternity making
a healthy transition from the following of its charismatic foundress to

the government of others who might give a different expression to the spirit of the Fraternity. She had never, in any case, looked upon the Fraternity as 'hers', and her resignation as General Responsible and what she had thought to be her final parting from her Little Sisters in 1957 had already demonstrated an extraordinary capacity for detachment from a creation into which she had poured her whole life. The gradual progress away from undue emphasis on her personality and personal wishes, for which the Apostolic Visit had highlighted the need, albeit perhaps with unnecessary harshness, was one which Little Sister Magdeleine welcomed. Following the Apostolic Visit, however, she found it difficult for a while to rediscover her spontaneity. In the life of the Fraternity a certain rigidity set in and for a while something of an intractable atmosphere lingered on.

What the Visit had also highlighted was that there had been an attempt by some young and inexperienced superiors to interpret the detailed and copious directives Little Sister Magdeleine sent out to the various fraternities too literally and rigidly. It was not a problem of which she was unaware. What she had set out to found was a 'nomad' fraternity. In 1942 she had invited the handful of Little Sisters who first joined her at Le Tubet to be like the nomads to whom she had drawn so close in Algeria. They did not worry but put their trust in God:

> If they don't arrive at their appointed place in three days, they
> do so in eight, and if they don't find a camel to make the
> journey, they wait. 'God is Master', they say.

For her such surrender to the will of God meant that there was nothing rigid or implacable even about an act of obedience. Indeed, paradoxically, flexibility was a prime characteristic of obedience. In 1942 she wrote to her sisters:

> How much flexibility is needed in a foundation such as ours,
> in order to be able to adapt to the changing circumstances of our
> life. It may have been decided to follow a particular rule, then
> next day something unforeseen destroys all your fine
> projects. . . . If you are not supple, it means you have understood
> nothing about what I want above all else: obedience in
> surrender, love and gentleness. . . .
>
> You must be prepared to do the opposite of what you have
> heard me say, without worrying.

'The written law condemns to death, but the spirit gives life,' in 1951 she had reminded her Little Sisters of the words of 2 Corinthians 3:6. Yet it seemed that there were still those who had not absorbed this message. It should be said that a certain ambivalence seemed to manifest itself even in Little Sister Magdeleine's approach to directives. When questioned about information she had already supplied in a previous one, she was not above writing another under the underlined heading of 'Important Directive' and starting it with obvious irritation: 'I don't know whether people are not receiving my directives or whether they do not understand them but . . .' On the whole, however, she was the first to recognise the need to give two apparently opposing directives to two Little Sisters of different temperaments.

Finally, in 1962, she asked for all her directives to be sent back to her and made them the subject of a questionnaire. She was amazed, to the point of not recognising in the answers her original intention, at the extent to which they had been deformed and rendered implacable. When, during the Apostolic Visit, she had been obliged to defend herself against the allegation that she was presenting the devotion to the infant Jesus to her sisters in terms that were too absolute, she had pointed out that it was impossible to avoid all distortion. Her teaching on the infant Jesus had been exonerated but it was true that there had been an element of deformation. By 1991 there would still be some Little Sisters who thought that the carrying of models of the infant Jesus had been obligatory. In fact this had never been the case.

At Christmas 1966, as part of an initiative for the renewal of the Fraternity inspired by the Second Vatican Council, she also sent out a letter inviting the Little Sisters all over the world to write to her in complete confidence about their experience of obedience within the Fraternity. She asked them to tell her without any animosity towards their superiors what difficulties they had encountered or even what had simply surprised them about the written directives or orders given to them or to other Little Sisters by their superiors. She received nearly a thousand letters in response and in May 1968 shut herself away in the tiny little room she occupied together with Little Sister Jeanne at Tre Fontane to write a seventy-five page letter in reply. The answers to her questionnaire should, she felt, be a source of reassurance to the Fraternity as a whole for, despite their general frankness and the bitterness of three or four arising largely out of mutual misunderstanding, none of them had been offensive. They did, however, give rise to a healthy airing of the whole issue of obedience and to the problems which seemed to derive not so much from the directives given by superiors as from the manner in which they were given. They arose too, it was pointed out, from the fact that 'responsibles' sometimes had difficulty in commanding obedience because they did not themselves set an adequate example.

Together Little Sister Magdeleine and Little Sister Jeanne handled the process with delicacy, without recriminations and without allowing the responsibles, many of whom, they emphasised, had themselves expressed an awareness of their own deficiencies, to carry the burden of guilt alone. Certain deficiencies such as the pressure arising from an excess of work must be accepted until such time as God saw fit to increase their numbers to meet the needs of all the fraternities throughout the world. At the 1964 Chapter the need had been felt to have four Little Sisters per fraternity: two to earn a living, one to work in the house and welcome people and the fourth to serve the neighbourhood; but the gap between recognition of an ideal and its actual implementation was a wide one. The vocations were still coming in but not in sufficient numbers to make such a plan possible in all the fraternities. Little Sister Magdeleine knew that it was hard to balance the requirements of manual work, study and prayer. As far as she was concerned the ideal fraternity would actually be made up of four or five Little Sisters: with two Little Sisters the relationship was potentially too intimate, in the case of three, one tended to be left out, four still meant that if one fell ill or was subject to strain, the burden on the others was considerable. Four to five in a fraternity was really the theoretical ideal but in practice, the number of available sisters still ordained otherwise. She and Little Sister Jeanne knew also that in despatching their Little Sisters around the world, expecting them to be as 'light as the soap bubbles that a child might blow', they had not always adequately taken into account their individual human needs. Some of this, she reassured them, would sort itself out with time. At very least, the airing of such problems brought with it the resolution to go forward with a more mature understanding of authority.

For a long time Little Sister Magdeleine had herself been inclined to express her views on what the Little Sisters should or should not do in terms of her own emotions. 'It would cause me too much pain' or 'it would upset me too much' were expressions she often used to dissuade people from a particular course of action. It was perhaps small wonder then that others adopted the same expression on her behalf. At one time it had become common practice in the fraternities to exercise authority on the grounds that a particular action would 'upset' Little Sister Magdeleine. Similarly, her personal likes and dislikes were sometimes used as instruments of justification or negation, and distorted. Long before 1968, and on more than one occasion, she had asked the Little Sisters not to use her personal preferences in this way. Little Sister Magdeleine's real affinity with animals and her love for them was no secret. She had even once asked a Little Sister from India to bring her a monkey back to keep in the courtyard of the General Fraternity. Animals had their place in the fraternity, particularly as a source of joy to the elderly. Even this affection, however, had become in some fraternities the pretext for what Little Sister Magdeleine herself regarded as over-indulgence of animals. The letter she wrote in 1958, stressing the fact that 'filling the fraternities with over-familiar dogs and cats' was a misrepresentation of her attitude, was a good indication of the tightrope which at times she was obliged to walk:

> I cannot accept all this sentimentality over dogs, and especially cats. For a long time I have been asking people not to stroke the cats as they used to in certain fraternities, not to have them on their laps, not to let them lick the plates. . . .
> Sentimentality about animals can have unhealthy repercussions and, even if not, it can still be a cause of scandal in certain regions, in Muslim countries for example.
> But as there are always two ditches, on either side of the road, don't let this recommendation become grounds for increased incomprehension, indifference and roughness towards animals. No sentimentality over cats and dogs, but no kicks either.

The letter which went out to all the fraternities in 1968 reiterated unambiguously Little Sister Magdeleine's request that the Little Sisters no longer resort to reinforcing their authority with phrases such as 'Little Sister Magdeleine said', 'Little Sister Jeanne asks', 'Little Sister Magdeleine will be upset if you do it', 'Little Sister Jeanne doesn't like that'. She understood that it was done out of a desire to comply as far as possible with the ideal that had been set out for them but there was a danger of it becoming an abuse of the freedom of certain sisters and of misrepresenting the concept of obedience.

Obedience, Little Sister Magdeleine insisted, must be, as the Vatican Council had intimated, 'responsible and active' and it was in the light of this understanding that superiors should exercise their authority: always with respect for the dignity of the human person and the freedom of the children of God. In 1969, at the opening of the Special Chapter of Aggiornamento she stated quite clearly that she was prepared to let all of her directives drop. In fact she was quite simply astonished that the Little Sisters had allowed themselves to become entrenched by them. Her introductory address at the same Chapter opened with the admission that for months she had been praying for the grace to take part in the Chapter from heaven because she felt she could help the participants better from there and because her presence would not then constitute a threat to their freedom of expression.

The third General Chapter which followed hard upon the heels of the Special Chapter substantially altered Little Sister Magdeleine's position within the Fraternity. At the opening elections a new General Responsible was appointed. Little Sister Annie belonged to the generation of French people who had been at school during the war. She had seen her Jewish schoolfriends taken away to concentration camps never to return, and she had gone through a period of despair during which it had seemed to her as if 'evil and death had the last word'. Then she had read 'This is my last will and testament'. The title had made her believe its author was dead but in it she had found something which she had not herself been able to express – a way of living which corresponded with what she was seeking. At the age of nineteen she had met Little Sister Magdeleine for the first time and been overwhelmed by the fact that, despite her experience of suffering, the older woman still believed in love and knew how to nurture love around her. Little Sister Annie had joined the Fraternity in February 1948. She had worked for a while in a factory in a Parisian suburb. She had accompanied Little Sister Magdeleine for much of her grand tour round the world, had started the fraternity in Varanasi, India, and had subsequently supported the foundations in South-East Asia before serving for many years as assistant to the General Responsible and as first General Councillor. Her first letter to her sisters as General Responsible expressed her full appreciation of the unity which had existed between Little Sisters Jeanne and Magdeleine and her own need for their continued collaboration:

I cannot envisage bearing this responsibility other than in total union of thought and heart, and in constant collaboration with Little Sister Magdeleine and Little Sister Jeanne. The unity there has been between them for more than twenty years has been and must remain a grace for the Fraternity. Consequently I am sure that I am expressing the unanimous desire of the Little Sisters by asking that both continue to advise us and show us the path to follow.

Little Sister Jeanne, who had lived through so much in such proximity to Little Sister Magdeleine, had wanted her at her side whenever possible. After twenty years of faithful service to the Fraternity as General Responsible the relinquishing of the role was something of a release. Now she would have greater freedom to travel with Little Sister Magdeleine in the 'Shooting Star', work with her on the Constitutions which were due for revision in 1971, and labour alongside her on the work site at Tre Fontane. The election of Little Sister Annie, for all her closeness to the two people who had previously held the ultimate responsibility for the Fraternity and her desire for their guidance, was a movement towards greater independence in its government.

For Little Sister Magdeleine the General Responsible was always the representative of God. 'I shall always give you my viewpoint but it must never restrict your freedom. You must retain your freedom of conscience,' she told Little Sister Annie who was to be re-elected General Responsible at the Fraternity's fourth General Chapter in December 1975. For Little Sister Annie and indeed for her successors this attitude was vital and appreciated. It afforded them the liberty to make decisions, even if it did not eliminate conflict altogether. Intuitive, unpredictable and given to expressing her views in the most forthright terms, the foundress was still very much a force to be reckoned with. Little Sister Magdeleine could be angry to the point of getting out of the vehicle in which she was being driven before it arrived at its intended destination. Such displays were instantly regretted but hand in hand with her spontaneity went the occasional outburst of impulsive impatience.

In her advancing years the foundress remained sensitive to the changing requirements of modern society. She had an insatiable appetite for listening to the world news, and for reading newspapers, magazines and books of all kinds. Indeed, she was often teased for making a point of reading the cartoon strips in the newspapers first and on the rare occasions on which she watched television manifestly had difficulty in tearing herself away from the screen. Her interest in contemporary concerns and in the most recent publications was a reflection of her love for life. It was also very much part of her overall view of modernity which like her response to youth was never one of negative resistance. If, however, she was in many respects open to 'progress' and ahead of her time in the vision she brought to the Church, and indeed perhaps even in the role she adopted as a woman, in some respects she belonged to her generation. Among her Little Sisters there were those who maintained that she had helped them to become more fully women, who were struck above all by the stand she had taken in relation to the male hierarchy of the Church. She enjoyed the company of men but, in the case of churchmen in particular, she did not hesitate to speak out respectfully but undaunted in their presence. Why was it that in Church parlance superiors of congregations were always referred to in the masculine form 'superieurs generaux', she would query, and supply the answer herself: 'Because it is always the men who matter'. At the same time her understanding of male and female roles and qualities was essentially traditional. Females were prone to excessive imagination. Their modesty was something to be safeguarded.

Amongst the motley assortment of expressions Little Sister Magdeleine did not like was the term 'psychological illness'. To her the suggestion that an illness was 'psychological' was comparable to calling it 'imaginary' and so in some way to negate its validity and not to afford the sufferer the sympathy and understanding he or she warranted. She was suspected by some of being frightened of the psychological approach which, in the century of Freud, found its way even into religious life, and of having an attitude to psychological problems that was nervous of the human or failed adequately to understand it, preferring rather to idealise the spiritual dimension. Certainly she was not one to probe the workings of the human psyche too deeply. The idea so central to her own life of blindly following a God who had taken her by the hand allowed no scope for it. Instead she was inclined to comments such as 'she's got a bad temper' or 'it's time you pulled your socks up'. She had difficulty in accepting that jealousy was a reality of human relationships. As a young woman, she had been shocked when a novice she had known committed murder out of jealousy. Her way of dealing with that shock was not to accept the

218

motivating emotion as a part of human life. Hers was not a blanket condemnation of psychology, however. In May 1953 she had written an article on the subject of psychoanalysis, stating that the religious life was based on too sacred and too intimate a relationship between the soul and God for its inner workings to be probed in the name of modern medicine. Psychoanalysis was no means by which to establish whether or not a person had a religious vocation. The spiritual and religious life transcended the boundaries of psychoanalysis because the latter took no cognisance of the unlimited potential of divine grace. For her such grace, which could quite suddenly and rationally unaccountably illuminate the soul or otherwise gradually transform it, was an irrefutable reality. It is not hard to discern the roots of such conviction in her own psyche and it was one which she maintained throughout her life.

By the time the Fraternity held its fourth General Chapter in 1975 there were thirty-seven capitulars of twenty-one different nationalities from all five continents. The firsthand experience of Little Sisters who had had years of insertion into the different countries of the world found a growing voice at Tre Fontane, albeit still in the French language. Little Sister Magdeleine welcomed this input as she welcomed the input of the Little Sisters into the Constitutions on which she was still working, submitting them to the Fraternity for ideas and approval. In some respects she showed remarkable understanding. She understood the problems of the Kenyan fraternities where the Little Sisters lived amongst the Masai tribes, some of them struggling to grow their food and finding it difficult to balance the requirements of hard labour, prayer and being present to the local people. She understood too that whilst the nomadic people of the Masai had very few needs, her Little Sisters in sharing the poverty would nonetheless have need of support from their sisters elsewhere. In Bombay the fraternity was housed in very confined accommodation in a slum area. Its door was always open and so the children from the overcrowded neighbouring houses often came to play there. Concerned that it was turning into a kindergarten, she had wanted the Little Sisters to close their door, but she listened and admitted she was wrong, when it was explained that in the Indian context it was important that the door to a place where women lived alone and where male priests sometimes visited was kept open. If children were present at the time, all the better.

She was always prepared to listen and always wanted to be fair. There was too something charming about the childlike quality of

219

Little Sister Magdeleine's simplicity. Given a new pair of secateurs to prune the trees she loved so much, she at once invited all the sisters on the Council to go outside and try them. Presented with a pig's trotter, one of her favourite dishes, she wanted to share it with those around her, persuaded that they must love it just as much as she did. The joy she could derive from everyday things was infectious and engaging. All the same it was perhaps inevitable that there were times when her young sisters, particularly those who had not had much direct personal contact with her more endearing ways, felt that she did not fully understand the requirements of the particular culture in which they were trying to live out the ideal of the Fraternity.

For those who had not lived through the earliest foundation years, it was not always easy to comprehend the Fraternity's continuing special consecration to the world of Islam. Amongst a new generation of Little Sisters there were some who were more inclined to be critical of the established Church than their foundress. There were those too who felt that she confused the idea of being international with the concept of universality and that for her unity meant merely the absence of conflict. In Latin America where, in defiance of all the oppression and injustice perpetrated by the military regime, the Church as a whole had given clear expression to its preferential option for the poor, it was felt that the poverty of the fraternity, the poverty of the working classes, did not correspond with that of the local people. In the aftermath of the Algerian war of independence there came a point where the Little Sisters in Algeria felt it inappropriate to maintain the size of property which had not seemed quite so self-indulgent in the days of French colonialism. Then the Little Sisters had in any case come in large numbers and at regular intervals for the sessions at El Abiodh but once it became impossible for the Little Sisters to maintain anything but a small, discreet presence in Algeria, El Abiodh seemed far too large for a handful of them. Similarly, at Sidi Boujnan the accommodation and courtyards began to seem too much like luxury to those actually living there. Little Sister Magdeleine held on to the idea that a minimum of space was necessary wherever possible for the spiritual and mental well-being of the fraternities, particularly in relation to the potential need to welcome others. She was deeply attached to the idea of retaining an area which would accommodate nomads, both the nomad sisters when they returned from the desert and the Arab nomads when they needed to pitch their tents and care for their flocks. She was also concerned about the effects on the surrounding villages of giving parts of the fraternity's property to friends and neighbours. 'Are you telling me', she wrote to the regional superior at the time, 'that I don't know the Algerian situation?' Gradually, however, more and more of the fraternities' accommodation was given away.

There were those outside the Fraternity who were struck by her capacity to comprehend the difficulties of marriage and the divisions of family life. She had what one Little Sister referred to as the 'psychology of charity', and yet, in the case of her Little Sisters, sometimes differences of viewpoint were compounded by what might appear to some as a lack of basic human psychology, but which had something of the two-edged sword of St Paul (Hebrews 4:12) about it. In order that her sisters might be shaped and grow, they must be 'pruned' and corrected; and Little Sister Magdeleine had a way of bringing her exceptional memory to bear when it came to their misdemeanours. Often those who came to Tre Fontane from distant fraternities for a session or a meeting would see her only just before they left. On such occasions she would remind them of things that they had written or not done quite as they should have done. Having pointed out the error of their ways, she would direct them to go with the assurance, 'We'll forget all about it.' There was nothing mean about her temperament. On the contrary, it was of crystal-like clarity. As far as she was concerned, the slate was wiped clean. They responded to her warmth and her charisma, but she was their foundress and her words were not so easily forgotten especially by people who did not know her well.

Those who knew her primarily through her writings were inclined to construct an image of a woman of great intuition whose ideas were nonetheless difficult to put into practice and whose own preoccupation with detail, verging as it sometimes did on the idiosyncratic, seemed at times to contradict the intended spirit. It was only when one sister came to serve on the General Council and so to spend six years in closer proximity to the foundress that she grew to understand her better: 'We were to be nomads amongst the nomads. We were to be really of the people of the country to which we were devoted, to learn the language and be inculturated. At the same time our skirts were to be of a certain length. She expected Little Sisters to come from France and renounce their French mentality and ways, to give up many things in order really to belong to that country. It was a way of respecting the local people, of not imposing an intrusive presence on them, but as a non-French person I could see that if Little Sisters from France really did all those things they would damage themselves. Afterwards when I really talked to her about it she understood completely and was in total agreement.'

Little Sister Magdeleine was capable of stating her views in the most emphatic terms and then being the first to change them, when she had an individual before her. Memories of her were punctuated with accounts of her readiness to listen and the resultant changes of opinion, often unexpected, frequently mercurial, sometimes disconcerting. She could change her mind within a space of minutes even when at Council meetings, invariably for very valid reasons. Sometimes the reaction she provoked in others was one of rebellion but often, when her sisters reflected on what she had said, there was in it an element of gospel truth even if the expression given to it was sometimes exaggerated. It was quite possible also to have a heated exchange about an issue with her and some months later meet her again only to find her voicing precisely the opinion which she had condemned completely on the previous occasion. Reproached for the fact that she had abandoned the viewpoint she had previously held so staunchly she would remark simply: 'Listen, only donkeys do not change their minds'.

When the Little Sisters in Oxford set fire to the fraternity and lost everything they had because they had hung up their washing to dry in the bathroom over a paraffin stove, Little Sister Magdeleine simply told them not to do it again. Far more trivial incidents could put relationships at risk. Those who really knew her learned to ignore the first explosive reaction. The purchase of some particularly cheap yellow chicken coops for the hens at Le Tubet was the occasion of such an outburst. Chancing upon a group of Little Sisters cleaning the newly acquired coops Little Sister Magdeleine informed them in no uncertain terms that it simply was not possible to have yellow chicken coops. One Little Sister, dismayed by Little Sister Magdeleine's vehemence, was at a loss as to how they were going to resell them and purchase others of a colour that Little Sister Magdeleine would find more acceptable. Another, who knew the foundress better, went to her next day. Her response in the exchange that followed was predictably tractable:

'What have you been saying about the yellow chicken coops?'
'I said that you might have chosen a different colour'

222

'But that was all I could find at the price.'

'You do what you can. Of course you must keep them.'

Sometimes it was as if she wanted people to disagree with her. One newly professed sister, travelling with her in a car in Yugoslavia to look for a suitable home for the fraternity there, was bemused to find herself being taken to an address in an unexpectedly affluent area. Eventually she mustered the courage to ask the foundress why they were going to look at a house in a district that was so obviously unsuitable. 'Because I'm not being shown anything else,' was the immediate reply. 'Show me something else.' At times she seemed to feel that opposition was a fertile ground for ideas. At others, if her Little Sisters did not show the faith she needed them to have in her, it was as if it was all too much for her, as if she could take no more obstacles on her apparently interminable climb. Sometimes, it seemed, things were by no means as clear or as easy for her as people might imagine and her sisters saying 'no' to her made her condition intolerable. At such times contradiction was hard for her to take. 'You are all against me,' she would protest, 'including Little Sister Jeanne. All of you.'

Alongside all the conviction of her faith went the self-questioning of a person who knew herself to be possessed of obvious human foibles. One responsible for a fraternity took it upon herself to alert Little Sister Magdeleine to the fact that her tendency to home straight in on such considerations as what she considered the imperfections of the decor, the fact that the door was too big for example, as soon as she arrived, was liable to alienate the sisters who lived there. On her subsequent visit to that fraternity Little Sister Magdeleine greeted everyone carefully without a word of criticism. Afterwards, she summoned the responsible to her: 'Why do you let that Little Sister go round with a habit like that?' she inquired. 'Her skirt is far too long,' then added, 'You see, I've made some progress. I didn't say anything in front of her.' She was over eighty at the time and still prepared to acknowledge to one who was far younger that she had to struggle with her own temperament.

She was in fact exceptional in her humility. It was humility which lay at the roots of her apparent lack of concern for what other people thought about her, and humility which enabled her to give way if she was shown to be in the wrong; and when the sparks did fly she was the first to seek reconciliation and forgiveness. After one such clash with a responsible over a Little Sister whom the foundress defended, the responsible went later to apologise for having been too harsh in her criticisms: 'She didn't say anything,' the responsible would afterwards recall, 'not even "Perhaps you don't know her well enough". She just looked at me and I understood in that moment how God might look at one who admits she is a sinner. I shall never forget it. She was recognising me as her Little Sister, the one who acknowledged her fault and knew how to ask for forgiveness.'

After more than eighty years of an almost obsessive aversion to a particular shade of yellow, in her very old age Little Sister Magdeleine was heard to wonder aloud whether there might not in fact be some medical condition which affected the manner in which one saw certain colours. Even later, shortly before her death, she would remark to Father Voillaume that there had been only three points on which God had clearly obliged her to act. In his own old age Father Voillaume failed to remember which three but he knew that whilst she believed in the signs God gave her and allowed them to guide her, she was denied the comfort of certainties.

Throughout the 1970s and 1980s Little Sister Magdeleine's time, when she was not travelling in the 'Shooting Star', was spent largely at Tre Fontane. The energy with which she undertook her journeys behind the Iron Curtain was a mystery even to Pope Paul VI. Following one of the general audiences which those Little Sisters who had made their final vows and all the Little Sisters from Tre Fontane attended annually, Little Sister Magdeleine and Little Sister Annie were invited together with a group of bishops into an adjoining room.

There the Pope, who maintained his affectionate interest in the Fraternity, addressed a few more personal words to each of them. 'I often think of you', he told Little Sister Magdeleine. 'I follow you on all your pilgrimages. I wonder how you have the spiritual and the physical resistance to do all that. You are carrying a spark there.'

For as long as her physical condition permitted she took part in the ongoing process of construction at Tre Fontane. Inspired by the peasant women she had seen labouring behind the Iron Curtain, she loved manual work and her enthusiasm for it communicated itself to her Little Sisters. To the barrack huts with their highly polished wooden floors, a chapel also constructed out of wood, and a home for parents, were gradually added a large kitchen and dining areas, housing for livestock such as rabbits which eventually found their way into the sisters' cooking pots, a vegetable garden, workshops from where the sisters' handiwork could be dispatched all over the world, and even a small gymnasium. A basement room was set aside as a chapel of the Sacred Heart in memory of Charles de Foucauld and on the wooded slopes, nestling amongst the trees and well apart from the growing number of main buildings, three small individual hermitages, each with its own study and sleeping area, bathroom, kitchenette and chapel, were eventually added. Here, on the outskirts of Rome, at intervals the Little Sisters could withdraw to rediscover the graces of the desert. There were those who recognised that even in the construction of Tre Fontane Little Sister Magdeleine was searching, seeking to express something: the idea of welcome, openness, a place where everyone could feel at home.

The Fraternity had become the focus of a certain public interest. Little Sister Magdeleine had at first declined to give interviews and could be quite awkward with journalists, but as time went on she did agree to be interviewed for written articles. Never entirely at ease with the inadequacy of words and their potential for distortion, and conscious perhaps of the pitfalls of the spontaneous way in which she spoke, she would not have her voice recorded. She would even ask that talks she gave to her Little Sisters, which she had not carefully prepared with notes and which were quite capable of roaming happily between the spiritual and the prosaic, be wiped from the tape if they had been recorded. She was not without a certain personal vanity, fighting shy of camera close-ups and not wanting her veil to reveal her ears, but when asked if this was not vanity, she would say disarmingly that probably it was. On the whole, however, she accepted the idea of photographs. She was quite at ease with the fact that photographs of her were displayed prominently in fraternities throughout the world. It was, after all, only natural for a daughter to have a photograph of her mother.

She was also writing herself. In 1981 she published the first volume of her history of the Fraternity entitled *Du Sahara au monde entier* (*He took me by the Hand*) which was followed two years later by a second volume: *D'un bout du monde a l'autre*. Both were made up of extracts from diaries and documents written at the time of the events described. In assembling them into book form, however, Little Sister Magdeleine was not able to resist making certain changes for the sake of greater clarity. They were accompanied by precise little notes providing background information or relaying to the reader such details as the fact that a series of dots in the text did not necessarily indicate that material had been left out but was more often simply a stylistic feature. Similar meticulous care went into her gathering together of what would eventually form a series of nine substantial volumes of 'Letters' relating to the development of the Fraternity. Mgr de Provenchères was instrumental in persuading Little Sister Magdeleine to supplement the two books available to the world at large, with a more intimate record based on the texts of her letters and those of others directly concerned in the Fraternity's history. The death of Mao Tse Tung in September 1976, visits to Tre Fontane by Mother Teresa and her Missionaries of Charity, by Jean Vanier and a group of people with mental handicaps, a talk given by Thérèse Vanier on the accompaniment of the sick, gatherings of young people organised by the Taizé Brothers and a multitude of other events of both international and personal interest also found their way on to the pages, for there was nothing which could really be considered beyond the realms of concern of Little Sister Magdeleine and the Fraternity. News of the death of Pope Paul VI reached her via the Russian Orthodox Metropolitan, Mgr Nikodim, when they met at the heart of a pine forest near Leningrad on 7 August 1978. The demise of a man whose friendship she had valued both for his understanding of the Fraternity and on a more personal level touched her deeply. As a tribute to him she included in the fifth volume of her letters his testament and last writings.

The 'Letters' would, as Mgr de Provenchères pointed out, 'illuminate the Fraternity from within' and be of great spiritual value to the Little Sisters in that they would show how its ideal had actually been lived in particular circumstances. They also reflected the diversity and the universality of Little Sister Magdeleine's interests and friendships. Largely because of the information they contained about the Fraternity's activities behind the Iron Curtain, they were reserved for the use of the Little Sisters of Jesus and were marked with a label which stated that they were not under any circumstances to be circulated outside the Fraternity; nor were they to be made accessible to all those within it. Together with Little Sister Jeanne and a group of secretaries who checked and read and typed, Little Sister Magdeleine would agonise over the clarity and editing of these texts in the same way that she continued to agonise over the wording of the Fraternity's Constitutions. No close approximations would do. Hours were spent searching for the right word with which to convey the intended meaning. Her desire for perfection pervaded everything she did. Often at meetings she would tell her Little Sisters, 'Ah you are not yet perfect Little Sisters. The perfect Little Sister is kind and gentle and you, you get angry.' Finally one day she was asked, 'Can't you accept that we are not perfect. After all who can ever be perfect?' 'Of course I realise that you can't be perfect,' was the instant rejoinder, 'but I have to tell you to be, so that you will be better.' At times she went so far as to demand a level of perfection that was impossible to achieve and that sometimes alienated those sisters who did not realise that it was really her way of telling them that they were not yet charitable enough.

Those who worked with her on a sustained basis grew accustomed to her eye for detail which would never accept a typing error or even a badly positioned piece of text. They coped with it because they were themselves for the most part perfectionists, and if at times they were disheartened by the need to retype whole pages to correct the tiniest error, Little Sister Magdeleine would tell them that they must work with joy. She didn't like to see them with long faces. In the early hours of one morning, after many hours of such labour, she announced to one of her helpers: 'I'd like to say nice things to you and the others, but it's two o'clock in the morning.' Hard taskmaster though she was, people enjoyed working with her. She had not surrounded herself with the kind of followers who needed a strong character upon which to lean. She would not tolerate such personal attachments at all. Nor was she one to pay compliments or show affection and yet, significantly, those close to her remained faithful to the last. Even those who had only brief contact with her in the course of the day, during which the conversation was exclusively about work, would come away from those apparently banal exchanges with renewed vigour. She had, it seemed, the capacity to communicate inner strength without anything special being said.

She liked to invite groups of her Little Sisters to have dinner with her at a large round table with a revolving centre in the Council Room. In one corner of the room in question stood a statue of 'Our Lady of the Whole World'. In another was a foldaway photograph frame with pictures of Little Sisters who had gone to 'paradise', and taking up the whole of one wall was a chart denoting with different coloured symbols the fraternities in each country, the Little Sisters in each fraternity and the type of fraternity. The sisters were invited to dine in categories. Thus those working on the Constitutions would enjoy some period of relaxation as a 'family' with her. Otherwise she had little time for small talk when work was in progress. In her tiny office at Tre Fontane which was little more than seven feet by five, she worked regularly late into the night before retiring into an equally tiny adjoining room just large enough to accommodate her bed and that of Little Sister Jeanne. Gradually the various editions of the Constitutions, carefully ranged in chronological order, came to occupy several rows of shelves specially made for the purpose. It was these same Constitutions, on which she had worked with such unrelenting dedication in such extraordinary conditions, that in 1981 were to present her with what might be regarded as a supreme test of her flexibility and her humility.

September 1981 saw the opening of the Fraternity's fifth General Chapter at which the number of countries represented by the capitulars increased to twenty-four and the elections produced for the first time a General Responsible who was not French. Little Sister Carla was Italian. The eldest of five children, she had lost both parents at an early age, an experience which raised in her serious doubts about her faith. Hungry for love herself, she had always felt drawn to those who seemed to her the least loved. At the age of twenty, she had contracted tuberculosis and spent four years in a sanatorium. It was there that, in her own words, she 'discovered Jesus as a living person to whom I felt called to give my life'. At the same time she discovered Jesus in the sick people around her. It seemed to her then that it was by sharing the lives of those whose illness rendered them among the poorest that she drew closest to Jesus. Cured of her tuberculosis, she remained in the sanatorium as a waitress until family commitments necessitated her taking other employment. It was the chance reading of Father Voillaume's book *Au coeur des masses* (*Seeds of the Desert*) which first introduced her to the Fraternity as a place in which she could realise a life of prayer and of presence amongst the uncared for. By then her 'circle' of the poorest of the poor included not only the sick or those who were poverty-stricken. Rather she felt particularly called to the world of atheism. There had been a point in her own life when she had been attracted to Marxism as a means of liberation for the poor. Afterwards, however, she had discovered the 'poverty of man left to his own resources and without a belief in God'. She had first met Little Sister Magdeleine in 1957 while doing a trial period with the congregation. The foundress had asked her whether she had an 'orientation' and she had found herself answering that she felt that lack of faith and hope was a very grave form of poverty. It had been a source of joy to Little Sister Carla to sense that her conviction found a chord of recognition. Little Sister Magdeleine's response to her as to so many others was swift and decisive: 'You can go to the Eastern bloc.' She had subsequently found herself canning gherkins in a factory in Austria where there were numerous refugees from behind the Iron Curtain. From there she had gone first to Paris to study Serbo-Croatian and Romanian and eventually to Yugoslavia. She was for many Little Sisters the embodiment of the smallness and the poverty that shaped the Fraternity's ideal. Her period as the first non-French General Responsible was a key one in underlining the universality of the Fraternity. By the time she was elected General Responsible of the Fraternity, Karol Wojtyla had been Pope for nearly three years. At his first encounter with Little Sister Magdeleine after his official inauguration he had remarked somewhat wistfully that as Pope he would no longer be able to tease her as he once had, but she would follow his journeys with as much interest as he followed hers and the Little Sisters' relationship with the Pope continued to be everything they might have hoped for. As an Italian, however, Little Sister Carla also had a particular role in cementing the Fraternity's relations with the wider Church in Rome.

By September 1981 Little Sister Magdeleine was still seeking the Church's formal approbation of the most recent version of the Constitutions. The text for them, which at that time still incorporated the Fraternity's Rule, was accordingly submitted once more to the Congregation for Religious. On 20 September Little Sister Magdeleine wrote on an optimistic note of how the Constitutions were still in the hands of the theologians but that the rules had been studied and, she thought, accepted. Four days later Little Sister Carla was called to the Congregation for Religious and Secular Institutes, as it was now called, only to be told that the current text of the Constitutions, though 'very beautiful and very spiritual', had not been accepted because it was too cumbersome. It was true that in working on the successive versions of the Constitutions in an attempt faithfully to shape a vocation in the footsteps of Charles de Foucauld but also to accommodate the new requirements of the developing congregation in all its diverse situations, they had become very substantial. Over the years, in the course of her life's journey, searching always for exactly the right mode of expression, Little Sister Magdeleine had added not only quotations from Charles de Foucauld but also quotations from the Gospels, from papal encyclicals, and from the Acts of the Second Vatican Council. It was Little Sister Magdeleine's life's work. Ever since her noviciate in 1939 when first Mgr Nouet had asked her to set down the guidelines for the congregation she was to found, she had laboured on them, she had prayed them and she had lived them; and in the end the fruits of all her efforts were pronounced too long and detailed.

Knowing all that the Constitutions meant to the foundress, Little Sister Carla returned to the Fraternity with a heavy heart to relay the response of the Congregation for Religious and Secular Institutes. She read on the face of Little Sister Magdeleine enormous suffering but the older woman said simply: 'If that is the Congregation's opinion, they must be reworked.' 'I am a little emotional', she wrote in the note she added to her collection of 'Letters', 'at the thought of rewriting another text when the Little Sisters have been waiting for it for so long, but it is the will of God.'

In fact the Congregation for Religious and Secular Institutes required that an international Commission compile a more concise text. A Commission, made up of Little Sister Carla, her Assistants and Councillors, Little Sister Annie and two Little Sisters from Asia because Asia was not at the time represented on the Council elected by the Chapter, was to set to work in collaboration with Little Sister Magdeleine. On 23 October Mgr de Provenchères called together all the Little Sisters at Tre Fontane to explain to them that the Commission, in extracting from Little Sister Magdeleine's work the essential points, was not to go into the details of their application but to confine itself to what canonists called the foundations of spirituality and government. The new Constitutions were also to exclude an article which was particularly close to Little Sister Magdeleine's heart concerning Little Sisters who were Christian but non-Catholics. The Curia had ordained that what in her simplicity Little Sister Magdeleine had long believed possible and what had been explored on an experimental basis, namely the full participation in the Fraternity of Little Sisters of other denominations united in their love for God and their respect for others, was not canonically possible. Difficulties arose not least because non-Catholics could not make their vows to the Catholic Church. For Little Sister Magdeleine such difficulties were not insurmountable. Nor was the solution conversion. For her the union of diversity was too valuable. 'Whatever happens they mustn't become Catholic,' she would say of those non-Catholics who sought to live the vocation of a Little Sister. Such questions, it was ordained in 1981, however, could only be resolved by official commissions dealing with relations between the Christian Churches.

The suppression of this article was, as Mgr de Provenchères pointed out, a source of real suffering to Little Sister Magdeleine. She accepted the disappointment as positively as possible with her customary enormous faith in the truth issuing from the Church but with considerable concern for those non-Catholic Little Sisters who had already joined the congregation. The relinquishing of the Constitutions, as she had seen them, required even greater surrender and yet, when in January 1983, at the suggestion of Mgr de Provenchères, 'her' work was presented to the Fraternity as its 'Rule of Life', in a foreword explaining why the texts that followed were no longer to be regarded as the Fraternity's Constitutions and stressing that it was the Constitutions which had received the official approval of the Church, she wrote of how she had worked 'with joy, in a fraternal collaboration with the international Commission'. Furthermore, those who worked with her would vouch for the fact that this was true. At over eighty years of age Little Sister Magdeleine, having put behind her the labour of a lifetime, listened and contributed with all the enthusiasm and vigour of one coming fresh to the venture.

About certain elements in the life of the Fraternity Little Sister Magdeleine remained insistent. One such issue was the importance of the fraternities of adoration. As early as the second General Chapter in the winter of 1963, she had seen fit to stress the need to have real fraternities of adoration in each of the regions. By then they had been formed but were gradually being put to other uses. Their importance was something which she continued to emphasise precisely, as she privately acknowledged, because she knew that they were something which her sisters might well allow to slide if she did not. She was not, however, one to hold on to less important considerations for the sake of it.

On 2 June 1984 Mgr de Provenchères, the Archbishop who had remained such a faithful guide and friend to Little Sister Magdeleine, died at Le Tubet where he had spent the last years of his life in the home for parents. On the day of his death he expressed the view that his work for Little Sister Magdeleine was concluded. He had had an agreement with God that he would remain on earth for as long as she needed him. 'There was always grace,' he said, speaking of the human folly of the earlier days of the Fraternity. 'The Fraternity must remain faithful to its first enthusiasm.' Then after a moment's pause he added with a smile: 'Not to the methods'. A Little Sister who was with him during these last hours recorded how he was no doubt thinking of the Little Sisters going out two by two, of their youth and the streak of madness that they had needed in the foundation years. Little Sister Magdeleine's record of the death of the man who had shown her so much confidence over the years and who had understood the lights that guided her because he too sought always to be guided by intimations of the Holy Spirit, was made up largely of the tributes of others. Of her own grief she wrote little in her 'Letters' but she undoubtedly felt the loss deeply. 'I can guess your deep pain,' Father Voillaume wrote to her from the tiny village of Cepie in France where he had spent much of his time since his retirement as Prior General of the Little Brothers of Jesus. 'Monsignor was always so close to you, as your light and sure guide. I feel a great peace and serenity because I know Monsignor went peacefully. It is as if a page has been turned in the history and life of our fraternities.'

There came a time in Little Sister Magdeleine's own life when the phenomenal energy which had given even Paul VI cause to marvel, began to wane. In her mid-eighties she still insisted on kneeling at the consecration during mass, despite the fact that it meant her Little Sisters coming to her aid. Asked why she insisted on doing so when it caused considerable disruption and other worshippers of a similar age were content to remain seated, she admitted simply: 'You know, if once I give up, I shall never manage it again.' With similar determination, in June and July 1986, she made her usual annual visit behind the Iron Curtain, this time to East Germany, Poland and Czechoslovakia. The journey began well with a preliminary visit to the Austrian fraternities in Regelsbrunn and Linz where the Little Sisters who lived and worked with a circus happened to be at the time. The circus was always a source of joy to Little Sister Magdeleine. She watched enthralled as a woman from a Polish troupe performed extraordinary acrobatics at the top of a high perch precariously balanced on her brother-in-law's shoulders. She feared for their safety. She derived pleasure from the fact that one of the Little Sisters' jobs was to help mount a number of children on small ponies in readiness for their act. In the sisters' circus caravan a chimpanzee was brought to sit next to her. It put its arms round her neck and she was captivated. 'It is really striking to see how like human beings these creatures are,' she recorded afterwards. In the tiny chapel in the Little Sisters' van she was 'so touched to see the Lord in this circus where so many people risked their lives, seeking to give joy to others . . . some of whom were going through real trials in their health or family life at the same time.'

From Linz the 'Shooting Star' went on to visit the four Little Sisters in East Berlin and then to Warsaw where the Bishop of Szczecin brought a group of priests and young people to meet her. They were starting a secular institute and helping him to found a theology faculty for lay people. She spoke to them from the heart of universal love, of her desire that Little Sisters from all over the world should live together, united in mutual love, and of the world of Islam, of the Muslims of Afghanistan who let themselves be killed rather than cease their cries of 'Allah akbar'. She spoke to them too of the love that should prevail between members of a religious community, institute or seminary, the love for which Jesus and Mary in Nazareth were the models.

At the Little Sisters' fraternity in Szewna Little Sister Magdeleine had difficulty in climbing the stairs to the chapel in the attic. It was only later, however, on her return to the 'Shooting Star' that instead of sitting down on a bunk as intended, she sat down on nothing and fell, supporting her whole bodyweight on her right hand. Her right arm was fractured. In considerable pain, and with her arm in a bandage rather than a plaster because of her age and her fatigue, she travelled on to Czestochowa, noting with satisfaction that this was her twenty-fifth visit. Some of her plans for the Polish visit had to be curtailed. She had also hoped to visit Yugoslavia that year but this was not to be. There was consolation to be drawn from the fact that she had at least managed to see her Little Sisters in East Germany and Poland and in fact she would manage to visit East Germany, Poland, Czechoslovakia and Yugoslavia during the following year, but the accident in Poland undoubtedly marked the beginning of a difficult period of her life. The arm recovered slowly but she had increasing difficulty in walking and had to resort to a wheelchair. There was no longer enough air or space for her in the tiny 'cell' she shared with Little Sister Jeanne at Tre Fontane and so she was obliged to move into a larger room next to the meeting room, which she had originally placed at the disposal of her hippy friends. She still found cause for joy. Tahar and his wife, faithful friends of so many years, came to stay for a while at the General Fraternity, but Little Sister Magdeleine was exhausted and the joy of their visit was tempered by sadness that this might be their last encounter and by her concern that they should not be too worried at leaving her in such poor physical condition.

The year 1986 brought another of her long-standing aspirations a step nearer to fruition. Little Sister Magdeleine had always wanted to make it possible for those with a vocation to become Little Sisters who were for one reason or another, such as for serious family reasons, prevented from living in community, to pursue that calling. In 1954 she had conceived the idea of 'Lay Little Sisters' but the project had proved to be premature. Later it was taken up again under the title of 'Auxiliary Little Sisters' but Little Sister Magdeleine had never been keen on the idea of 'helping' associated with the word 'auxiliary'. Various people had tried to live out Little Sister Magdeleine's idea of the spirit of the Fraternity intimately linked to the lay world but they had done so only on a more or less temporary basis. She had maintained her attachment, however, to the idea of Little Sisters living outside the Fraternity but making the same commitments as any other Little Sister to union with God, poverty, the state of spiritual childhood, smallness and a preferential love for the poor. In 1986 two Little Sisters began their lives as 'External Little Sisters'. It was a source of considerable satisfaction to Little Sister Magdeleine, as was the profession of the first Little Sister from the Reformed Church. Shortly after Little Sisters came to Rome from Brazil, Korea, France, Sri Lanka and Switzerland to make their final profession in the crypt of St Peter's in September 1986, the first Little Sister from the Swiss Reformed Church made her final commitment at Tre Fontane. An arrangement had been reached whereby the vows were made not 'into the hands' of the General Responsible but in her presence. Few non-Catholics had in fact been able to participate as fully as Little Sister Magdeleine had hoped in the life of the Fraternity, but that made the final commitment of the first all the more precious to her. On the eve of the ceremony Little Sister Magdeleine was so ill that she received the Sacrament of the Sick. From her sick bed, with the aid of a sound system, she followed the event which took place next day at Tre Fontane, presided over by Pastor Markus from the Evangelic Church. She considered it such an important step in the history of the Fraternity, however, that suddenly it came to her that she must make a supreme effort to get up and have herself wheeled into the chapel. She had hoped to do so discreetly but her arrival was greeted with a burst of applause.

Notwithstanding the resources she could still muster when the occasion demanded, she was very frail. A severe attack of influenza turned into bronchial pneumonia which confined her to her bed for four months – a fact which she reported to Pope John Paul II when she wrote to him at Christmas to extend him the love, gratitude and prayers of the Fraternity. Nor was she exempt from all the natural human anguish and frustration of old age. Her heart went out with even greater empathy to the old people who occupied the parents homes at Le Tubet or in Rome. She wished them patience 'because you need it when you are elderly and can no longer do for yourself the things you would like to'. Yet she continued to keep track of events that were going on in the world: of the violent conflict between Iran and Iraq, the elections in South Africa, the trial of the Nazi war criminal Klaus Barbie in Lyon which evoked for her so many tragic memories, and the demonstrations in South Korea. When General Jaruzelski came from Poland to visit the Pope the event did not go unrecorded in Little Sister Magdeleine's book of 'Letters', nor did the opening of Mother Teresa's home for the poor of Rome inside the walls of the Vatican, and nor did the papal reception of Dr Kurt Waldheim, the Austrian President. Indeed, John Paul II's every major step was closely followed, as was the progress of the case for the beatification of 'Brother Charles'. Even when confined to bed, Little Sister Magdeleine would still write up to fifty letters on the one day of the week she set aside to deal with the mail that poured in to her from all over the world. She wrote to her Little Sisters, to Father Voillaume, to clerics and religious of all denominations, to Salvation Army members, and to friends of all nationalities and faiths. Her fidelity in friendship was a characteristic for which many would remember her. She would go out of her way staunchly to defend the reputation of a friend even when others were critical and she would travel many miles just to renew an old acquaintance. Her 1987 visits behind the Iron Curtain were made in a state of dependence on the power that was made perfect in weakness. Her lung was by this time causing her difficulties to the extent that she was obliged to carry an oxygen cylinder with her on her travels, but she went on regardless, praying resolutely for the strength to be able to see all those who waited for her so expectantly each year.

By the time September 1987 brought the Fraternity's Sixth General Chapter, Little Sister Magdeleine was doubtful about her ability to read to the assembly a letter she had written on 26 June during an interlude of quiet and rest she had spent at Regelsbrunn. She felt too tired even to attend some of the opening meetings but, like any other Little Sister, she had the right to draw the attention of the Chapter to those issues she considered important, and when the moment came and the capitulars gathered in a room close to hers so that she would not have to go out to another building she discovered 'an unbelievable vigour' which enabled her to read the letter, especially the passages which were closest to her heart. Essentially the letter, which she also sent out to the fraternities throughout the world in order that they might be united with the Chapter in prayer, was a reassertion of the spirit and form she had called for on many previous occasions. Her life's journey had not been marked by any obvious evolution of her message. It had, it seemed, been received in all its simplicity and its profundity in the earliest days of the Fraternity. In many respects she was calling for greater fidelity to the Constitutions and the legacy of Charles de Foucauld, for open-armed hospitality, for the joy of obedience in faith and love. She spoke of how it saddened her when she heard her Little Sisters judging harshly the Church which was the body of Christ and the people of God. If there were deficiencies in the Church, she informed them, they must be attributed to the human limitations of the people of which it was compiled. She told them also and by no means for the first time that, whilst they had no mission to teach, that did not mean they did not have one to evangelise. She defended the Fraternity's special consecration to their Islamic brothers and the idea of 'substitution', of offering prayers and suffering in the name of others. Louis Massignon, one of the first disciples of Charles de Foucauld, had founded the *Badaliya* – the Arabic word for 'substitution' – members of which offered their prayers and their suffering in the name of their Muslim brothers and sisters. It was an idea based on a theology of the redemption according to which Christ had been the first to substitute himself for humankind by offering his suffering unto death for the salvation of humanity. In this spirit the Little Sisters in factories and elsewhere had the opportunity to offer themselves in lieu of others to undertake the roughest, most dangerous work or at least to assume in their hearts the difficulties and the suffering of others and carry them to God.

There were delicate issues to be tackled in the course of the Chapter. Given the not unlimited availability of Little Sisters, for a long time now there had been a conflict of interests between the requirements of the sections and those of the regions. The subject had become a contentious one, but Little Sister Magdeleine held fast to her conviction that the sections and section assistants who would represent them in the government of the Fraternity had an irreplaceable role to play in its life. She had words of praise for her Little Sisters also. She spoke to them of her joy at all the positive things she had encountered in her journeys to visit them and in the letters they wrote from the four corners of the world. There were, however, some Little Sisters who felt that she was resistant to the changes that were taking place in the religious life as a whole, particularly in relation to the wearing of the habit and to the authority of superiors. In the twilight of her life she felt obliged to point out that from its very initiation the Fraternity had been in the forefront of change to the point of being adjudged scandalous and that she herself walked gladly along the pathway of the evolution that was taking place in the modern world provided people remained alert to possible deviations. What she could not accept as part of that evolution was the gradual erosion of the role of responsibles, judged by some to be unnecessary in the light of the maturity of the groups in their charge. Nor could she accept the rejection of the religious habit, particularly when the motive for abandoning it was the desire not to be associated with the institutional Church. For a Little Sister it should rather be a question of being the means by which the Church of the poor, the Church of Helder Camara, Oscar Romero and so many others, came to be loved. She wanted the Fraternity to correspond ever more closely with the mentality of different countries and changing epoques but above all she wanted it to be a clear reflection of the face of the God of love. Characteristically Little Sister Magdeleine's letter concluded with 'A Little Remark'. The Little Sisters' practice of calling her 'Mother' was becoming a source of growing embarrassment to her. She was constantly having to explain the appellation to members of the public, but she was tired of these daily explanations. Could they not, at least in public, address her as 'Little Sister Magdeleine'?

Some of the changes that were introduced at the 1987 General Chapter were a source of personal regret to her. One of the ideas to which she had always been deeply attached was that of the Little Sisters from all over the world making their final professions in Rome, at the heart of the Church. Many of the Little Sisters were content to complete their noviciate there but they also expressed the wish to go back to their own countries to make their final vows where their families, their parishes and their villages could all be fully part of their commitment. For a long time Little Sister Magdeleine herself had been saddened that parents from distant continents could not always come to Rome for the occasion of their daughters' profession. She recorded in her 'Letters',

> And suddenly it seemed to me that the Lord was asking me to sacrifice what, in my great love for the Church and the Holy Father, I had been so attached to since the beginning of the foundation: the final profession of all the Little Sisters in Rome. It really seemed that this was what the Lord was asking me to do and that it was one of the consequences and requirements of our universality.

Her sisters knew what a sacrifice this was for her. They had never really dreamt that she would agree to it and when she did there was long applause from the capitulars and a whole procession of Little Sisters from distant continents came to embrace her.

Other changes were possibly even harder for Little Sister Magdeleine to accept. Although, after much discussion, the Chapter ratified most of the sections, there were nuances of change implied in some instances by a change of vocabulary. The section for the 'diffusion' of the heritage of Charles de Foucauld, the history of the Fraternity and the Christmas message, for example, became a 'service'. To Little Sister Magdeleine's undoubted disappointment, however, the section for the sick was suppressed. It was with regret also that she accepted the relinquishing of the habit in certain instances, with the approval of the regional Responsible and the General Responsible. Some of the Little Sisters had arrived for the Chapter without their veils. Their foundress was at ease with considerable diversity in the style of the habit provided it was of a particular blue, and made up of ordinary, simple material. She considered trousers with a long top which came to within a few inches of the knee, for example, as eminently suitable attire for her Little Sisters, but as far as she was concerned the absence of the veil meant they were in civilian clothes. In the end the Constitutions which had once more to be revised to accommodate the changes of the Chapter retained the wearing of the religious habit with the modification that in certain circumstances 'civilian clothes' could be worn provided they were simple and preferably blue. Little Sister Magdeleine insisted on the expression 'civilian clothes' because, as she put it, 'when Little Sisters are without a veil, with different blouses in the same fraternity, you cannot talk about a "religious habit".' She asked too that those Little Sisters who wished to retain the habit should not be pressurised into abandoning it. The foundress accepted the decisions of the Chapter as the will of God for the Fraternity at that point. Afterwards she wrote a very gracious and characteristic letter, reflecting her hurt and simultaneously her joy, acknowledging that her acceptance had not been without tears but reaffirming her acquiescence:

> Despite those things that were a little painful for me, I did not lose a sense of peace and joy for a single moment. The Lord helped me and Charles (de Provenchères) accompanied me.
>
> . . . Furthermore I have the impression that this Chapter has drawn the Little Sisters and me closer together, even though I dared to tell them everything that was in my heart. My hand so frequently put up to ask to speak didn't seem to make anyone impatient.

If there was great humility in Little Sister Magdeleine, there was also a deep desire not to alienate her Little Sisters. In the past she had shown that unity of the Council was to her something so beautiful that it was worthy of preservation even when it went counter to her own wishes. At General Chapter meetings participants voted by means of red and white balls. On one particular issue the count after the vote revealed that the white balls far outnumbered the red. In front of everyone present, Little Sister Magdeleine admitted, 'Oh, I put a red ball but count me with the white.' On another occasion when everyone apart from Little Sister Magdeleine was in agreement with the General Responsible, their foundress told them: 'Even if I don't agree with you, if you are all in agreement, I shall join you. Unity is important.'

She wanted to be one with them and to that end a certain wisdom came into play. 'She suffered but she kept quiet,' Father Voillaume elaborated some time after the 1987 Chapter. He had himself been tempted in the course of his talks to the sisters to speak out about the movement towards secularisation but Little Sister Magdeleine was listening from her bed in the adjoining room. She warned him to be careful: 'Don't burn your bridges. You must maintain the influence you have. You have to know when to keep quiet about certain things. When you know that people will not follow what you say, it is better not to speak.' When the point came where Little Sister Magdeleine was too ill to take part in meetings and work went on on the Constitutions without her, some of the Little Sisters would go and report to her in the evening. Sometimes Little Sister Jeanne would ask her: 'Does that word really convey what you would have liked to say?' 'Leave them,' she replied. 'They like that sort of word'.

It was a source of particular joy to her that the elections held at the 1987 Chapter resulted in the appointment of the first non-European General Responsible. Little Sister Iris-Mary was a South African who had grown up in Cape Town's coloured area, 'District Six'. She was one of two children who, because her father suffered from tuberculosis, went to work at an early age in order that her brother might have the education considered more important to him because he was a boy. She hated the work altering dresses in a shop, but never resented her supportive role. Rather she was proud of it. Her first contact with the Fraternity was through three Little Sisters she came to know in her area. It was only after some time, however, that she discovered that 'I was the poor they had come to live with.' She was drawn to Little Sister Magdeleine's vision of the Fraternity as a place where there was no apartheid in any sense of the word and that belief was never to be dispelled. She had completed her noviciate in Europe, spent some time in England, working at one point in a jam factory in Leeds, and then returned to South Africa where for some years she had served as regional responsible in the sisters' house in Johannesburg.

'I am very conscious', she said in response to Little Sister Carla's enquiry whether she was willing to accept the responsibility the Fraternity wanted to entrust to her, 'of the fact that the Fraternity was begun by Little Sister Magdeleine, and that Little Sister Jeanne, and then Little Sister Annie and Little Sister Carla have given it everything that they are. And now I arrive . . . I am bound to be a bit different.' Little Sister Iris-Mary believed that the fact that different expressions had been brought to the spirit of the Fraternity by successive General Responsibles while Little Sister Magdeleine was still alive was of considerable value. Even if there were those who felt that in reality Little Sister Magdeleine still held on to her authority, the fact that the foundress had officially ceased to hold overall responsibility for the Fraternity and submitted to different ways of expressing its ideal was important. The manner in which she could write supporting alterations to the Constitutions which were not of her instigation underlined the fact that Little Sister Magdeleine was not one to resent 'differences'. That did not prevent her, even as she approached her ninetieth birthday, from having heated disagreements with her General Responsible, but she was still swift to insist that as far as she was concerned no lasting shadows had been cast and to ask forgiveness of one whose will she was glad to obey out of love for God and for her. 'Don't worry,' she wrote after one such clash, in handwriting that was still remarkable for its neatness, 'you are still the one who represents the Lord for me. Have no more fear. I ask your forgiveness. I was not fully aware. I shall try to do better.'

Little Sister Magdeleine spent her ninetieth birthday at Tre Fontane. As midnight struck on the eve of 26 April the sound of the Little Sisters singing a Latin American birthday song resounded from the meeting room. An early-morning religious broadcast on Italian radio took as its subject that day a sister who had walked with a great deal of difficulty but who still exuded surprising vitality: 'Bent in her chair,' it reported, 'she writes, responds to so many letters, receives people, plans, dreams. She would still like to go to the ends of the earth . . .' Throughout that day there were garlands, bouquets, embraces, greetings from the Little Sisters, their parents and families, from friends at the Luna Park, and from countless others. At the conclusion of a celebratory mass a blessing and birthday wishes from Pope John Paul II were read aloud. The festivities continued with a celebration by the various generations of Little Sisters of the history of the Fraternity and the life of its foundress. Next day she received yet another blessing from the Pope, written in his own hand on a picture of Our Lady of the Whole World. It was true that she was still ready to go to the ends of the earth. 'Don't ask that I live for much longer,' she had told her sisters in thanking them for their tribute, 'I long so much for paradise. . . . I have lived so much that I am exhausted.' Nevertheless she wrote immediately to thank the Pope for his double benediction because the very next day she was leaving in the 'Shooting Star' for Le Tubet where her birthday celebrations were to continue. From there she planned to go on to Poland, the Soviet Union and Yugoslavia passing through East Germany and Czechoslovakia. The North Korean ambassador had also offered her a visa for his country, she informed Pope John Paul II. It was a country which she had long wanted to visit and where she would like to see a fraternity opened but she did not know whether it was the will of God, '. . . because of my state of health, because one can't go there in a car'.

Wherever her 'Shooting Star' could go, however, she was still prepared to go there with it. In 1988 she spent a month on the road visiting sisters and friends behind the Iron Curtain and rejoicing in the change of political climate in the Soviet Union. The rigours of the journey brought on another bout of bronchial pneumonia from which she doubted whether she would recover. By 8 January 1989, however, she was able to write that she had been as far as the gates of paradise but that they had not yet opened to receive her. Gradually she recovered. Her time was divided largely between her bed and her wheelchair, 'but working more than ever because my head is ever more active'. She went on applying herself assiduously to the history of the Fraternity as recorded in the 'Letters'. On 31 January she was delighted at last to be able to announce to her Little Sisters that the Congregation for Religious and Secular Institutes had given its definitive approval to the Fraternity's Constitutions. After fifty years she had at last seen a version which could be presented to her Little Sisters as something more than provisional.

Still people came to see her. In March she received a visit from Chiara Lubich, foundress of the Focolare movement, whom she had long wanted to meet and with whom she shared a commitment to the spirituality of Nazareth and the ideal of unity. 'I felt', Chiara Lubich afterwards told the Little Sisters, 'that we have the same spirituality in many things but in different forms.' Little Sister Magdeleine continued to keep her finger on the pulse of world affairs. At a gathering of the Association of the Spiritual Families of Charles de Foucauld on 29 March she spoke of the 'extraordinary transformations Gorbachev was gradually bringing about'. 'How is your health?' one of the White Sisters, who had been a novice with Little Sister Magdeleine at Saint Charles-Birmandreis so many years previously, wrote to her in April 1989. 'It didn't seem brilliant to me during the noviciate, and yet you remain so full of vigour.'

Her ninety-first birthday came and went, again with much festivity, and in June 1989 Little Sister Magdeleine made her thirty-third journey behind the Iron Curtain, and her eighteenth to the Soviet Union. The muscles in her neck had lost their strength years before. She frequently had to prop her head up with her hand but the will to do whatever was required of her was still undaunted. Travelling stretched out on a bunk, she went armed with her letter to President Gorbachev and the reply from the deputy director of customs. On the Little Sisters' entry into the USSR a customs officer in heavy boots accidentally broke the skylight of the 'Shooting Star' as he clambered down from the roof in the process of searching the vehicle.

The skylight had to be repaired with adhesive tape but the journey continued across Russia with the drivers taking it in two-hour relays. Now they could meet openly with the Little Sisters there. On the streets of Moscow musicians and poets were openly extolling the virtues of *perestroika* or criticising the government. Craftwork on religious subjects was on sale. Religious belonging to the Ukrainian Uniate Church dressed in habits held up placards inscribed with the words: 'We demand the rehabilitation and legalisation of the Ukrainian Catholic Church and the reopening of our churches'. Father Alexander Men, the Orthodox priest who had served as the Little Sisters' priest in Moscow, prayed aloud in Little Sister Magdeleine's presence, then turning to face her, he told her: 'There is a Russian proverb that says: "You recognise your friends when times are hard" . . . You came to us several times when times were hard and we know that you have been our friend for a long time.' He went on to point out that now that the Church was in the process of being reconstructed in Russia, now that great spiritual strength was needed, her visit was even more important. The fact that the young people of Russia could at least wear their crosses openly meant that the time had come for them to show that they were worthy of doing so. The time of trial had really come. On leaving Russia the Little Sisters took the precaution this time of showing their two letters to the officer in charge of customs. In consequence there was no security check, no one climbed on the roof or looked inside the vehicle. 'This was definitely the first time we have crossed a Soviet frontier in this way,' noted Little Sister Magdeleine. 'Then we went through the barrier, a little moved to be leaving a country so dear to us.'

She had intended to go on from Austria to make her annual visits to Yugoslavia and Hungary, but it was not to be. The extreme cold during her journey across Poland from the Soviet Union affected her badly. For a while she remained in Regelsbrunn. Tired and running a fever, while the Little Sisters of Regelsbrunn set about bringing in their harvest of straw, she worked on at her writing table. The jubilee of the Fraternity was approaching. In August 1989 the Fraternity would be fifty years old. There would be celebrations at Le Tubet on 3 September and at Tre Fontane on the 8th, and she wanted to write a letter to her Little Sisters to mark the occasion. It was to a large extent a letter outlining the early history of the Fraternity for the benefit of those generations of Little Sisters who had not lived through it. It reiterated the importance of the spiritual values which Little

Sister Magdeleine had always emphasised, and it gave thanks to God for all the achievements that were so manifestly his. Its author claimed it was a rambling letter. She liked to write letters, she maintained, as she spoke, without too much preparation, spontaneously so that God could bring the necessary light. By then she was obviously looking to the future of the Fraternity without her. Could her Little Sisters not give her a present on the fiftieth anniversary of her profession: the promise that they would make a generous effort with regard to obedience? she wrote,

> I have no recollection of any real disobedience, but your obedience is not always as joyous, as light as that of a young wife who is so happy to fulfil the least desire of the one she loves . . . and who can be loved more than the Lord?

After she had gone, she assured them, they would have Father Voillaume, who had aided and comforted her through difficult moments, to guide them along the path of Brother Charles. They would also have Little Sister Jeanne without whom she could have done nothing and who was her second self. She asked for the Little Sisters to show special affection for those who had been amongst the first ten who had shared with her the arduous and sometimes quite incomprehensible years of the foundation, and for the General Responsibles who carried the responsibility of government. To all her Little Sisters she expressed her thanks for their love and understanding. There were very few things that she felt they had not understood, very few that they had not granted her.

It seemed she could not resist the opportunity, however, to enumerate those things which she felt had been denied her and to make a further attempt at stressing their importance. Still the need for sections and for the wearing of the habit manifestly preyed upon her mind. She had also long wanted a fraternity reopening amongst the pygmies of Mbao and new ones founding in Barcelona and Bordeaux. The war that had followed the independence of Zaire, in which several Little Brothers had been killed, had necessitated the closure of the original fraternity in Mbao. The Little Sisters understood their foundress's attachment to the pygmies but to date another foundation had not been practicable. Little Sister Magdeleine's preoccupation with Barcelona and Bordeaux was less readily comprehensible. In the case of Barcelona, she had simply resolved that once there were ten Little Sisters from Barcelona, a fraternity should be opened there. There were now ten Little Sisters from Barcelona but the Fraternity could not see any other, more rational reason for opening a fraternity there. In the case of Bordeaux, she had looked at the map one day and noticed that there were fraternities in the West and South of France but that they were conspicuously absent from the South-west region of Bordeaux. Her Sisters, however, were less inclined to stretch their resources merely to fill in a gap on the map of France. Perhaps Little Sister Magdeleine had other reasons yet to be revealed for what was something of an obsession, for often her real intuitions found expression in very practical desires. On her death-bed, scarcely able to speak, she would raise three fingers in an attempt finally to make her point. 'Mbao, Barcelona and Bordeaux?' Little Sister Iris-Mary would enquire, and the foundress nodded then in confirmation. For the moment, however, she asked for them as a gift to mark her jubilee year before she left her sisters for paradise.

On her arrival at Le Tubet, confined as she was for the most part to her room, she could only sense the mounting excitement as the days of celebration approached. Little Sisters poured in from all over the world but she had only the energy to see a few of them privately. On 2 September after a mass celebrated by Father Le Sourd, she joined her sisters in a meeting room. It had been decorated with paper flowers in a multitude of colours and with a large inscription of the phrase that was the leitmotiv of her whole life: 'The Lord took me by the hand and I followed him blindly.' She started to read her jubilee letter but her strength failed her and Little Sister Jeanne had to finish the task for her. Next day a celebratory mass was held outside in the shade of the plane trees. From her wheelchair positioned so that she could see the proceedings from a first storey window, Little Sister Magdeleine joined in the mass, watched as fifty balloons were launched into the air and finally, by means of a microphone system, thanked all those who had come to take part in the festivities. Some of them had even helped with the foundation of Le Tubet in 1941. Some were friends she had come to know through the fraternity for prostitutes in Marseille, whose recognition of her preferential love for them had brought them to join in the thanksgiving celebrations. From the ground below Little Sister Iris-Mary responded by thanking the foundress for having had the courage to continue 'even when it was very difficult . . . even when we were very difficult'.

There were a multitude of farewells to be paid as the Little Sisters returned to their fraternities throughout the world. Finally, on 5

September Little Sister Magdeleine herself left Le Tubet to continue the jubilee festivities in Rome. Before doing so she was taken to the stables to meet two calves that had been born for the festival and a goose which impressed her with its tameness. She left apparently content. Her previous departures had all borne the hallmark of her insatiable desire for perfection. She would praise the Little Sisters for their kindness but there had always been a qualifying 'but': 'but you don't love each other enough'; 'but you have left a dead leaf on the table and it shouldn't be there'; 'but you should really remove those decaying branches from that tree'. This time the qualification, even one that might be considered trivial by those less exacting in their horticultural or domestic requirements, was conspicuously absent.

❧ 10 ❧

If a Friendship is of God . . .

'IF I HAD TO START my life all over again,' Little Sister Magdeleine once told a journalist, 'I would do the same, with, I hope, much more love and without the tactlessness and mistakes.' In her old age she felt as young at heart as she had ever done, perhaps even younger because now she was full of confidence in those who had replaced her in the position of command. As to the prospect of death: 'Why should the heart tremble when the Lord is sustaining it and when one is approaching a meeting which one has yearned and waited for, for so long?' In the last months of her life Little Sister Magdeleine was called upon to live in an ever more explicit way the message of the Nativity and the Passion on which she had centred her being. The journey back to Rome from Le Tubet was an arduous one. En route on 5 September she paused for a while at Tassy in the south of France where Mgr Mercier, who as Apostolic Prefect of the Sahara had played a crucial role in the birth of the Fraternity, was now living in a home for elderly priests. The old man wept for joy at the reunion and when, finally, the time came for Little Sister Magdeleine to leave, he said he would see her again in paradise. 'I can't wait,' she replied with conviction. That same evening as she stepped out of the 'Shooting Star' at the fraternity in Carnoles where she was due to spend the night, she fell without quite knowing how, and fractured her right femur. In extreme pain but without complaint, she made the journey back to Tre Fontane. There it was decided that in view of her age it would be inadvisable to operate. Her Little Sisters did not want to subject her to the trauma of admission to hospital. They were also fearful that a general anaesthetic might impair the lucidity of her mind. Instead, in the hope that the bones would weld, her right leg was placed in traction, but the process undoubtedly caused her dreadful discomfort. By then she weighed little more than thirty kilos. A four-

247

kilo weight was applied to her leg and for someone as thin as she was the consequences of enforced immobility were considerable.

Obliged at last to accept that she would never return, as she had always wanted, to the tiny cell adjacent to her office, she resolved that what had once been the room reserved for hippies should be her *Thebaide*, a word associated with the fourth-century desert fathers, implying a hermitage of prayer and retreat. Since 1 October of the previous year the Blessed Sacrament had been reserved in that room behind an icon of Our Lady of Vladimir. Above it hung a cross made by a Russian prisoner which had been given to her in the Soviet Union, and beside it was suspended a lamp sent to her by the Little Sisters in Greece. The hippies' room became indeed a place of contemplation and surrender. As her helplessness increased, her sisters asked her what they could do to relieve her condition. 'We must accept,' she told them and it was a peaceful and undramatic acceptance in which the ordinary and the everyday still had its place. Little Sister Magdeleine had long been someone who lived the transcendent even whilst being fully present on earth, one in whom holiness and union with God was so completely absorbed into daily life that to some it was not even noticeable. Some Little Sisters had even been known to ask whether their foundress prayed because even before she was actually confined to her bed she had so rarely appeared in chapel other than for mass. A woman of faith and humility, her will was totally subordinated to the will of God and so her life had quite naturally become contemplative, without the need always to express the fact in articulated prayer. Reduced in height by twenty centimetres, hunched up in her bed, with her head continually falling forward on her strained neck, in quiet moments when she was not sleeping her eyes would focus on the Reserved Sacrament. Asked then as she looked back on her life how she had coped with the enormous problems she had encountered, she replied with a gesture towards the little tabernacle in the wall, 'There was always the Lord.' Then, when it was put to her that God did not always make problems disappear just like that, she added: 'There was Little Sister Jeanne too . . .' As always there was no separation between the supernatural and the natural.

Not long before her death, a service to mark the end of a year of formation for those making their final vows was held at St Peter's, but not as usual in the crypt at the tomb of St Peter. Instead, it was held in the Hungarian Chapel, set a little apart, behind a closed grille.

There the Little Sisters were removed from the noise and bustle of sightseers looking round the church. It was a quiet and beautiful ceremony, but when Little Sister Iris-Mary returned to Tre Fontane Little Sister Magdeleine had already received reports of the peace and tranquillity of the occasion: 'I hope you too are not going to tell me that it was a very beautiful ceremony.' 'Yes, it was very beautiful,' responded the General Responsible, only to be told by the foundress that she had not initiated the Fraternity so that the Little Sisters could be comfortable together. The Fraternity's vocation was not to be cloistered but to be religious in the midst of the world. 'Our ceremonies may not always be very ordered, but so what!' Out of consideration for those of her Little Sisters for whom French was a foreign language Little Sister Magdeleine rarely resorted to slang but she did so on this occasion to reinforce the strength of her feeling.

In her weakness and her pain she remained as alert as ever to all kinds of things. When Little Sister Iris-Mary mistakenly referred to a cat of which the foundress was particularly fond with the feminine article, the error was still not allowed to pass uncorrected: 'It's not a she, it's a he,' came the sharp rejoinder. When a meal was not cooked as she felt it should have been, she did not hesitate to try and remedy the situation: 'You cooked the brains for too long,' she instructed the Little Sister responsible. 'Go and fetch my mother's cookery book.' She had carefully kept Madame Hutin's cookery book for all those years and knew exactly where it was to be found.

She still wanted to express her thanks personally for all the letters and gifts she had received for the jubilee. Choosing a phrase herself, she had it photocopied. To this, one of her Little Sisters added a personalised note but then, asked whether her name should just be typed at the end, Little Sister Magdeleine insisted on trying to sign it herself. Six times she tried with desperate tenacity until she finally achieved a signature which satisfied her and which could then be photocopied. To the last, she wanted her work table to be as carefully ordered as it always had been and gave directions from a distance as to how it should be arranged. At the same time her attitude was very much that of a child turning to her Father. Her sisters saw in the way she reached out her arms to them to be raised up on her pillows the reflection of the gesture she had so frequently called upon them to emulate, that of the infant Jesus whom she loved and who was constantly before her.

On 19 September Little Sister Magdeleine received the Sacrament of the Sick from Father Voillaume. At the moment of absolution she asked forgiveness of all her Little Sisters for the suffering she may have caused them during her life. She asked forgiveness of those who had been closest to her and she asked God to forgive her for all the occasions on which she had lacked charity, love or patience. Until 10 October, despite her obvious fatigue, the sisters held on to hope of her recovery. On 10 October the doctor removed the weight from her leg. The release brought her temporary relief but the bones had not welded and her strength continued to drain away from her. Despite solicitous care, it had been impossible to prevent her emaciated body from developing sores. On the 20th she suffered an attack of pulmonary oedema which was subsequently arrested but thereafter she often had difficulty in breathing. Too tired now to see her Little Sisters, she asked for their understanding. She wanted only to be alone with God. For the two medically qualified sisters to whose constant care she was entrusted it was hard to watch this decline. They knew that she was not receiving enough nourishment in the small quantity of food that she consumed but she did not want to be sustained by artificial means. As far as Little Sister Magdeleine was concerned her moment had come. She accepted the attentiveness afforded her because this was the care that she had always maintained the Little Sisters should give to their elderly parents, but she did not want to delay any longer the moment when the hidden presence of the tabernacle which she had revered in fraternities throughout the world would be at last unveiled. Even Father Voillaume, who took the general view that on medical matters doctors should make the decisions, after talking to Little Sister Magdeleine herself, felt that she should have her way.

At several points during the beginning of November she thought the gates of paradise were at last about to open for her. Several times, in Father Voillaume's absence, she asked for Father Le Sourd to come and bless her. On 1 November, when those around her thought that she was about to leave them, another Little Sister died elsewhere. The Little Sister engaged in changing Little Sister Magdeleine's dressings at the time afterwards recalled how that very day, her patient had inquired of her: 'Who has died? Are you hiding something from me?' She took the presentiment as a measure of the foundress's love. Little Sister Magdeleine knew her Little Sisters, even those whom she saw only briefly before they left for distant destinations. She loved each one of them profoundly and she wanted them to know that. She

250

also wanted them to love one another. A few days before her death, when Little Sister Iris-Mary was obliged to leave for Africa and the two women thought they would never see each other again, the foundress's farewell directions were: 'You must love Father Voillaume. Love this house, love Little Sister Jeanne because I could not have done anything without her. . . .' She could have spoken of the necessity to be childlike in heart, of obedience or other spiritual matters. Instead, she spoke of concrete things.

It was somehow particularly appropriate that, on 5 November after praying with a small group of Little Sisters gathered in her room, she should have expressed her spiritual legacy for the Fraternity in a series of almost wordless gestures. In the last weeks of her life when she was able to speak only with difficulty it was remarkable to some how everything she could not actually say passed through her eyes. Little Sister Magdeleine had a beautiful profile but her sisters acknowledged that in life they had scarcely noticed it because of the striking quality of her eyes. In 1992 one who had been a Little Sister for eight years but who subsequently left and married, wrote of how Little Sister Magdeleine's whole being was consumed with love and of how 'Her face had become quite small but her eyes transmitted such a force of love which was no longer hers: Jesus was speaking through her.' With hands that were also still remarkably expressive, she pointed to the statue of Our Lady of the Whole World which stood on a table in her room, to a statue of Saint Joseph with the child Jesus on her cupboard, and to a photograph of the Pope with Our Lady of Fátima.

That night, as Little Sister Iris-Mary, having returned from Africa, went with others to say goodnight to her, she took the General Responsible's hand and kissed it in a gesture that was not, it seemed to Little Sister Jeanne, simply one of affection but an expression of her remission of everything into the hands of the one in whose charge she was leaving the Fraternity. That night also she made a point of thanking various Little Sisters. 'Are you leaving us?' Little Sister Jeanne finally asked. 'I've no idea,' was the simple reply. Later, as she struggled to breathe in the early morning hours, she told Little Sister Jeanne that she was happy to be going. Next morning she was manifestly astonished to be still there but, since she had not died, for her it was immediately a question of resuming life. She gave directions to be put in her chair at her table, and asked for a lamp and a notebook: 'I shall need at least four days of peace to recuperate. Make me some light dishes . . .' In fact that afternoon her breathing became laboured again. Several times she was heard to say that she had never thought it would take so long, that she could wait no longer, and that she wanted to go to paradise. Her wish was finally granted that evening as those nursing her were in the process of arranging her bed and her dressings for the night. In the words of Little Sister Iris-Mary, her death was 'ordinary . . . unspectacular, nothing special, a moment between her and her Lord'.

At Tre Fontane the night of 6 to 7 November 1989 was spent informing the Little Sisters throughout the world of the demise of their foundress. Father Voillaume, who was on his way to Morocco at the time, was notified via the fraternity at El Abiodh. As the news spread to newspapers, radio and television, messages of sympathy, friendship and thanksgiving for the life of Little Sister Magdeleine poured in from the Pope, from Brother Roger of Taizé and a multitude of others. Little Sisters began to arrive from all directions. So too did friends from far and wide. One cardinal came on foot 'as if on pilgrimage' to pray beside her body. Beside it stood the paschal candle; before it was a bas relief of the infant Jesus made by one of the Little Sisters which Little Sister Magdeleine had asked to have placed upon her tomb. A sand rose from Touggourt called to mind the many friends in Algeria and the beginnings of the Fraternity; some ears of corn came from the sisters at Grandchamp; a bouquet of roses was the gift of a long-standing friend whose family were among the neighbours of a fraternity in a sprawling concrete jungle of highrise flats erected to house the former slum dwellers of Rome. A group of Russian seminarists from the Russicum came to sing their office for the dead. Later members of the Greek College in Rome came to take their turn. In all offices were sung in Arabic, Russian, Ukrainian and Greek.

The farewell mass was held next morning in the open air because even the sizeable chapel at Tre Fontane could not accommodate the number of Little Sisters and friends present. The coffin was placed outside on a bed of sand and surrounded by mats on which some three hundred Little Sisters took their places. Little Sister Magdeleine had left a will which she had requested be circulated to all the Little Sisters immediately upon her death. She had written it first at Easter 1982, revised it in September 1988, and then again in August 1989. In doing so she knew she ran the risk of being criticised for attaching too much importance to what she believed God wanted for the Fraternity. She acknowledged this in her opening remarks, 'But to this day I have never taken any notice of what people thought of me in this respect, because I know only too well my poverty and wretchedness. If I believe that God has lit my way it is because it was he who obliged me to found . . .' And so she had gone on to outline those things to which she felt the Fraternity must remain faithful.

They were the same essentials: the Jesus of the manger; Our Lady of the Whole World; love for the heart of Jesus after the example of Charles de Foucauld; the imitation of Jesus the humble carpenter of Nazareth; love for the Church and the Pope; daily adoration of the exposed Blessed Sacrament; veneration for the Gospels; unity; special consecration to the people of Islam; universality; attachment to the Churches of the Eastern Rite; poverty; blind obedience; charity; solidarity with the indigent, the oppressed, with the victims of racial discrimination; insertion among prostitutes, prisoners, lepers and the mentally handicapped; the gratuitousness of hospitality; community life lived in small fraternities; love for parents . . . There were those who might have expected something fresh or in some respects more striking by way of a testament for their foundress, who were disappointed to find in it the same insistence on the importance of sections and section assistants to ensure the representation of the interests of the most forgotten in the Fraternity, and even the reiteration of the need for the religious habit that was very simple and poor and 'approximately 25 centimetres from the ground, even though you do not like the precise specification of numbers'. But Little Sister Magdeleine had never regarded such considerations as secondary. 'Secondary!' she had once put an interviewer, who had dared to query the manner in which one who had in many ways been in the vanguard of the Church could be so attached to such apparently secondary concerns, firmly in his place. 'The habit is not a secondary consideration for the Little Sisters,' she informed him. 'It is the evidence of their consecration to Christ in the Church and of their belonging to the world of the poor. It is the proof that this "institutional" Church which is so decried today, and of which the habit is the sign, once allowed a foundation, which in 1939 was not exactly traditional, to live inserted amongst the poor.' Unpredictable, apparently contradictory, spontaneous, faithful, trusting, ready to defend her corner but equally ready to ask forgiveness and never disheartened, she had sometimes offended, but more often, with a love that recognised no barriers, she had opened doors. Her testament was as true to herself as she had always been and the extraordinary assembly of people who gathered for her funeral was possibly her most eloquent defence.

The mass over which Father Voillaume presided was concelebrated by more than eighty priests from different continents and countries, some of them members of the spiritual family of Charles de Foucauld, many of them friends of numerous years. Among the cardinals present was a special representative of the Pope. A Greek Orthodox representative of the ecumenical Patriarch Dimitrios I, brothers from Taizé, sisters from Grandchamp, members of the Salvation Army, people from l'Arche and 'friends' from all walks of life bore witness to the extraordinary diversity and universality of the friendships born of a lifetime devoted to unity through love. Amongst the multitude of bouquets and funeral sheaves were flowers sent by 'all the Trappists of the world'. There were flowers too from the 'Management of the Luna Park'.

In a way that was quite unexpected Father Alexander Men, who less than a year later, on 9 September 1990, would lose his own life, assassinated in Moscow, was also able to be present. He had never previously left the Soviet Union. Prior to *perestroika* it had been impossible, and after it he had been in such demand to speak in his own country that he had chosen not to. Receiving an invitation to a symposium in Italy, he had made an exception, however, and chanced to hear of Little Sister Magdeleine's death from the Russian priests who had sung at the office for the dead. For the Little Sisters the unexpected presence of one who had formed so staunch a link with the country that had so called to Little Sister Magdeleine was something of a miracle. Nor did they fail to take into account the joy their foundress would have derived from the events that were happening in the Eastern bloc countries. On the eve of Little Sister Magdeleine's death the church bells rang in Red Square for the first time for seventy years. With the faith that 'could move mountains', she had always believed that the Berlin Wall would come down and on the day of her funeral it did.

Little Sister Magdeleine had wanted to be buried at Tre Fontane. The land there had once encompassed a form of catacombs and so a subterranean chapel had been constructed and permission had been granted for a number of Little Sisters to be laid to rest there. The permission for such entombments had subsequently been withdrawn, however, and had to be reapplied for after Little Sister Magdeleine's death. On 14 November her body was carried by her Little Sisters down to the cemetery grotto in the hillside at Tre Fontane but even then the wall which the Little Sisters built in front of the tomb had been a provisional one. Permission for them to keep Little Sister Magdeleine there was slow in coming and on 2 December they were informed that the Director of the Verano Cemetery required the body to be transported there and kept in the cemetery until such time as the demands of Italian bureaucracy had been met. Followed by some of her Little Sisters in cars and a van, Little Sister Magdeleine made yet another journey, this time through the noisy congestion of Rome's morning rush hour. She had made provision for most eventualities, even setting down the broad outline for the completion, after her death, of the ninth volume of her 'Letters' and choosing the cover picture – a photograph of herself waving a smiling goodbye. The thought that this somewhat unceremonial crossing of the metropolis was one journey that she had not foreseen was not without its mischievous appeal for the writer putting the finishing touches to that last volume. Finally, on 26 April 1990, Little Sister Magdeleine's birthday, her sisters were able to return her to Tre Fontane and lay her to rest in the spot which she had personally chosen. That same day Little Sister Iris Mary received a visa for Russia in her South African passport. Two years earlier she had been told by the foundress that one day she must go to Moscow. The General Responsible had pointed out to Little Sister Magdeleine that such a visit would not be possible for her, either with her South African passport or with a Vatican passport, but the older woman had simply continued, undeterred: 'And you will see how beautiful it is.'

Little Sister Magdeleine had left behind her a total of 280 fraternities comprising some sixty regions with 1,400 Little Sisters from sixty-four different nations. Her determination to break through every form of 'iron curtain' she encountered had in a multitude of instances produced tangible results. The very existence of Little Sisters who were native to the country and now bearing open witness to the love of God in Yugoslavia, Hungary, Czechoslovakia, Poland, East Germany, the Soviet Union and Romania was powerful evidence of this fact. Only North Korea remained as a target she had not quite reached. Such statistics had given Little Sister Magdeleine satisfaction. The joy had been visible on her face when she saw large numbers of Little Sisters with smiling faces gathered around her. There had been cause for sadness over the years. Fifty-two Little Sisters had died before her. Others had left the Fraternity they had helped to build. For a variety of reasons it had been necessary to close some fraternities: in certain slum areas properties occupied by the Little Sisters had had to be demolished; the opening of new fraternities in response to pressing priorities had sometimes necessitated the closure of others. The Little Sisters had had to live through and share all the consequences of war, revolution, division, injustice and inhumanity, but in this as in a multitude of other ways Little Sister Magdeleine had seen her intuition realised. In the Lebanon her sisters lived amongst people subjected to constant bombardment. Much of their time was spent in bomb shelters where some eighty people, babies, children, the elderly and the infirm, huddled together through nights rendered interminably long by gunfire and constant noise. The only respite came between the hours of seven and eight each evening when the men turned off their radios and people gathered to sit or kneel on the mattresses to pray. In Nicaragua where war and economic blockades were rendering the life of the poor even more intolerable the Little Sisters were involved with a group of poor peasants in a government project designed to restore the land. In North America and the more affluent countries of the West where the pursuit of materialism, the breakdown of family life and all the consequences of advancing technology served often to marginalise even further the weak, the lonely and the most vulnerable, the Little Sisters were there to bear witness to a life that was poor yet joyous and fulfilled. In the dreary-looking and often vandalised flats of the 'developed' world they were unemployed with the unemployed, and a witness to unity in cosmopolitan communities where even the gift of a home-made Christmas cake could be rejected by white neighbours because 'it came from a West Indian woman's kitchen'.

In Algiers, as political unrest divided local communities and a Christian presence was required to be increasingly discreet, the Little Sisters continued to live in an area where even taxi drivers frequently would not venture, creating deep bonds of friendship through mutual respect and shared vulnerability. Amongst the sick, they shared the poverty of dependence. Amongst the prisoners, prostitutes, homosexuals, transexuals, those caught up in the 'moral marginalisation' often inextricably bound up with other forms of poverty, in cities ranging from Bern to Amsterdam to Tokyo, they were there to recognise that the weakness that pervaded the lives of the morally vulnerable was also inherent in their own; and the closer they came to the people whose lives they shared the more they realised also that in lives that were often full of violence, the deliberate attempt to change them would be just one more violation of something very precious to humanity: individual freedom. In the snows of Alaska, in the tropical forests of Africa, amongst the Aborigines of Australia, in the *favellas* of South America, and the urban jungles of the West, amongst the hungry for bread and the hungry for spiritual food, the Little Sisters were affording the poorest and the least considered the respect they seldom found elsewhere. Furthermore, in solidarity with the pain of the world they were endeavouring to assume that suffering in prayer and bear witness to the love of God for all created beings. In tiny fraternities in slum dwellings, caravans and tents the Blessed Sacrament and the prayer of the Little Sisters radiated the presence of Jesus.

Little Sister Magdeleine had shown them a way of work and prayer and love. What was more she had left a Fraternity which was fully approved by the Church to which she had been so constantly obedient but which she had undoubtedly challenged. In the course of her lifetime she had seen nine successive Popes come and go, from Leo XIII to John Paul II, and as far as she was concerned they had all in their different ways reflected a desire to render the Church ever more present in the world of their day and more attentive to the dignity of the human person. She had witnessed so many signs of progress: the search for unity through ecumenism had become an ongoing one; the Eucharist had become the daily nourishment available to all, even little children; the understanding of the Church as the people of God had deepened and allowed for a greater collaboration of the laiety, both men and women; concelebration was permitted, as was the celebration of mass in the local language; the Bible was now accessible to all; the Pope, instead of remaining in the Vatican, walked in the streets and travelled the world. None of this had been the case in her childhood years. In the face of all these transformations, she had reasoned in 1983, how could she not believe in the progress of the Church and trust that it would continue to want to render the message of the gospel ever more accessible. She had always believed and hoped in the Church, and as far as she was concerned the Church had not let her down. 'The Little Sisters of Jesus', Pope John Paul II had said, 'have received from God the grace of inventing a new and original presence in the world of the poor, in the manner of Charles de Foucauld.' The Church had finally accepted the Fraternity as a new form of religious life.

257

If she had craved this recognition from the Church, she had wanted, too, a family spirit to prevail amongst the Little Sisters whom she had looked upon, not without a certain pride, as her daughters. She had seen them as a family and there were few, if any, in the Fraternity who would deny that she had succeeded. The fact that the Fraternity had retained French as its common language had undoubtedly contributed to this fact. Little Sister Magdeleine herself had wanted English to be a second language of the congregation but the number of Little Sisters who spoke English as their first language was limited, and those who came from 'Third World' countries for whom English was not actually their native tongue were often all too happy to learn French. All Little Sister Magdeleine's writings were in French, and the struggle to learn the language frequently created a bond amongst Little Sisters of wide-ranging nationalities first embarking on their studies. The diaries from the fraternities, although now only circulated once a year, still carried the news around the world and people still responded to their contents when they touched upon the 'family spirit'. What had appeared to some an eccentricity had shown itself to be of value. When Little Sisters visited or moved to other fraternities, they already knew the local people by proxy and 'friends' felt valued by such interest. In general there was a closeness between members of the Fraternity which meant that people who had not seen each other for many years or who had never met before were somehow immediately at ease with one another. That was not to suggest that there were not times when people in fraternities did not have enough of each other or indeed of the whole way of life, but that was only human. Certain Little Sisters at Tre Fontane might be peeved for a while when someone mistook their precious cheese for soap and placed it in the laundry, but that was all part of family life.

Pope John Paul II, on the occasion of the fiftieth anniversary of this 'family', had pointed out that its history was only just beginning. Saddened by the absence of Little Sister Magdeleine's physical presence, the Fraternity must nonetheless continue the work their foundress had begun. At a 'family gathering' shortly after her death, Little Sister Iris-Mary pointed out that each of the Little Sisters had joined the Fraternity because of an intuition which had stemmed from Little Sister Magdeleine and taken hold of their hearts, 'And we want to live that to the limits not because Little Sister Magdeleine said it but because we believe in it ourselves. Now the Fraternity is made by us all.' Little Sister Magdeleine's face, peaceful but strong in death as in life, had seemed to the General Responsible to say, 'I have done the running, I've done everything I could, now it's up to you.' The foundress had on more than one occasion assured her sisters that she would still be close to them in paradise. 'If you lack charity after my death,' she would tell them, 'I shall come and pinch you.' As early as 1947 she had written to Father Voillaume:

> If one fine day I die, at a moment when it is least expected . . .
> I entrust my Little Sisters to you. I shall be so close to them and
> you in heaven. I shall be able to be everywhere at once: in the
> Sahara, in the Ahaggar, in France, in Transjordania, in Russia,
> in Japan, amongst the Eskimos, in central Africa. . . . Father, if
> I could go, it would be so much more beautiful afterwards.
> The Little Sisters would suddenly grow and replace me so well.
> I would always be at their side, much more effectively than on
> earth.

There was no doubt in Father Voillaume's mind, as in the minds of many others, that Little Sister Magdeleine was still actively present to the Fraternity. What he revealed in response to the Little Sisters' expectations of a letter about his memories of more than fifty years of intimate collaboration with their foundress, in relation to 'her intimate life and the supernatural manifestations which marked her relations with God profoundly', shed further light upon the dynamic that had operated in her. The booklet entitled 'Jesus and Little Sister Magdeleine' which he put together in 1991 and its sequel 'Little Sister Magdeleine and the consummation of her love for Jesus', completed in 1992, explained many things. If for some these revelations were slightly shocking, and if others felt they might lead to the pursuit of precisely those 'extraordinary ways' from which Little Sister Magdeleine had consistently endeavoured to divert them, for yet others they were an illumination and the missing factor in the equation of her life. They explained the unrelenting insistence with which Little Sister Magdeleine had spoken of the Infant Jesus received from the hands of the Virgin Mary. They explained why Little Sister Magdeleine had sought to recapture this gesture in pictures and statues without ever really finding total satisfaction. Her Little Sisters had sometimes treated this quest lightly – after all, the works of art were beautiful – but she had been distressed and they had not always understood. The experiences she had kept such a closely guarded secret explained, also, all that she had written about the importance of being childlike at heart. It was not, she had maintained, by any effort solely on their part that they would manage to become like little children. Instead, it would be given to them to conceive within themselves and to become the infant of the gospel, the infant, simultaneously God and man, which contained Christ in his entirety . . . Christ the carpenter, the Christ of the Passion, the glorious Christ of the resurrection. They explained what she herself had become and what she had wanted them to be.

Referring to the supernatural manifestations which had so marked Little Sister Magdeleine, in 1991 Father Voillaume wrote to the Little Sisters: 'I felt myself all the more impelled to speak to you about them because it was by means of these graces that God showed what the Fraternity, its mission and its soul should be.' The challenge after the death of the foundress was how to go forward, not with that which related to her personality, but with the vital dynamic that had operated through her. In many respects the world had changed since first she had started building at Sidi Boujnan. The very nomadic way of life which had so captured her heart in the Sahara was under threat and increasingly people were abandoning an existence so precariously dependent on waterholes, grazing and the availability of salt. In the villages of the Ahaggar the men worked for at least part of the year on building sites. Their homes had gardens in which they kept a few sheep. The world of Islam, to which the Fraternity had been dedicated in a special way from the very beginning, was in considerable turmoil. *Perestroika* and the breakdown of Communist power had brought significant changes to the Fraternity's calling to be a hidden presence of prayer behind the Iron Curtain. Indeed, the idea of the 'hidden life' in general was not one which now enjoyed the appeal that it once had. The feeling amongst Christians in France in particular but in other countries also was that the time had come to be visible and to speak out. The pressure to become more overt and active became particularly pronounced in countries where there was manifestly much to be done. In places where many people were in desperate need of education and other forms of assistance, it was hard to resist the call to more tangible ways of meeting that need.

Vocations from Europe were not now as readily forthcoming as in the early days of the Fraternity. Viewed from the perspective of one Little Sister from the Orient, in relatively stable materialistic societies, people did not have their dependency on God brought home to them quite so obviously as those who contended daily with the suffering of war and famine. It was a mark of the insecurity of the times, however, that those in Europe who did feel called to follow God in the religious life were being attracted now to more structured communities. It was also a reality that the Fraternity's life had never been as firmly established in the English-speaking world as elsewhere.

Little Sister Magdeleine had never considered the possibility of the Fraternity not continuing. She had never spoken or written as if the eventuality entered into her thinking. Little Sister Iris-Mary, who did not believe that the Fraternity's apostolate should be changed for something more overtly active, held the conviction that precisely because it did not have a very specific apostolate and because its calling was to be as close to the gospel as possible, it would always have some form of future. The number of Little Sisters might not be so large, the Fraternity might have to adapt in many ways, but she believed deeply in the spirituality on which it was founded, in the fact that one did not have to preach the gospel in order to evangelise. She believed that the poor and the vulnerable, whether they mentioned the name of God or not, frequently lived very close to him, and she believed in the Little Sisters' role to recognise the dignity in all people and to befriend them.

There were still some who failed to recognise the value of such a vocation. It was, after all, a life that defied evaluation. In the gypsy fraternity in France one Little Sister looked so very like a gypsy that when she walked into a department store, an announcement was made to shoppers to take particular care of their wallets and handbags. Being one with the travelling people to whom she had consecrated her life meant knowing what it was to be taken for a thief on the strength of her appearance alone. The growth of understanding arising from experiences such as this, the assumption of another's suffering, the effect of the leaven in the dough, was frequently immeasurable. It was hard at times for the Little Sisters themselves to believe in the value of knowing what it was to walk the streets of Leeds in winter and gaze in at warmly lit windows, knowing that a cold fraternity awaited them. It was hard to witness the often relentless downward spiral of poverty, drugs and prostitution and still be a 'smile upon the world'; and hard to hold on to the conviction that the making of little tortoises with wobbling heads out of walnut shells and pieces of fir cone, to sell on market stalls or even just to bring laughter and happiness to passers-by, was in some way to contribute to the salvation of humanity. It required, above all, blind faith in the capacity of love

261

to transform even the smallest of things and in the power made perfect in weakness and littleness.

There were times when the sisters' faith was vindicated in obvious ways. In everyday situations they never tired of discovering the beauty hidden in so many people who were frequently ignored or condemned by society at large as being of no value. In seeking to love as Jesus loved they were often the recipients. In places such as Iraq or the Lebanon they knew that they quite simply could not survive if the people did not love them. And if at times their life of self-surrender appeared to bear no obvious fruits, it was precisely by experiencing apparent failure that Little Sister Magdeleine had maintained they would become true disciples of Jesus who died on the cross, 'betrayed and forsaken by those he had loved and called his friends, those he had guided and prepared by sharing everything with them and keeping them close to him in his love'. Those who tried to do great and beautiful things, believing that they were disinterested, but unable to resist being proud and happy if they felt they had in some way succeeded, she had pointed firmly back to the way of the Gospels:

> You wanted to present the Lord the results of your enterprises, coming happily to him, your hands full. But you forgot to turn towards Jesus, your only Model. He could show you only hands pierced by the nails of the cross, or the calloused hands of a workman, or again the tiny, helpless hands of a newborn baby in a crib.

There were those outside the Fraternity who believed resolutely in the continuing importance of its message of solidarity with the poorest and the most forgotten, those who recognised the value of walking up five flights of dirty stairs in a squalid apartment block in the black areas of Boston or Chicago, or into a wooden house built on stilts in Papua New Guinea, to find a door with a cross on it, and beyond it a smiling welcome and a tiny chapel containing the Blessed Sacrament. For Jean Vanier, who had discovered through a life of communion with people with mental handicaps the beauty there was in fragility, this was 'a pearl of the religious life'. 'Since 1948 when you came to our hill, we have followed you and understood. The Little Sisters' vocation counts so much more than you imagine,' Brother Roger of Taizé wrote to Little Sister Magdeleine in 1986. 'It has left its mark on us.' There were many others who were prepared to express similar views. 'Often, I repeat,' wrote one priest in Rome of the Little Sisters' calling, 'that it is a very particular charism of which the Church had great need; that of the contemplative life in friendship with all men and women, through the sharing of their lives, especially the lives of the poor. Friendship is your apostolate, which no-one can resist.' 'The religious life today owes a great deal to her,' wrote the Secretary General on behalf of the General Council of the Sacred Heart Sisters on the occasion of Little Sister Magdeleine's death. 'For us also and not only for the family which she founded, she was a source of inspiration, a call to renew ourselves and come back to the origins and to the charism of our own foundress.' 'They are doing very beautiful work for Jesus,' was Mother Teresa's comment on the congregation which had been founded only eight years before her own. Above all, however, it was those whom Little Sister Magdeleine had persisted in calling 'friends' who knew the value of the Fraternity. 'Now that she has gone,' asked one such friend in Algeria after hearing of her death, 'who will think of me in the way that she did?' Abdou, whose father Little Sister Magdeleine had sought to rescue from the desert years ago, supplied the answer. 'She has raised you, shown you the way,' he told the Little Sisters, 'the way of love between people, and has planted you in all countries. Now she can go. You are there. Continue on the path she had traced for you.'

'If a friendship is of God, it lasts,' Tahar, whose elder brother Athman had died some years previously, spoke with all the certainty of his devout Muslim faith. At Sidi Boujnan, the 'cradle of the fraternity', in the building which, as a young man, he had helped to construct, Little Sister Magdeleine's rooms next to the chapel had been preserved much as she had left them. In a corner of what was once her study, there still remained the plaster representation of the infant Jesus given to her in 1939. Its outstretched broken limbs repaired, it lay on a red woven cushion, beneath which Little Sister Magdeleine had tucked a carefully written little note:

> This Infant Jesus is a precious souvenir of the beginnings of the foundation. He has brought numerous graces. Let us keep him, even if he isn't very artistic.

Appendix A

Little Sister Magdeleine's Journey Round the World

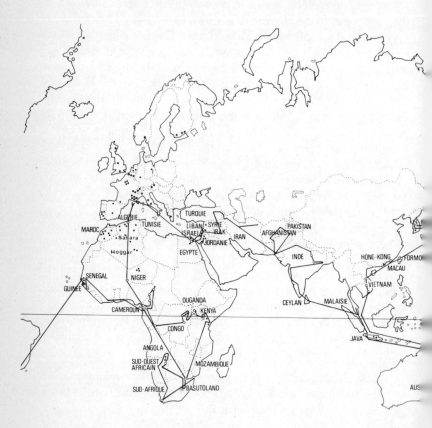

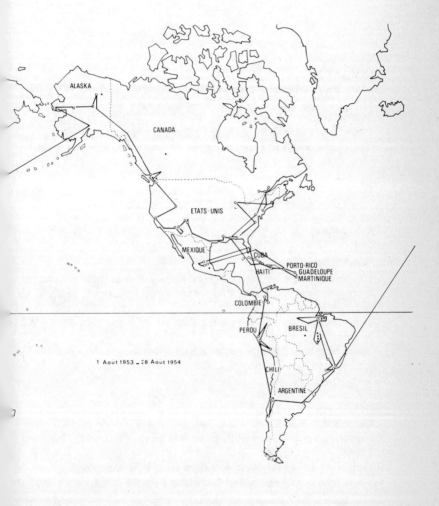

ALASKA

CANADA

ETATS-UNIS

MEXIQUE

CUBA

PORTO-RICO
GUADELOUPE
HAITI
MARTINIQUE

COLOMBIE

PEROU

BRESIL

1 Aout 1953 – 28 Aout 1954

CHILI

ARGENTINE

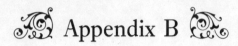

Appendix B

The extension of the Fraternity to the Eastern Bloc

1956
YUGOSLAVIA
- Little Sister Magdeleine made her first journey there in 1956, then returned every year from 1958 onwards except 1960, 1962, 1986 and 1989
- Little Sisters from the West have been present there since 1956
- There have been Little Sisters originating from the country since 1961

HUNGARY
- Little Sister Magdeleine made her first journey there in 1956, then returned in 1964, 1965, 1977, 1978, 1979 and 1985
- Little Sisters from the West were there in 1964, 1965 and 1966
- There have been Little Sisters originating from the country since 1969

CZECHOSLOVAKIA
- Little Sister Magdeleine made her first journey there in 1956 and returned every year from 1957 until 1989 except 1960, 1967, 1969, 1980, 1983 and 1984
- Little Sisters from the West were there in 1957 and then from 1967 onwards
- There have been Little Sisters originating from the country since 1973

1957
POLAND
- Little Sister Magdeleine made her first journey there in 1957, then returned every year from 1959 until 1989 except 1960, 1967, 1968 and 1969
- Little Sisters from the West were there from 1957 until 1961
- There have been Little Sisters originating from the country since 1962

1958

BULGARIA

- Little Sister Magdeleine made her first journey there in 1958, then returned every year from 1965 until 1975 except 1974
- Little Sisters from the West were there from 1967 until 1977

1959

GERMAN DEMOCRATIC REPUBLIC

- Little Sister Magdeleine first drove through the GDR in 1959, then in 1961, 1962, 1965, 1971, 1974, 1976, 1980 and each year from 1982 until 1989
- She made her first journey to East Berlin in 1973, then returned in 1980, 1983, 1984, 1985 and 1986
- Little Sisters from the West made temporary stays there from 1965 onwards
- There have been Little Sisters originating from the country since 1981

1964

USSR

- Little Sister Magdeleine made her first journey there in 1964 and returned in 1965, 1966, 1969, 1970, 1971, every year between 1973 and 1982, then in 1988 and 1989
- Little Sisters from the West have been there since 1974
- There have been Little Sisters originating from the country since 1979

1965

ROMANIA

- Little Sister Magdeleine made her first journey there in 1965 and returned in 1968, 1969, 1973, 1974, 1975 and 1977
- There have been Little Sisters from the West there from 1966 until 1970, from 1974 until 1983, and since 1991
- There have been Little Sisters originating from the country since 1992

✦ Index ✦

271